Inventing Intelligence

This book is dedicated to the memory of

my father Alfred and
my sister Lynda Privateer,

and to

André, Renee, and Lilas Privateer
for their unconditional love and unique intelligence

Paul Michael Privateer

Inventing
Intelligence

A Social History of Smart

BLACKWELL PUBLISHING
350 Main Street, Malden, MA 02148-5020, USA
9600 Garsington Road, Oxford OX4 2DQ, UK
550 Swanston Street, Carlton, Victoria 3053, Australia

The right of Paul Michael Privateer to be identified as the Author of this Work has been asserted in accordance with the UK Copyright, Designs, and Patents Act 1988.

First published 2006 by Blackwell Publishing Ltd

1   2006

Library of Congress Cataloging-in-Publication Data

Privateer, Paul Michael, 1946–
    Inventing intelligence : a social history of smart / Paul Michael Privateer.
        p.   cm.
    Includes bibliographical references (p.) and index.
ISBN-13: 978-1-4051-1216-1 (hardcover)
ISBN-10: 1-4051-1216-6 (hardcover)
1. Intellect—History.   2. Intellect—Social aspects.   I. Title.

BF431.P688 2006
153.909—dc22

                                              2005024957

A catalogue record for this title is available from the British Library.

Set in 10 on 12.5 pt Dante
by SNP Best-set Typesetter Ltd, Hong Kong
Printed and bound in India
by Replika Press Pvt. Ltd, Kundli

The publisher's policy is to use permanent paper from mills that operate a sustainable forestry policy, and which has been manufactured from pulp processed using acid-free and elementary chlorine-free practices. Furthermore, the publisher ensures that the text paper and cover board used have met acceptable environmental accreditation standards.

For further information on
Blackwell Publishing, visit our website:
www.blackwellpublishing.com

Contents

Contents

Acknowledgments

Many colleagues, friends, librarians, and governmental agencies are responsible for bringing this book to life. First, I would like to thank those who helped me during my sabbatical year.

I am indebted to Roe Smith of the Science, Technology, and Culture Program at Massachusetts Institute of Technology for providing me with a visiting professorship. The MIT environment presented opportunities to meet with Steven Pinker and Media Lab faculty and research staff, as well as with Rosalind Williams and other STS faculty engaged in regular seminars. Those sessions helped to expand my thinking about the nature, history, and science of intelligence. Christophe Lécuyer could not have been a better MIT office mate, never once complaining about frequent interruptions, while Debbie Meinbresse consistently pointed me in the right direction around Cambridge. I also want to thank David Palumbo-Liu and Monica Moore of the Modern Thought and Literature Program and Tim Lenoir of the Program in History and Philosophy of Science at Stanford University for their support and discussions.

Then there were those who gathered materials: Diana Pardue and Jeffrey Dosik of the Museum Services and Department of Interior at Ellis Island, Dr Tomoko Steen of the Science, Technology and Business Division of the Library of Congress, Alan Kraut of American University, Dorothy Gruich of the Archives of the History of American Psychology at the University of Akron, and the research staff of the British Library, The Bancroft Library at the University of California, the Green Library at Stanford University, the McHenry Library at the University of California at Santa Cruz, the Hayden Library at Arizona State University, the Barton Library at MIT, and the Widener Library at Harvard University. David A. Parthenheimer of the Public Affairs Office of the American Psychological Association and Alan Zonderman of the National Institutes of Health were equally helpful.

Acknowledgments

Then there were others who made me think in different ways. Robert Markley at the University of Illinois, Urbana-Champaign, and Michael Adas of Rutgers University offered insights from their books and e-mails, as did ongoing conversations with Kent Wright of the History Department at Arizona State University. Nora Taylor of Arizona State University and Andre Privateer helped me with important French translations. Professor Sandy Cohn at Arizona State University tutored me on the history and methods of psychometrics. And I would like to thank Peter Lehman and my colleagues and staff of the new Film and Media Studies Program at Arizona State University for their kind help and generous support. I would like to especially thank Ms Melanie Mierzejewski at Arizona State University for her professionalism and diligence in editing this manuscript.

Next I would like to thank Dr Jack Moran, Charles Lynch, Mick Mortlock and Ann Scott, John and Jennifer Tangney, Bill Blymiller, Professor David Conz, Susan Ledlow, Steve Salik, Thomas Kester, Dr Ron and Marilyn Gordon, Dr Richard and Susan Loveless, Gary Calendar, and Tom Broderick for their very special and kind support during a very difficult time. Dr David Friedman kept me motivated with his always inspiring doubt and good humor. And then there were my students. Their questions and insights made this project worthwhile.

Finally, I want to thank the staff at Blackwell for their advice and assistance. And for my Blackwell editors, Jayne Fargnoli and Ken Provencher, I have nothing but the greatest respect and admiration. They consistently matched their faith in this project with unlimited energy.

Introduction

Girl . . . 17 . . . IQ 72 . . . is a fairly capable houseworker when she tries . . . he [IQ 72] is fairly industrious when he gets a job as an errand or delivery boy . . . he [IQ 72] is generally called queer . . . delinquents and criminals often belong to this class.

Lewis Terman, *The Measurement of Intelligence*, 1916

Autonomous (*intelligent*) weapons can select their own aimpoints and are available in quantity. Even though redundant kills reduce efficiency, overall kill rates can be high.

Institute for National Strategic Studies, www.ndu.edu/inss/

This book explores the emergence and cultural effects of new ideas of human intelligence in Western culture. It analyzes how those notions contributed to the rise of new modes of power shaping contemporary culture. Rather than revisiting the more familiar terrains of intelligence – those like the cognitive sciences or educational or governmental policy – my goal is to investigate the socioeconomic and material world of intelligence. The central question is how certain representations of intelligence took historical form and functioned ideologically. The ultimate purpose invites readers to re-examine the very nature of intelligence – *of why the term even exists* – and to think of intelligence not simply as a human attribute but as a complex and powerful cultural practice.

This history of human intelligence begins with the problematic idea that although it is everywhere – from being a Greek planetary manager to the most contemporary of "smart" technologies – intelligence may and may not exist; that is, intelligence may be as much a social construction as it is a proven scientific phenomenon. But rather than creating an impasse, this paradox allows us to trace the evolution of ideas of intelligence by exploring how their past representations have functioned ideologically. Its capacity to construct beliefs is tied to the malleability of intelligence, to its being an *indeterminate metaphor* capable of producing varied and significant meanings. Metaphors of intelligence have operated within various Western knowledge systems, including Greek cosmological

1

models, medieval spiritual typographies, various Renaissance, eighteenth-century, and modern scientific theories, post-Renaissance economic and mathematical theories, and Enlightenment nation state policies. In essence intelligence has played a significant but generally unexplored role in shaping social epistemologies and hierarchies of power.

Their symbolic status have allowed new and competing ideas of intelligence to help to produce social policies, institutional practices, identity formations, economic modalities, specific technologies, and social norms. Tracing that history explains why certain notions of intelligence are more privileged than others, with most engaged in the production of knowledge and power systems. More importantly, these tracings also reveal the *other* story of intelligence, those accounts absent from traditional ways of knowing intelligence. Foucault's purpose in writing *Madness and Civilization* speaks to this absence: "The language of psychiatry, which is a *monologue* of reason about madness, has been established only on the basis of such a silence. I have not tried to write the history of that language, but rather the archeology of that silence" (Foucault, 1965, p. xi). This book attempts to make audible the *silences* embedded in, but silenced by, conventional notions of intelligence. Dominant representations of intelligence have created these silences by virtue of how construction contents minimize ideological resistance to them. For instance, how do we know intelligence as a continuous *monologue* formed by habitual ways of thinking? Arguably the cultural effects of those habits cannot be uncovered without interrogating how representations of intelligence and the forces of material history intersect. My interest is in connecting dominant era-sustaining ideologies to their discursive use of intelligence. Robert Serpell argues that in their efforts to "operationalize the construct of intelligence" practitioners and scientists "have drawn unselfconsciously on the topical preoccupations of their particular historical epoch" (Sternberg, 2000).

To uncover these "topical preoccupations" this book has had to loosen familiar concepts of intelligence from their protective disciplinary moorings. This approach is critically important because it is not enough to say that *any* study of intelligence would be incomplete if it ignored those disciplines because that ignoring *is the history of intelligence; the intelligence we know exists primarily because of certain absences and deficiencies*. Ideas of intelligence have historically helped to produce privileged social values and to insure conformance to them. For instance, they have legitimized notions of *superior* intellects and superior kinds of knowledge different from ordinary minds and inferior knowledge. In this way they have helped to construct epistemological filters through which the very conditions and limits of knowability are determined by superior intellects. These minds usually discover "truth" consistent with the ideology informing that knowledge. The minds of "geniuses" determining how the knowable is constructed and mapped have indeed an amazing power. What other human attribute has the authority to determine what is or isn't knowable, or what knowledge is more valuable primarily because of the caliber or class of the mind producing it?

There are two broad types of intelligence: *ubiquitous* intelligence and the *other* intelligence. Ubiquitous intelligence is about learning and coping with difficult situations. It is reason skillfully deployed, the application of knowledge and abstract thought. It is also about creating models: "[Bill Gates's intelligence has] incredible processing power, and unlimited bandwidth, an agility at parallel processing and multitasking" (*Time*, January 1977, volume 149, p. 2). The *other* intelligence deconstructs the ubiquitous: "Why did the measurement of individual differences and the assessment of hereditary influences commence when they did? . . . Once individual differences were successfully measured and the potency of heredity was established, how was this knowledge incorporated into the fabric of society?" (Evans and Waites, 1981, p. 131). It is about underscoring and problematizing the essentialness of ubiquitous intelligence: "studying the 'problematization' of madness, crime, or sexuality . . . is not a way of denying the reality of such phenomena. On the contrary, I have tried to show that it was precisely some real existent in the world which was the target of social regulation at a given moment" (Foucault, 2001, p. 84). The problematizing of ubiquitous intelligence reveals how its various constructions are related to historical aggregations of cultural power. To understand the intelligence of the *other* we need to explore the powerful cultural spaces occupied and epistemologically controlled by ubiquitous intelligence.

The World of Ubiquitous Intelligence

Ubiquitous intelligence resides in nine cultural sites: the legal, the educational, the biological (race and gender), the aesthetic, the mathematical, the scientific, the technological, the clinical, and the economic (as a commodity). Dominant notions of intelligence within these sites are continually being reinforced through a process of "intelligences of difference," constructions that continually reaffirm ideological values that affect different populations. In all nine, intelligence is not simply a human capability, as ubiquitous intelligence would lead us to believe. I now review these sites.

The legal

In the legal world intelligence is a matter of life and death. Intelligence *operates within the law* to regulate, order, include, and exclude. Thirty-eight US states

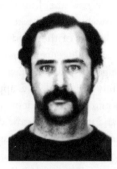

Figure 1   Robert Alton Harris, executed 1992, fetal alcohol syndrome, IQ 64, 73, 83 (taken over a fifteen-year period).

practice capital punishment. Twenty-six executed mentally retarded inmates between 1976 and June 25, 2002, when the Supreme Court held that these executions violated the Eighth Amendment. Prior to 2002, more than half of all states executed prisoners with IQs below 70, with the majority executing prisoners who performed adequately on the Binet 4, the Cattell B, the Savicki Culture Free, and the Wechsler (WISC III) tests. In 52 percent of these cases the condemned were executed regardless of what they scored. Thirty-five mentally retarded prisoners were executed in the USA between the reinstatement of the death penalty in 1976 and the recent Supreme Court decision. Of the thirty-five, eight were given a single IQ test, seventeen were tested twice, with scores ranging from 55 to 76 (two of these prisoners were diagnosed as being mentally retarded and insane) and one inmate was tested three times, scoring 68, 77, and 81. Six were never tested, and three were diagnosed as being medically retarded before being executed.

On April 21, 1992, California executed Robert Alton Harris in the San Quentin gas chamber (figure 1). Harris had suffered from fetal alcohol syndrome since birth. John Earl Bush, executed four years later, had severe brain damage from birth (Bonner and Rimer, 2000) and was tested with low borderline retardation (www.coadp.org/thepublications/pub-2002–5-ExecuteRetarded.html). Ricky Ray Rector, executed in Arkansas in 1992, was radically lobotomized prior to his crime and his brain was half its normal size because of an inadvertent self-inflicted gunshot wound. Bonner and Rimer (2000) claim that the lobotomized Rector "was so mentally impaired that he did not even know he was about to be executed." His final statement was a request that half of his uneaten pecan pie be saved "for after."

In 1985, Morris Mason asked four guards strapping him into the electric chair if they would tell his inmate friend that he wanted to continue playing basketball after the execution. The severity of Mason's retardation was never adequately assessed, and his IQ scores were 70 and 66. In 1988, Jerome Bowden said he wanted to thank everybody at the Georgia institution as he too was being strapped into the electric chair. Bowden had an IQ of 59 (www.advocacyone.org/deathpenalty.html).

The unregulated and inconsistent use of intelligence tests at the federal level extends to state legislatures. One would suppose that uniform criteria exist for states to determine whether an IQ score proves a prisoner sufficiently intelligent to be morally culpable, but there are no such universal criteria. Why do some states use scores below 70 while others use 75? In Nevada, for instance, a legislator argued that 70 would be an acceptable IQ number because it has been used to determine eligibility for social services.

Presumably IQ numbers reflect a certitude legislation neither enforces nor guarantees. What safeguards, for instance, insure that prisoners will be given similar tests under similar conditions? Are all court-appointed psychologists similarly trained? Do they use the same tests, the same computational and assessment processes? Do they use similar interpretative methods? These questions are important because no state decides whether the Binet 4, Wechsler (WISC-III), Rorschach, TAT, or any other test will be used on the basis of any mandated or studied objective. The absence of such standards of analysis raises the obvious question of whether a difference between scoring a 70 on the Binet 4 or a 70 on the Wechsler has any bearing on determining whether a prisoner is mentally retarded. Nor has any state conducted a scientific comparison of the relative validity of the range of tests used by court-appointed psychologists. Nor are there any mandated standards for psychological procedures or methods used in prisoner evaluations.

More importantly, why is a person's *intelligence* being tested if the legal question is whether a prisoner understands morality or reasons morally? What is the unstated connection between what an IQ score means and a person's capacity to be moral, assuming there is no organic illness that causes a person to make immoral choices? What is the connection between intelligence and morality, a linkage never contested from the beginning when Alfred Binet and Louis Terman tested for "moral intelligence." The problematic correlation between aptitude and morality is embedded in modern theories of intelligence but rarely explored. This absence of analysis is truly striking given a history in which there have been several manifestos linking mental superiority to moral superiority: "The view, common among those of superior intellect, that the poor are by nature a little mad, comes considerably closer to the truth than does the still commoner view that they are more than a little wicked" (Burt, 1918, p. 54).

What is the significance of the disparity between trusting IQ tests to determine who should be put to death and distrusting them as indicators of academic success? Individuals can be executed if they score 70, while others are spared with scores of 68. This two-point difference is not statistically reliable yet it can be used to determine a person's moral culpability. These inconsistencies are historical, part of an "intelligence of difference."

A case in point – after several appeals, Oliver Cruz (figure 2) was executed by lethal injection at 6 p.m. on August 9, 2000, in Huntsville, Texas, after having been convicted of raping and murdering Kelly Donovan in San Antonio two years earlier. Substantial evidence of Cruz's mental retardation did not spare his life. His mother was a diagnosed paranoid schizophrenic, Cruz failed seventh grade three times, supported himself with menial work, was barely literate, failed the Army test three times, was twice committed to a psychiatric hospital, suffered from severe drug dependency, and scored 64 on a court-ordered IQ test. He had scored 73 and 83 on earlier tests. Defense psychologists argued that his school records and test scores proved conclusive retardation. But rather than disputing this evidence, the Bexar County prosecutor, Susan D. Reed, used it, arguing that Cruz's lack of intelligence was indeed the aggravating factor warranting his execution:

> The Defense may tell you that . . . he is not very smart. And they may try to show you that this should be mitigation of punishment. . . . But the main issue that you have to look at, does the fact that the defendant was intoxicated or the fact that he may not be very smart, does that make him any less dangerous? Does that make him any less of a threat to the rest of society? . . . And I would submit to you, it's the opposite. It makes him in fact, more dangerous. It's part of the outlook of Oliver Cruz that makes him what he is. And that's not going to change. And society cannot take the chance of having him on the streets again, or having him out in prison where there is other people that associate with him, also, for their safety. (Makeig, 1995)

A similar rhetoric was used in the trial of Tony Tyrone Dixon, charged with murdering Elizabeth Peavy in Houston in 1994. Dixon had an IQ of 64. To prove that Dixon was smarter than any test, the prosecutor created a different kind of intelligence standard:

> there is a certain measure of street smarts that you can't measure on those standard examinations. . . . [Dixon] clearly has strong survival skills and can engage in criminal conduct and operate with a *predator's mind* on the streets. . . . I submit to you that Tony Dixon has what it takes to make the decisions that scare you to death when you're on the street. (Liebraum, 1995)

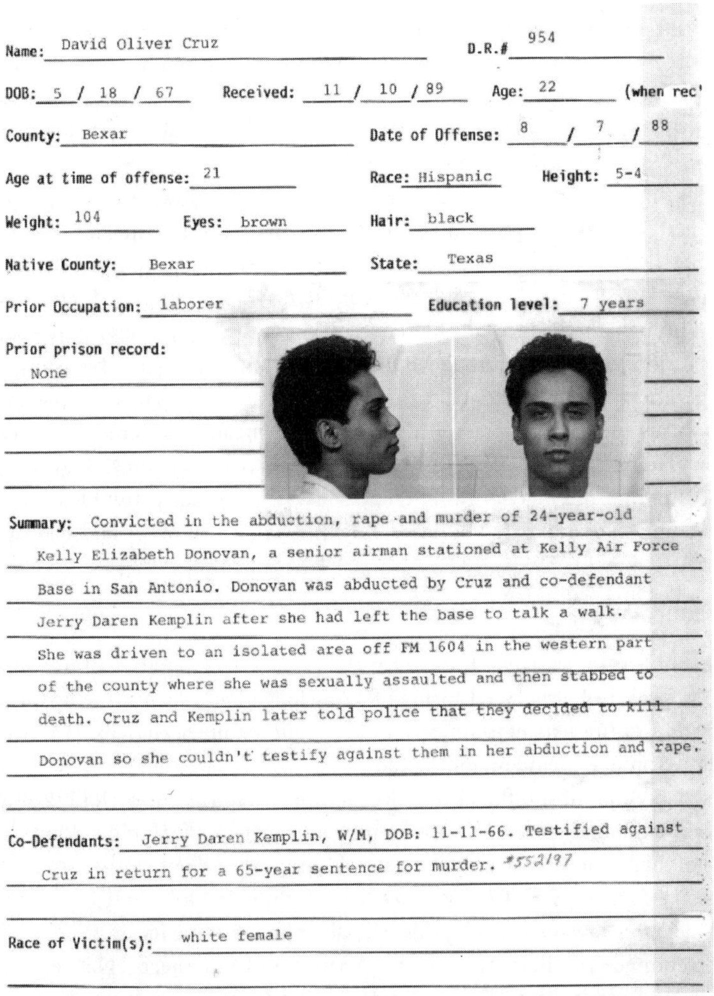

Name: David Oliver Cruz   D.R.# 954

DOB: 5 / 18 / 67   Received: 11 / 10 / 89   Age: 22   (when rec'

County: Bexar   Date of Offense: 8 / 7 / 88

Age at time of offense: 21   Race: Hispanic   Height: 5-4

Weight: 104   Eyes: brown   Hair: black

Native County: Bexar   State: Texas

Prior Occupation: laborer   Education level: 7 years

Prior prison record:
  None

Summary: Convicted in the abduction, rape and murder of 24-year-old
  Kelly Elizabeth Donovan, a senior airman stationed at Kelly Air Force
  Base in San Antonio. Donovan was abducted by Cruz and co-defendant
  Jerry Daren Kemplin after she had left the base to talk a walk.
  She was driven to an isolated area off FM 1604 in the western part
  of the county where she was sexually assaulted and then stabbed to
  death. Cruz and Kemplin later told police that they decided to kill
  Donovan so she couldn't testify against them in her abduction and rape.

Co-Defendants: Jerry Daren Kemplin, W/M, DOB: 11-11-66. Testified against
  Cruz in return for a 65-year sentence for murder. #552197

Race of Victim(s):   white female

Figure 2 Oliver Cruz, executed 2000 (www.tdcj.state.tx.us/deathrow/drowlist/cruz.jpg).

These arguments invite us into a dark, apocalyptic place, scaring the jury with a nightmarish world of midnight predators. The word "predator" is ideologically loaded, referring to a perverse genius "smarter" than "standard examinations" can detect, the traditional "trickster" who defies "normal" classification, linking Dixon to the machine-like monster of the 1987 film *Predator*. Moreover, it forms an unconscious mental menagerie, a zoo of sharks, wolves, tigers, mass murderers, and aliens, all of whom the jury would know as precision killers, keen-eyed predators hunting down the weakest and most innocent. According to the prosecutor, Dixon's intelligence could not be measured by "normal" means. Dixon's intelligence, he argued, came from another culture; it came from the uncontrollable, the unclassifiable, those dark streets filled with all kinds of "Others," of minority predators and sociopaths.

These images and arguments are not new. Descriptions of the dangerously deformed, the retarded, the alien, colonial natives, the uneducated, the unemployable, the defective, the sick, and the insane are as old as they are rhetorically plentiful. This is a community of the marginalized, its members drawn together by a cunning "intelligence of difference." They are part of a historical discourse of exclusion, of prohibition and homophobia, of social hierarchies configured on a geometry of breeding, cultural differences, and intelligence levels supporting policies of segregation, most of which delineate relations of power and mastery along socioeconomic, gender, racial, or scientific lines. This discourse constitutes the "intelligence of difference" – ways of looking, thinking, or behaving needing to be repressed because they threaten social order and security.

The educational

Intelligence is not strictly a human capability; it is also a matter of acquiring or being deprived of privileged forms of knowledge and power. Intelligence *operates within institutions of training, thinking, and learning*, and, like the legal, it regulates, orders, includes, and excludes.

Arguably the most difficult of colonial tasks is replication, a cloning and conversion of the indigenous into the homogeneity of the invading culture. This is why colonial schools played a critical role in conquest enterprises. Gustave Le Bon's *The Psychology of Peoples* (1899) and Arthur de Gobineau's *Essai sur l'inégalite des races humaines* (1853) praise the discipline, rationality, and virtue of hard work required for their African and Asian colonial subjects. Native passivity, passion, indolence, and carelessness presented problems in acquiring imperial wealth. These characteristics sharply contrast with those central to the modern Western epistemology, with its emphasis on speed and production, and the privileging of reason, mental agility, and methodical accuracy – the criteria for most IQ tests. Its influence is indeed significant, not simply directing and shaping the scientific economy of technocapitalism, but also determining how modern culture constructed notions of intelligence helping to regulate and assure social order. Imagine any modern intelligence test or analysis of intelligence that does not require orderly, quick, and rational responses to questions about abstract spatial, mathematical, and linguistic processes. This presumably *objective* criterion constituting and representing modern intelligence is the same as that driving contemporary alliances between science, technology, and capitalism. In fact, some modern definitions of both intelligence and modern techocapitalism share the value of optimizing limited resources – stressing the sanctity of problem-solving – which effectively produces new commodities. Even the popularity of terms like "intellectual capital" reveals intriguing ideological correspondences formed between modern economics and the claiming of the human interior and representation of it as scientific space.

As part of the "white man's burden," European colonial educators developed programs to "civilize" indigenous populations. Their goal was to identify the kind of education locals needed due to their "native" intelligence and its adequacy in understanding Western mathematics and science. Colonial pedagogy illuminates the ideological roles ideas of intelligence played in imperial thinking. In fact, two dominant ideas had the greatest impact on determining the direction of colonial education policy: the Western devaluation of "primitive" science and the scientific "proof" that intelligence was racially determined. Michael Adas argues that these two ideas determined "both the quality and amount of instruction different colonized peoples received," and, more importantly, "what purported to be scientific proofs of varying mental capacity of different human groups increasingly stifled or blocked altogether the dissemination of advanced scientific knowledge and methodologies to subject populations" (Adas, 1991, p. 15).

This colonial intelligence of difference also appears later in the libraries of early twentieth-century American educational policy and social theory. Writing in *American Medicine*, Dr Bean stated that he had discerned "the anatomical basis for the complete failure of negro schools to impart the higher studies – the brain cannot comprehend them any more than a horse can understand the rule of three. Leaders . . . now acknowledge the error of human equality." The threat, he insisted, was "a large electorate without brains" (*American Medicine*, April 1907, p. 36).

Other voices, visions, and discourses have prevented African-Americans from gaining access to higher education, their supposed intelligence a ready-made target for justified repression. A 1922 *Atlantic Monthly* article argued that because 89 percent of African-Americans scored at the deficient level on US Army intelligence tests,

emphasis must necessarily be laid on the development of the primary schools, on the training in activities, habits, occupations which do not demand the more evolved faculties. . . . A public school system, preparing for life young people of a race, 50 percent of whom never reach a mental age of 10, is a system yet to be perfected. (Chase, 1977, p. 262)

Introduction

The assumption that intelligence is a scalable human capability has reinforced the authority of imperial knowledge and power since the eighteenth century.

The aesthetic

More than a human capability, intelligence been attributed to the beautiful; it resides within the aesthetic, the sexual, the taboo, and the insatiable and like the legal and education it regulates.

In his *Observations Concerning the Increase of Mankind* (1751), Benjamin Franklin asks

> why should we in the Sight of Superior Beings, darken its People? why increase the Sons of *Africa*, by Planting them in *America*, where we have so fair an Opportunity, by excluding all Blacks and Tawneys, of increasing the lovely White and Red? But perhaps I am partial to the Compexion of my Country, for such Kind of Partiality is natural to Mankind. (http://bc.barnard.columbia.edu/~lgordis/earlyAC/documents/observations.html)

In his *Account of the Regular Gradation in Man* (1799), the surgeon Charles White describes ultimate beauty in terms of a female Caucasian: "a nobly arched head, containing *such a quantity of brain* . . . in what other quarter of the globe shall we find the blush that overspreads the soft features of the beautiful women of Europe" (Stanton, 1960, p. 17).

While the aesthetics of Western intelligence constitutes perfection and order, anything "lower" merely approximates the simian, the apish, the "thick lips," and the "grimacing teeth" of predators. Ideas of intelligence stabilize and order, part of an aesthetics of facial elevations, arches, and bridges guaranteeing a "highly elevated" intelligent social architecture. In Western culture, intelligence and beauty form a politics of the symmetrical.

The mathematical, the scientific, the technological, and the clinical

Intelligence operates ubiquitously by the authority of computation and ordering. But despite claims of absolute certainty, mathematical calculations are often inexplicable. For instance, in his *Method of Measuring the Development of the Intelligence of Young Children* (1911, p. 42), Binet observed that in mental testing it "matters very little what the tests *are* so long as they are *numerous*." Calculations also create significant but problematic connections. Lewis Terman, the American "father" of IQ testing, insisted that great minds may not be all that great. In a moment of excess, if not absurdity, he assigned the "father" of mental testing, Galton, an IQ score of 200 while giving Copernicus a mere score of 100. Galton, Darwin's cousin, enjoyed classifying people into "good, medium, and bad," using a hidden pricker needle to poke out corresponding holes on early punch cards: "I used this plan for my beauty data, classifying the girls I passed in the streets . . . as attractive, indifferent or repellent" (Galton, 1909, p. 316).

Computations also prove contradictory. T. Bischoff studied the brains of 119 thieves, assassins, and murderers and discovered that criminal brains outweighed genius brains by an average of 11 grams (Gould, 1987, p. 94). And computations sometime make the contradictory inexplicably true. When Broca studied 125 skulls from different aged cadavers from various centuries, he concluded that:

> the cranial capacity of Parisians has really diminished during centuries following the 12th. Now during this period . . . intellectual and social progress has been considerable, and even if we are not yet certain that the development of civilization makes the brain grow as a consequence, no one, without doubt, would want to consider this cause as capable of making the brain decrease in size. (Broca, n.d., p. 106)

Samuel George Morton, physician and scientist, gathered 600 skulls in the 1820s to test his theory that brain size objectively proved the intelligence of various races. The frail man turned the skulls upside down and poured both mustard seeds and small diameter BB shots into their brain cavities. From these and other tests, he published a table of size differences, with Caucasians scoring 92, Mongolians 82, Malays 85, Native Americans 79, and the Native African Family within the Negro Group 83 (Gould, 1987, p. 55).

Computations sometimes reduce or translate complex phenomenon into simple rules. H. H. Goddard, research director at the Vineland Training School for Feeble-Minded Girls and Boys, used numbers to simplify certain diagnostic goals: "when we measure the intelligence of an individual and learn that he has so much less than normal as to come within the group that we call feeble-minded, we have ascertained by far the most important fact about him" (Goddard, 1919, p. 272). Inversely, he told his Princeton students that the "fact is that workmen may have a 10 year intelligence while you have a 20. To demand for him such a home as you enjoy is as absurd as it would be to insist that every laborer should receive a graduate fellowship. How can there be such a thing as social equality with this wide range of mental capacity." Democracy, he insisted, "means that the people rule by selecting the wisest, most intelligent and most human to tell them what to do to be happy" (ibid., p. 237).

Computations sometimes create their own standards. Lewis Terman once theorized about race and mathematical abilities: "Ethnology shows that racial progress has been closely paralleled by development of the ability to deal with mathematical concepts and relations" (Terman, 1906, p. 309). Computations of intelligence often appear in the world of capitalism: "Is intellectual ability a bank account, on which we can draw for any desired purpose, or is it rather a bundle of separate drafts, each drawn for a specific purpose and inconvertible?" (ibid., p. 9).

Computations of intelligence sustain socioeconomic ways of constructing and knowing the world. Terman argued that "the near future of intelligence tests will bring tens of thousands of these high-grade defectives under the surveillance and protection of society . . . curtailing the reproduction of feeble-mindedness and in the elimination of an enormous amount of crime, pauperism, and industrial inefficiency" (Terman, 1916, pp. 6–7). His view of the relationship between intelligence and productivity is enhanced with the observation that "moral judgement, like business judgement, social judgement, or any other kind of higher thought process, is a function of intelligence" (ibid., p. 11). Elsewhere he argues that "the evolution of modern industrial organization together with the mechanization of processes by machinery is making possible the larger and larger utilization of inferior mentality. One man with ability to think and plan guides the labor of ten or twenty laborers, who do what they are told to do and have little need for resourcefulness or initiative" (Terman, 1919, p. 276).

Computations require speed, reason, mental agility, and methodicalness, the criteria of modern intelligence. The four had an instrumental role in Binet's most famous tests. Actually Binet called his tests "tasks," the metaphoric linkage between intelligence and productivity being unmistakable. Binet's linkage converts an examination, a diagnosis that corrects an unstated defect, into a task, a labor-based duty.

When a "mental test" becomes a "task" several ideological alliances are revealed. For instance, as science is given the power to identify and correct nature's mistakes, it also "solves" labor problems by mathematically identifying underachievers and non-conformists. This "test-as-task" connects the scalability of intelligence to work, to hierarchies of performance and appropriate rewards. Doing well on Binet's various "tasks," as with all IQ tests, produced certain rewards for certain students, while a poor performance enabled "non-standardized" children to receive "special tuition" and remedial services.

Computations may not be as objective as the psychometric industry assumes. As the computational science of intelligence, psychometrics is concerned with the design and analysis of human characteristics in terms of mathematical systems. Its origins assemble a number of familiar names – Binet, Spearman,

Galton, and Thurstone being the most well known. At its core are statistical and quantitative methods giving psychology and the cognitive sciences the objectivity needed to become modern sciences.

Psychometrics relies on mathematical objectivity and certitude for its validity. During its existence a number of challenges to classical mathematics have occurred that have been neither acknowledged nor refuted by the psychometric community. For even if we ignore Fermat's seventeenth-century *last theorem* ($x^n + y^n = z^n$), we are still stuck with the implications of theories proposed by Gödel, Wittgenstein, and Heisenberg, as well as recent developments in chaos and entropy theory. When these theories challenge the objectivity of mathematics, they also put into question the validity of any mathematical systemization or model of human behavior.

In 1931, Kurt Gödel published his *incompleteness theorem* in *Monatshefte für Mathematik und Physik*, volume 38. The Czech mathematician argued that certain propositions within any branch of mathematics can never be proven either true or false by using rules and axioms from within that given branch. Here Gödel was referring to the fact that mathematicians have traditionally proven all statements about numbers within a system by essentially going *outside* it. Yet this production of new rules or axioms has only generated a larger system fraught with unproven statements. Gödel proved that all logical systems of any degree of complexity are incomplete because they contain more true statements than they can ever possibly prove according to the limitations imposed by their own set of rules. And there are those who speak of a "crisis" in mathematics, especially as a method of modeling human behavior:

> We are less certain than ever about the ultimate foundations of [logic and] mathematics. Like everybody and everything in the world today, we have our crisis. We have had it for nearly fifty years. Outwardly it does not seem to hamper our daily work, and yet I for one confess that it has had a considerable practical influence on my mathematical life: it directed my interests to fields I considered relatively safe, and has been a constant drain on the enthusiasm and determination with which I pursued my research work. This experience is probably shared by other mathematicians who are not indifferent to what their scientific endeavors mean in the context of man's whole caring and knowing, suffering and creative existence in the world. (Hermann Weyl, 1946, www.cs.auckland.ac.nz/CDMTCS/chaitin/georgia.html)

And then

> there have been within the experience of people now living at least three serious crises. . . . There have been two such crises in physics – namely, the conceptual soul-

searching connected with the discovery of relativity and the conceptual difficulties connected with discoveries in quantum theory. . . . The third crisis was in mathematics. It was a very serious conceptual crisis, dealing with rigor and the proper way to carry out a correct mathematical proof. (John von Neumann, 1963, www.cs.auckland.ac.nz/CDMTCS/chaitin/georgia.html)

The failure of psychometric sciences to address the implications of contemporary mathematical theory puts the validity of what science produces into serious question.

There are other modern ideas that challenge mathematical objectivity. For example, in all their complications, Wittgenstein's major works – *Tractatus Logico-Philosophicus* (1921) and *Philosophical Investigations* (1953) – focused on philosophical questions dealing with the foundations of mathematics, logic, and certitude. His work on language, scientific methodology, and psychology reveals a persistent doubt about the value of essentialist meanings and metaphysical doctrines. Wittgenstein spent a lifetime deconstructing the claims of traditional philosophy and mathematics, in the end articulating essentially a non-systematic and non truth based epistemology. More importantly, his work challenges the basic invention of Enlightenment humanism, particularly the validity of a science dealing with the human subject. This agenda is made clear with the argument that

Mathematics is a logical method. . . . Mathematical propositions express no thoughts. In life it is never a mathematical proposition which we need, but we use mathematical propositions only in order to infer from propositions which do not belong to mathematics to others which equally do not belong to mathematics. (Wittgenstein, 1961, p. 169)

Contemporary social applications of mathematics cannot claim validity if they ignore the implications of Heisenberg's uncertainty principle and modern developments in chaos and entropy theory. When Heisenberg argued that "the more precisely the position is determined, the less precisely the momentum is known in this instant, and vice versa," he constructed the uncertainty principle. Prior to the discovery of quantum mechanics, scientists and mathematicians generally believed that the precision of any measurement – such as an IQ score – was determined by the accuracy of instruments. What Heisenberg proved was that no matter the accuracy of an instrument, quantum mechanics denies the possibility of precision whenever two properties are measured at the same time as variables having special equation relationships. When the foundations of classical mathematics are contested, the power of mathematics to be "right" about human intelligence is also challenged.

These sites are explored in more detail throughout this study.

Key Terms

In this book the term *ideology* refers to value constructions derived from complex cultural systems of representation – media images, ideas, myths, or concepts, or any symbolic construct of value and truth – that produce social power and organizations sustaining them. Ideologies determine the relations humans have with certain constructions of reality, their way of perceiving of and complying with "reality." Human belief in a set of representations that are "true" functions by a process of interpellations, whereby they become subjects of a given ideology. More important, however, to my analysis of the history of ideas of intelligence is the relationship between these individual performances and state power. Ideologies, Althusser reminds us, function best when individuals believe they are free from anything ideological, that their thinking is their own. Ideas of intelligence – the ideology of intelligence, if you will – describe precisely what this book seeks to explore. Likewise, I explore historical representations of intelligence precisely as control mechanisms rather than as numerical indicators of a person's mind and potential, or as a mark of divine genius, or as a gift, a corporate asset, or a mechanism explaining how the universe functions symmetrically. The goal is to demonstrate that before intelligence is a human attribute, it is a historical discourse, the means by which knowledge is produced, and accessible in terms of relations of power.

To explore the ideology of intelligence means exposing the generally closed *scientization* of intelligence to cultural and political analysis. The fact that within this scientization there are so many contrary definitions of intelligence does not simply prove that there are so many different ways of being intelligent. The more interesting idea is that these differences reflect differences among competing conceptualizations, cultural control mechanisms, and different domains of power rather than proving differences of a unique inner intelligence. Competing representations of intelligence can be traced to various power alliances operating with different controlling mechanisms (differences in practices) and behavioral objectives (differences in how institutions and individuals respond to those practices). In turn this tracing can clarify why ideas of intelligence have taken different form in ancient Greek philosophy, medieval Platonism, Renaissance culture, the new Enlightenment political economy, Romanticism's creative genius theories, nineteenth-century utilitarian social theory, hereditary sciences, and psychometrics. It also explains why there is little agreement as to what intelligence is among contemporary cognitive scientists, clinical practitioners, robotic and AI technologists, and educational policy-makers. Lastly, the Geertz–Foucault approach creates other contexts for insights, those obscured by two centuries of ideologically charged debate about what *objectively* defines, measures, and determines human intelligence.

Building upon Sternberg's *Metaphors of Mind: Conceptions of the Nature of Intelligence* (1990) and Gould's *The Mismeasure of Man* (1987), this book argues that the ideological DNA of contemporary ideas of intelligence can be traced to socioeconomic, political, and institutional forces arising in sixteenth-century Europe. Moreover, these same forces can be shown to be responsible for the symbolic transformation of intelligence into a postmodern commodity, capital, and equity. This postmodern trend began to take form with eighteenth-century use of myths, symbolic systems, institutions, and various discourses to form knowledge systems driven by techniques of grouping, exclusion, suppression, surveillance, ordered competitions, performance measurements, reinforcement rewards, and other bureaucratic processes.

It may not be enough to say that ideas of intelligence have functioned as ideologically supportive mechanisms. That would not explain how their conceptual differences have impacted different historical knowledge systems. For example, our era of intelligence differs significantly from earlier eras, with our current ideas of intelligence having been invented during the past three hundred years to facilitate the institutionalization of new social modes of organization, to stabilize new political systems, and to generate and profit handsomely from new kinds of scientific and technological knowledge. All three are the *modernist political economy*. Throughout this study I use the term *investment* to refer to various ideological commitments Western culture has made to identify, rank, promote, institutionalize, and regulate intelligence as a means of controlling and privileging certain behaviors and values. Restricting intelligence studies to the history of the measurable – to the monologue – misses the promise of exploring the *other* intelligence, and how its various historical representations constitute dense knowledge networks forming modern cultural history.

From here on, my goal is to examine certain documents and ideas that have enabled ideas of intelligence to generate ideological content. My desire is to drop ideas of intelligence into the flow of history, observing such ideological turns and twists as:

1 The slow disintegration of the idea of a "collective" human destiny.
2 The emergence of modern individualism and the nation state.
3 Changes in what constitutes work and art, New World expansions, and industrialization.
4 The emergence of global commodity capitalism.

My method is to trace ideas of intelligence as they move from discourse to practice, from ideation to materiality. Rather than remaining in the realm of the abstract, asking *what intelligence is*, this study explores *why* intelligence consumes us, and, in turn, what social controls, practices, and technologies have made intelligence so easily consumable. Clearly its ideological history reveals the significant role that representations of intelligence have played in creating dominant modes of social power in European and American cultural "history of the present." Nikolas Rose's idea adds focus to what this book intends: "A historian of the present needs to think of thought as itself 'technical'; the task is not one of interpreting 'discourse' in terms of the meanings embodied in systems of representation, but of analyzing the *intellectual technologies* by which thought renders being amenable to being thought" (Jones and Porter, 1994, p. 63). The later chapters of this book focus on how *intellectual technologies* have rendered institutional, scientific, and medical practices thinkable.

Stated Purpose and Outline

My intention is not to prove or disprove the existence of intelligence. The ontological question fascinates me far less than its epistemological relative. Nor do I want to debate whether Western culture *invented* intelligence, the word a mantra some writers use to homogenize their method, assuming *invention* means that nothing is real and, therefore, everything exists simply as a cultural construct. This is nonsensical because it ignores what analyses of representations can yield, preferring instead to be mired in the metaphysical muck of a dead philosophical dualism. The real job of cultural studies is not to argue what is real, but to trace claims of real through a study of the relationship between cultural ideologies, cultural behavior, and various productions of power. Cultural studies seemed an appropriate tool for my interest in exploring how certain Western knowledge systems have used intelligence to support ideas of race theory fortifying the sovereignty of capitalism, the tradition of progress, the appropriation of nature as a resource for productions of power, the creation of essentialist identity, and state-reinforced self-production strategies. Each of these trends has appropriated representations of intelligence for its ideological scaffolding. This study is also unapologetically speculative. Nevertheless, it hopes to show that intelligence is above all else a metaphoric idea, a multidiscursive concept embedded in and woven through philosophical, mathematical, sociopolitical, economic, legal, educational, and medical texts.

The book is divided into three parts tracing the evolution of various historical representations of intelligence. Each part has chapters that situate intelligence within the social practices of the period studied. For example, part I explores the relationship between Renaissance constructions of radically new notions of intelligence, the emergence of modern capitalism, various New World expeditions, the development of new technologies, and the invention of new information repository systems. Likewise, part II explores Enlightenment intelligence in terms of a new political myth, the rise of utilitarian social theory, and the invention of human "normalization" models and "political arithmetic." Part III explores our contemporary "smart" world, investigating the ideas of modern architects of intelligence, as well as the technologies and practices that make it possible and its complex commodification activities. I conclude with speculation about the future of intelligence.

I should like to apologize in advance for my mix of ambitiousness and short-sightedness. This book would have been impossible had it not been for the work of previous cultural historians. I thank them. Much of this book might suggest that I have a guarded rebellious attitude. Several colleagues have said that it is a "radical" book. What other word, they insist, defines someone who denies that intelligence exists. My answer again is that I do not want to prove or disprove the *existence* of intelligence. This book is not about the *what* of intelligence, but its cultural behaviors. All I can do is apologize in advance if my assumptions, ideas, and methods fall short of that goal. However, if I am successful then two important accomplishments are achieved: I will have served cultural studies goals by providing new examples of how truth construction activities function as cultural organizing systems; and I will demonstrate that modern notions of intelligence are just as much about certain forces in material history as they are about objective science. Modern notions of intelligence evolved in accord with significant changes in the nature, definition, and technologies of Western power, fueled by the development of utilitarian science, capitalistic reproduction, a legalized individual identity, and the nation state. Understanding these correspondences is finally a matter of understanding the relationship between ideology and artifice.

I like using structural metaphors to guide my research: the palimpsest is particularly apropos. The cost of medieval parchment proved so prohibitive that scholars often washed ink off from previous manuscripts to recycle them. However, after time, prior writings bled through and blended with the most recent text. The palimpsest is intriguing because of its magical refusal to forget. It is a memory without the intentional consciousness that fabricates rules and regulations. It ignores the attraction of repression. The palimpsest is a solid transparency, a stage on which the normally hidden collisions of competing ideas emerge from the shadows of time, illuminating how the "original" and the "new" contest their presence.

All I can hope is that this book behaves like a palimpsest, offering readers a different story of intelligence, a history that is really "there," written over thousands and thousands of times, obscured by the ink of dominant thought and submerged in forgotten girders of social power, the two having so much to do with shaping the cultural truths that define us.

The Renaissance Economy of Intelligence

> . . . from whence
> You owe this strange intelligence?
> *Macbeth*, Act 1, Scene 3

O Aristotle! If you had the advantage of being "the freshest modern," instead of the greatest ancient, would you not have mingled your praise of metaphorical speech, as a sign of high intelligence, with a lamentation that *intelligence so rarely shows itself in speech without metaphor* – that we can seldom declare what a thing is, except by saying it is something else.

George Eliot, *The Mill on the Floss*

After all, intelligence clearly isn't in the brain; it is the brain. It's less like the oil in the engine and more like the efficiency of the engine . . . every aspect of the engine affects its efficiency.

http://encarta.msn.com/column_iqmain_tamimhome/

He was no Einstein . . . not intelligent but just a nice neighborhood guy.

Dennis Neely, CNN Report, referring to Paul Johnson,
an American executed in Saudi Arabia in 2004

1 The Pre-Renaissance Tradition of Intelligence

Renaissance philosophers, scientists, sociopolitical essayists, and religious clerics contributing to expressly modern notions of intelligence inherited a tradition of ideas of intelligence. Prior to the sixteenth century, ideas of intelligence had already circulated through nearly three thousand years of Western thought. The idea of intelligence appears in the writings of many pre-Socratic philosophers (Thales, Anaximander, Anaximenes, Xenophanes, Heraclitus, Parmenides, Alcmaeon of Crotona, Empedocles, Anaxagoras, Diogenes of Apollonia, Diogenes of Sinope, Democritus, and Leucippus), as well as in the writings of Plato and Aristotle. Research suggests that the Greeks produced three notions of intelligence: intelligence as a divine, absolute entity, proving that a stable and rational universe made certitude possible; intelligence as a divine gift given to humans; intelligence personified, with the divine nature of intelligence incarnated as *"sophos, sophistes,* or *sophia,"* the clever, wise, skilled, or highly knowledgeable person. These ideas of intelligence occur in the following disciplines:

1 Metaphysics: intelligence constructed in terms of or associated with a divine soul or gift, a protecting god, immortality, an ideal world of abstract form, a perfect form in mathematics and geometry, permanence, the absolute good, and a higher intelligence.
2 Astronomy: intelligence associated with the regularity of circular planetary motion, the center of all things, stars, predictable celestial revolutions, and perfect spheres.
3 Physics: intelligence associated with light, matter, inertia, and force.
4 Human physiology: a lack of intelligence can be identified by specific body defects.
5 Epistemology: intelligence can be a way of knowing (*phronesis*).
6 Ontology and figuration: intelligence can be anything objectified.

This list suggests that as early as 300 BCE intelligence was associated with the celestial, the divine, the rational, the mysterious, the unknown, the abstract, and human dependency upon an absent, abstract, and rational deity, all of them central to the evolution of intelligence in Western thought.

The Greeks provided modern Western culture with the idea of divine intelligence that immigrated through many medieval philosophical texts. The list of contributors and sources is too lengthy to include, but names like Plotinus, Boethius, John Duns Scotus, Thomas Aquinas, Anselm, Pierre Abelard, William of Ockham (Occam), Aegidius Colonna, Albert the Great, and Roger Bacon certainly contributed to the discourse on intelligence in medieval culture. Nor can the School of Chartres and Scholasticism be overlooked, especially since they tended to revalidate Platonic and neo-Platonic notions of a spiritual and cosmic "Intelligence." The tradition of intelligence preceding the Renaissance plays an important part in the ideological history of intelligence in so far as its ideas helped to construct the conditions of certainty and authority that were appropriated by the Church, the monarchy, theology, and early science. When the Greeks associated intelligence with a "divinity" of perfect forms, they also laid the groundwork for the future authority of science and abstract systemization methods. A power given celestial immensity, divine intelligence transcended the Heraclitean world of unstable forms and impossible knowledge and made possible mathematically produced certitude. The construct of a divine intelligence also helped to construct a new way of knowing that reduced tragedies linked to the instabilities of life. The formalization of abstract modes of cognition created a new fledgling epistemology promising that knowledge could, in fact, be precise, true, and exact. It is no accident that seventeen hundred years later Isaac Newton, like Augustine before him, would marvel at how the Creator's divine intelligence created mysterious laws of gravity and inertia illuminated by the flame of mathematical certitude and classical mechanics. Implicit in both Augustine's neo-Platonic theorizing and the mathematical rationalism of seventeenth-century thought is the assumption that mathematics provides the clearest illustration of the intelligence that achieves divine truth. This early relationship between mathematics and intelligence is arguably the most ideologically significant of all connections between intelligence and some other element.

The second and even more obvious ideological role divine intelligence played in early Western civilization comes with its part in providing the Church with the absolute authority and power to represent the whole of human existence. The power to define God and the authority to create, control, and manipulate stories that explained it all – the Creation, Nature, the meaning of human life, the need for death, and the spiritual delivery of every man or woman back to the Father – was a formidable power. Interestingly, the management of this myth was handed over to an intelligentsia trained organizationally to assure a continuation of ideological power gained from various institutionalizations of this master narrative. For nearly seventeen hundred years, philosophers, theologians, and Church officials capitalized on the authority derived from the idea that God or ultimate forms were divinely intelligence. Moreover, the monotheism of the Judeo-Christian God, his symbolic nature appropriated to regulate human behavior within social organizations, and his commercial value in helping to create economic profit may arguably be the very earliest version of the coming to ideological dominance of a myth that combines autonomous individuality, market capitalism, and the legitimacy of the state as a regulatory social agency, key elements in the modern hegemony.

Within a century, however, ancient and medieval epistemological agendas of ultimate forms, absolute certainty, abstract science, and divine intelligence would yield part of their power to a competing discourse of intelligence tied to social movements focused on rebirth and reform. These new ideological competitors would subvert the transcendental and ideological authority attributed to divine intelligence by replacing it with an "enlightened" intelligence derived from the strictly human power to reason.

Tracing how classical ideas of intelligence entered Renaissance thought proves a formidable challenge, solved, in part, by turning to the *Waning of the Renaissance: 1550–1640*, a study that describes two Renaissance historical movements: those following a single direction and those behaving in more "varied, complex, multi-directional, and even contradictory" ways, with the latter describing "a major alteration in the European cultural landscape . . . [in which] conflicting impulses were often simultaneously at work, without a clear resolution between the creativity and spontaneity of cultural freedom and a growing tendency toward order and restraint" (Bouwsma, 2000, pp. 259–60). This idea parallels Markley's (1993, p. 5) observation that the "history of representation [is] a complex and internally divided process rather than a linear sequence of progressive development." Bouwsma's notion of multidirectionality underscores the nature of Renaissance constructions of intelligence. This history is difficult to know; ideas of intelligence had no disciplinary home. In fact, ideas of intelligence wound themselves, like vines, through several Renaissance discourses. Writing this history is an extraction process, of unearthing socioeconomic patterns that affected ideas of intelligence.

Much of this surveys central Renaissance cultural productions, particularly humanism, the myth of individualism, advances in science and technology, and art, to explore the Renaissance "economy" of intelligence. This new economy – this new way of understanding and manipulating the world – was driven by the idea that intelligence created tools for wealth and social stability, an idea shaping modern thought. If the myth of individualism drove the Renaissance, then the economy of intelligence proved to be its engine.

Fashioned largely by economic forces, the economy of intelligence was a multidiscursive and "multidirectional" force that created ideological cohesions between ideas of capitalism, the new nation state, the scientific method, and the social value of applied material technologies. These collaborations not only produced new ways of knowing the world but began their institutionalization. In essence, intelligence had to be humanized – taken out of the ancient clouds and placed within the human body – if humanism was to achieve ideological success. Ultimately, by the mid-eighteenth century, the two forces were largely responsible for the victory of market capitalism and the new science over past religious orthodoxy. The next chapter explores the relationship between certain thought alliances and new representations of intelligence to show how the Renaissance *humanization* of intelligence helped to formulate the ideological core of modernist thought, its function being that of an essential component trafficking authority, knowledge, power, science, and capital into a single and ultimate construct – the constructed individual.

2 The New Landscape of Smart

The Renaissance produced two new intelligence models: a composite *divine – human* model and a more radical, totally *human* form, primarily empirical, material, natural, and scientific in nature. This latter model also coincided with the production of new criteria for truth, chief among them rationality and observation proving more valid than faith. How this shift in criteria cooperated with new ideas about intelligence becomes evident nearly a century later with David Hume's point "that the cause or causes of order in the universe probably bear some remote analogy to human intelligence" (Schlagel, 1996, p. 521). An earlier version is offered by LaPlace and Pierre (1951, p. 3):

> Given for one instant an intelligence which could comprehend all the forces by which nature is animated and the respective situation of the beings who compose it – an intelligence sufficiently vast to submit these data to analysis . . . for it nothing would be uncertain. . . . The human mind offers . . . a feeble idea of this intelligence.

Tame by comparison with the hip-mantra hype about postmodern *alienated, collective, commercialized,* or *globalized* intelligence, these analogies illustrate a revolutionary drift in historical representations of intelligence. Its radicality lies in its ascribing to human intelligence the power and privilege once given divine and celestial models. The gradual Renaissance replacing of divine mysteries with human reasoning, science, and measurement was a critical step in the construction of modern ideas of intelligence.

Hume's comment also illuminates how new notions of intelligence were consistent with the goals of Renaissance philosophy and science. Both disciplines essentially invented a new logistics of consciousness, moving from an interest in natural objects or systems to systematic interrogations into the very nature of consciousness itself. This shift is evident in several influential Renaissance philosophical texts, such as Descartes's *Discourse on Method* or Locke's *Essay Concerning Human Understanding*. Pervasive interest in the relationship between consciousness, identity, and knowledge provided new ideas about the nature of being human and the nature of intelligence. Both appeared in the texts dealing with individualism, books reflecting spiritual, scientific, and philosophical explorations of internal worlds. Modeled after Dante and Augustine, these adventurers included the likes of Petrarch, Piccolomini, Cardano, Boccaccio, Montaigne, Burton, and Cervantes. Arguably the most famous of these interior nomads, the Cartesian *cogito*, migrates from a world of doubt to a promised land of certainty, armed with reason, mathematics, and a rational *method* – criteria essential to the creation, administration, and evaluation of modern intelligence tests.

Themes of internal discovery wind through many Renaissance cultural productions. For example, interest in self-discovery, evident in proliferations of autobiographies dealing with the accumulation of wealth, paralleled scientific interest in prosthetic technologies, like microscopes and telescopes, that helped individuals to overcome physical limitations imposed by Nature. Sometimes the two strands intermingled, as is the case with Cardano's *De vita propria*, which frequently weaves interior psychological reflections with scientific and medical observations. Widespread interest in self-discovery also meant that the analysis of intelligence could now take form as a self-inventing narrative, intelligence becoming an *attribute* that an individual possesses and can use for self-profit. Given their analysis of various kinds of self-consciousness, various Renaissance thinkers had no other venue, nothing other than the metaphoric *within* from which they could explore the cognitive and physical world of the human. And to construct new knowledge systems for this landscape, writers appropriated, reconstructed, and repurposed earlier ideas. Hence the integration of human intelligence with a divine source, even in contemporary times, explains why popular culture touts "genius" in terms of a godlike, spiritual, or omniscient entity. Einstein often thought of his work as a reading of the mind of God, while countless articles praise his divine "genius."

Explorations of this new interior correspond with the discoveries of new exteriors – the *New World* of transoceanic explorations, international commerce, and market capitalism. Condorcet, a century later, explains how these expansions influenced the progress of the mind "that will last as long as man's destiny," bringing "wealth of resources for industry and intellect" (Baker, 1975, p. 360). Both journeys were inspired by the Renaissance economy of intelligence, triggered by the Copernican revolution, the decay of feudalism, and the invention of commercial technologies, like gunpowder, the mariner's compass, paper, and printing, all of which generated unprecedented productions of information. Another way of understanding the Renaissance is to see how it helped to revolutionize the nature, production, and technologies of information. In fact, at its most abstract level, the Renaissance represents the evolution of a new information dynamic, the creation of entirely new and economically driven information networks significantly different from earlier systems because of the increased amount of data converted into capital and wealth. The Renaissance was unique because it turned information into a commodity, not for Rome or a few families, but for middle-class consumption. This new commodity is central to the creation of the modernist hegemony.

Part of Renaissance increases in the capitalization of information networking can be linked to the mass production of books with large audience appeal and to the popularity of translations and reproductions of original manuscripts, supported by an abundance of print industry investment capital. For instance, in 1533, John Leland, Henry VIII's "King Antiquary," was given the capital to begin searching for classical manuscripts in convents, colleges, and monasteries with the "intent that the monuments of ancient writers . . . might be brought out of deadly darkness to lively light" and profit (Baugh, 1967, p. 334).

Printing became a modern business as early as 1400, with book dealers and entrepreneurs developing new inventory models (production-on-demand strategies replacing ready-to-sell manuscripts), creating modern supply and distribution channels, and reducing operation costs. In some British cases, as with William Caxton (1422–91), Wynkyn de Worde, Richard Pynson, and Robert Copland, printers were translators who produced a wide range of literature to meet market demand. The market for information and culture was aided by a lack of copyright protection and by censorship toleration. Other information production and networking increases can be attributed to a significant growth in the number, size, and diversity of modern university and public libraries. In addition, literature began appealing to new classes of Latin and vernacular readers interested in a new literary genre, the various self-expressive forms of writing in which unique authorial personalities explained their beliefs. Most importantly, behind this push of information commodification was a new social epistemology of individualism and liberation, which, a century later, would blend the political, the rational, the economic, the scientific, and the production of information into the creation of an "enlightened," if not more "intelligent," middle-class culture.

The human model of intelligence had far greater impact on Renaissance culture than its divine – human version. For instance, it supported the development of capital and individual authority by frequently being cited as the basis of entrepreneurialism. As we shall see, the argument was relatively simple: intelligent people created "special" or "profitable" knowledge. Although written accounts of entrepreneurialism differ, they nearly unanimously reflect the creation of a unique sixteenth-century *exploitative* intelligence, a way of thinking in which an explorer's or inventor's "superior" or adventuresome mind, together with his knowledge and use of technology, guaranteed unlimited riches and respect. Regardless of who they were – Columbus, Bacon, Descartes, Montaigne, Newton, Pascal, Magellan, Locke, Burton, Galileo, or thousands of less known individuals – the marriage of a humanized intelligence – the quality that makes us human – to new ways of discovering entrepreneurially revealed truth reflects the cultural power of this new *economy of intelligence*.

The human model of intelligence also helped to institutionalize many new political, economic, and class system ideas, those advanced most notably by social philosophers like Bacon, Hobbes, and Locke. The power of this new model of intelligence becomes apparent by virtue of the fact that we cannot, in contemporary times, conceive of intelligence as being anything other than a human attribute, unlike the Greeks, and by the fact that the modern political economy is maintained by institutional practices based, in part, on various notions and activities based on differences in human intelligence. These practices, moreover, are schematically consistent with the architecture of class-based hegemonies.

Before proceeding I would like to define two important terms. First off, I use the term capitalism to refer to a complex and abstract system of continually dynamic value responsible, in part, for the creation of the merchant, industrial, and information society, and historical alliances forged among them. The creation of capital consists of value productions implicit in the creation of "rational work practices . . . work discipline," "a mass working class," "market exchange," "object or service as pure commodity . . . a combination of acquisitive individualism, a "rational view of the productive process," and "colonial expansion" (Johnson, 1996, pp. 7–10). My second term, the nation state, refers to potentially "coercion-wielding organizations that . . . exercise clear priority . . . over all organizations within substantial territories . . . [whose] structure of power exists in a large, contiguous population" and consists of "relatively powerful, centralized, and differentiated sovereign organizations" (Tilly, 1990, pp. 1–2). Clark and Dear (1984, p. 4) argue that the modern nation state is derived "from the economic and political imperatives of capitalist commodity production. *The state is ultimately implicated in the generation and distribution of surplus value as it seeks to sustain its own power and wealth.*" These definitions are essential to understanding the modern emergence and social deployment of ideas of intelligence, concepts not simply housed in the vacuum of abstract science, but invented and institutionalized by bureaucratic, social, and clinical practices. My interest in capitalism and the nation state is driven by a curiosity as to how social systems are constructed and what determines their dynamic behaviors. Lastly, the term the Renaissance *economy of intelligence* refers to interrelated knowledge formations and practices whereby traditional ideas and information were transformed into new contexts through various ideational collaboration. My use of the word discourse refers to these formations, to assemblages of ideas and writing that uniquely create knowledge and power systems.

The Renaissance reordering of earlier notions of intelligence, knowledge, and nature and the human helped to invent middle-class wealth and profitability, which, in turn, created new resources and trade, laying the basis for later industrial expansion. This discourse of recontextualization, of shared and repurposed knowledge underlying the Renaissance economy of intelligence, was also largely responsible for an unprecedented increase in the production and consumption of goods and services presumably requiring even greater intelligence to sustain that energy. Or so the arguments went.

By the end of the era, Renaissance ideas of intelligence became ideological, more a matter of function than fate, arching across ancient skies animated by celestial forces and landing upon the new rational soil of European culture, where intelligence was something empirical and eventually measurable. This is no capital without measurement. The next chapter concentrates on how Renaissance ideas of intelligence operated within the first *economy of intelligence* to support the growing institutionalization of ideas related to invention, discovery, capital, and commercialization. Part of the success of this new economy can be attributed to the deployment of rational methods, the power of scientific "certainty," and the use of mathematics and instrumentation. This becomes obvious when we realize that it is literally inconceivable to think that modern notions of intelligence, validated by scientific and institutional practices, would be possible without the production of a knowledge system that developed measurement technologies to achieve "true" certitude.

3 The First *Smart* Economy

An analysis of the economic, business, educational, and institutional practices of Renaissance Europe suggests that many writers appropriated new concepts of intelligence in the same manner they understood capital. Both are open-ended tropes, with each having sufficient metaphoric malleability to assure the production of new meanings. Moreover, Renaissance ideas of intelligence functioned as diamond-like assets, with artists, intellectuals, writers, and entrepreneurs using its wealth-promising facets, which, in turn, illuminate the growing power of entrepreneurialism. No longer strictly metaphysical, intelligence became a human attribute that could be invested in, treasured, and understood as both a divine gift and a human asset. The Baconian and Hobbesian idea that unrestricted freedom given to the intelligent would improve the fortunes of the many became a popular one, finding its greatest expression in the utilitarian industrial world of Bentham and Mill. Arguably the most significant role new ideas of intelligence played in the Renaissance was the accumulation of unprecedented capital created by various investments in presumed materializations of intelligence.

The growth of Renaissance capital can be attributed to several factors: to abundant trade routes that increased silver and gold bullion production and importation; to the development of centralized banks that created money markets and maritime credit; and to private merchant bankers (Peruzzi, Medici, and Fuggers) who proved instrumental in mercantile expansion. Increased entrepreneur capital also came from the invention of modern stock exchanges, more capital distribution centers, and improved production processes. But arguably, as significant as the growth of access to capital was to the success of Renaissance culture, so too were those early steps toward the creation of national governments that operated as "collectors and redistributors of revenue," offered increased property protection, and established a centralized and controllable monetary system (Earle, 1989, p. 26). Robert Duplessis (1997, p. 10) attributes the development of Renaissance capital to asset and credit creation, to "landlords and tenant farmers who dispossessed impoverished aristocrats and peasants . . . [to] merchants who crushed artisan guilds, and [to] merchants and adventurers who operated the lucrative slave trade, exploited or outright looted colonies and practiced usury." These entrepreneurs "were assisted by government laws, monopolies, taxes and debts, far from the state being a brake on or enemy of capitalism."

There is a significant connection between modern ideas of intelligence and the state sponsorship of methods for capital accumulation, activities, laws, and policies helping fledgling governments to recover from internal instability or foreign unrest. For arguably the first time state-supported capitalism created a class whose wealth and control of knowledge separated inventors, thinkers, and the intelligentsia from peasant and artisan classes. This fact explains why knowing how market capitalism operates is not simply about economic performances – a Fortune 500 company's profit forecast not meeting street expectations – but is also about how different production dynamics operate, especially with regard to relationships between capital and labor (Prak, 2001, p. 17). The history of modern ideas of intelligence (content and institutional practices) can be traced to the creation of the modern state, to increased support for capital access, and to the emergence of a new "intelligent" class whose "genius" ultimately helped to generate that capital. This relationship between the Renaissance humanization of intelligence, the evolution of capitalism, and the invention of the modern state is intriguing.

While these factors helped to contribute to a capitalist economy, their primary impact was to put a premium on the cultivation, production, and management of new ideas. In fact, the growing demand for greater intelligence reveals certain similarities between Renaissance ideas of intelligence and the very fundamental nature of capitalism. Hernando De Soto (2000, p. 5) argues that "capital . . . creates the wealth of nations" because it is "the lifeblood of the capitalist system, the foundation of progress." Capital is more than material wealth; it is part of a "representational process" whereby assets (equipment, property, and ideas) are "represented in a property document that is the visible sign of a vast hidden process that connects all these assets to the rest of the economy" (ibid., pp. 6–7). The solving of the "mystery" of capital

requires an understanding of why Westerners, by representing assets with titles, are able to see and draw out capital from them. One of the greatest challenges to the human mind is to comprehend and to gain access to those things we know exist but cannot see. Not everything that is real and useful is tangible and visible. Time, for example, is real, but it can only be efficiently managed when it is represented by a clock or a calendar. Throughout history, human beings have invented representational systems . . . to grasp with the mind what human hands could never touch. In the same way, the great practitioners of capitalism . . . were able to reveal and extract capital where others saw only junk by devising new ways to represent the invisible potential that is locked up in the assets we accumulate. (Ibid., p. 7)

That capital is part of a "representational system" enabling individuals to invent an economy based on abstract value explains, in part, why an era that invented capital would have to characterize humanized intelligence in somewhat similar terms. Nor is it surprising that Renaissance ideas of intelligence were heavily metaphoric. Abstract ideas, by their nature, are metaphoric. What is different, however, is how Renaissance thinkers used the implicit capital-like economy of metaphor to define intelligence in terms of capital, assets, profits, gifts, investments, abundance, resources, consumption, deficits, and dividends: hence I have coined the term "economy of intelligence."

These metaphoric associations have continued for the past five hundred years. But more importantly, they were not an accident of history or merely coincidental. As suggested earlier, the word "intelligence" has always been more a metaphor than a concrete term describing an actual physical phenomenon. Intelligence has always been a metaphor, and what it has signified, like celestial angels, capital, or information, must remain invisible. And as Renaissance assets were created by their inscription in such documents as deeds, ledgers, contracts, and accounts – activities extracting the visible and valuable from a bank-like invisible – so too have post-Renaissance, more modern inscriptions of intelligence produced statistical tables, instruments, experiments, and demonstrations. In materializing the invisible, these documents literally construct some measure of a human asset. De Soto's idea that "one of the greatest challenges to the human mind is to comprehend and to gain access to those things we know exist but cannot see" could also serve as a motto for psychometricians, research psychologists, IQ test-makers, and clinicians, whose measuring of intelligence renders visible something that "unquestionably" exists but remains invisible. Moreover, intelligence tests are like the world of capital in that they too are constituted as a complex representation system, operating as a microcosm of all the values implicit in notions of standardization, rationality, reasoning, and logic.

There are other ways in which intelligence and capital have been culturally related because of Renaissance ideology. Both, for instance, are valuable because they make manifest a latent asset, a similarity operating in the human resource world of modern corporations. Fortune 500 companies are as busy harvesting "intellectual" or "intelligence" capital as they are deploying front-end and back-end "intelligent knowledge systems" to increase their "corporate IQ . . . the measure of how easily your company can share information broadly and of how well people . . . can build on each other's ideas" (Gates, 1999, p. 239). And in such recent works as *In Good Company: How Social Capital Makes Organizations Work, The Social Life of Information,* and *The Springboard: How Storytelling Ignites Action in Knowledge-era Organizations,* postmodern gurus pitch the virtue of making intelligence visible. Software applications – especially "killer" apps – automate intelligence in order to make visible what was previously incomprehensible. According to the Velosel corporation, its software application can produce "business intelligence":

> Insight into product data and product information processes is a must for making well-informed, timely business decisions. Information from Velosel5 can provide important data related to process improvement and enforcement, the identification of bottlenecks, and visibility into customer activity. Velosel5 can also make data available to existing reporting tools, thus simplifying the user experience and contributing to the ROI of these tools. (www.velosel.com/solutions/#integration)

It is no accident that Renaissance writers conceived of and constructed intelligence in terms of a capital asset given the fact that the emerging myth of individualism began to dominate Renaissance culture by promoting a political economy backed by a mercantile class of prosperous families. This major ideological transition would have been impossible without the creation of a new economic system driven by collaborations of individual efforts, international banking, the rise of city-states, mercantile enterprise, and military inventiveness, with intelligence – meaning both genius and strategic knowledge – becoming essential to those efforts. The rise of a merchant, artisan, and shopkeeper class is tied directly to the economic "logic" of individualism. The late agrarian Middle Ages had already seen significant peasant migrations. The poor knew where to seek wealth and the greater social freedom it promised. With improvements in communication and trade, typical citizens frequently challenged the status quo and began producing new charters, new laws, and new governmental roles, the three having a significant effect on the relationship between conceptions of individualism and ways of doing businesses. What brought new groups of merchants into power were not only their trading experiences with new cultures, but also the wealth made from Asian and American expeditions. Interestingly enough, this new class invented a new value standard: the accumulation of capital ultimately replaced the sanctity of property that for hundreds of years guaranteed aristocratic wealth and power.

This new merchant class also believed that, rather than being an accident, wealth production was the result of hard work and individual excellence. In fact, their often self-validating rhetoric reveals that their native business "intelligence" had a good deal more to do with success than did the inherited wealth of the landed gentry. This new class delivered the individualism touted by artists, philosophers, and scientists into a core cultural value, with an individual's ability to change the world the mantra of modernism. They became well known through their exploits, with the most notable – those like Paolo da Certaldo, Giovanni di Pagolo Morelli, Bonaccorso Pitti, Donato Velluti, and Lorenzo de' Medici – the authors of many "how to" autobiographies, texts outlining strategies for how self-capitalization and individual intelligence could lead to wealth accumulation. Their claim to authority was part of the unique discourse of recontextualization, a reformatting of the old into the new.

The merchant class was not alone in pushing the earliest form of capitalistic individualism. The first instance of its institutional support appears in several events, particularly with the English Statute of Monopolies in 1624, followed by the Copyright Act of 1710, both actions indicating a parliamentary willingness to accord the same legal protection to productions of intelligence that was given to physical property. European law sanctioned productions of intelligence, regardless of whether they were abstract or concrete ideas like van Drebbel's submarine (1620), Brunelleschi's clock (1418), fifteenth-century war rockets, Gutenberg's printing press (1450), Boyle's match (1662), Janssen's microscope (1595), or improvements made to the air pump, navigational chronometers, or the telescope.

As an economic force, the "intelligence – entrepreneurial alliance" also created virtual productions that ultimately defined *superior* intelligence in terms of what that intelligence created or produced. This construct parallels the expanded meanings given to intelligence during the sixteenth and seventeenth centuries. For instance, the *Oxford English Dictionary* defines intelligence as "a faculty of understanding," a "degree of superior understanding" or "quickness of mental apprehension" – yet adds the new late sixteenth-century definition of an "interchange of knowledge or information." This new meaning represents the modernization of the metaphor of intelligence, connecting "superior" thinking, knowledge, and information to *interchanges* or *exchanges* of commercial, military, and religious activities, this in an age in which the chance for profit brought merchant-class entrepreneurs together with those producing commercial art and technologies. The linkage of intelligence to information production also explains the more modern ideological habit of relating intelligence to "business." The multimillion dollar business of IQ testing and the billions made from various post-1990s Madison Avenue "smart" campaigns (e.g. the making of water "smart"), the hiring of corporate intellectual capitalists, and the making of films about misunderstood, tragic, or even psychotic "geniuses" reinforce how intelligence, information production, and capitalism have cooperated during the past four hundred years. More importantly, the most central of all unexamined contemporary assumptions about intelligence – that a person's intelligence level is proportionate to his or her potential productivity or wealth generation – has its earliest footprint in Renaissance linkages of superior knowledge to information production and capital gain.

As with any idea, the Renaissance economy of intelligence existed within a larger knowledge dynamic. For instance, intelligence became fully modern when it became a primarily *individualized* attribute, garnering divine respect for *smart* individuals whose *superior* insights produced institutional, national, and business advantages for an individual. Research indicates that the growing praise given to genius eventually knew no Renaissance limits given the fact that the economy of intelligence ultimately formed ideological partnerships between natural law and human agency theories, ideas creating a co-privileging of the empirical and human "nature." This partnership also tended to subject medieval philosophy and Papal orthodoxy to the growing scrutiny of reason. As ideas of intelligence and reason began to be more intertwined, seeds were sown for initiatives that would eventually help to shape the content of modern thought. This intertwining may also explain why popular culture continues to define genius in terms of a supernatural-like inventiveness, or why clinicians continue to assess the level of intelligence in terms of a person's abstract reasoning abilities. The marriage of intelligence with the reasoning implicit in the scientific method ideologically prepares the way for abstract mathematical, geometrical, logical, and semantic reasoning to define the totality of cognition, this ordering eventually becoming content criteria for contemporary intelligence "tools."

Western culture arguably became modern when its social epistemology linked the humanization of intelligence to Cartesianism and the scientific method, its goal being the unraveling and mending of the "irrational" basis of religious orthodoxy. The zealousness of the new appreciation for reason and the scientific method is illustrated in Henry Power's *Experimental Philosophy* (originally published 1664):

This is the Age wherein (me-thinks) Philosophy comes in with a Spring-tide; and the Peripateticks may as well hope to stop the Current of the Tide, or (with Xerxes) to fetter the Ocean, as hinder the overflowing of free Philosophy: Me-thinks, I see how all the old Rubbish must be thrown away, and the rotten Buildings be overthrown, and carried away with so powerful an Inundation. (Power, 1966, p. 26)

The Renaissance economy of intelligence, as I shall show, had a significant role in promoting the "overflowing of free Philosophy."

This new economic epistemology was driven by the idea that human intelligence could liberate the mind from superstition and the repression of orthodox authority. Although there are many examples of this reasoning, none may prove more representative than an idea presented in Locke's *Essay Concerning Human Understanding* (1690). Like other seventeenth-century philosophers, Locke pits empirically grounded ideas against conventional religious thought, challenging the logic of transcendental ideas by placing them in the material world of human behavior and the marketplace. With one eye looking back critically at Greek and medieval philosophy, and the other looking toward the promise of a new earthly Eden – as envisioned in Bacon's *New Atlantis* – Locke distinguishes two ways of doing the *business* of science; the first, unlike the second, is *worthless* because it is *unprofitable*:

> He that shall consider how little general maxims, precarious principles, and hypotheses laid down at pleasure, have promoted true knowledge, or helped to satisfy the inquiries of rational men after real improvements; how little, I say, the setting out at that end has, for many ages together, advanced men's progress, towards the knowledge of natural philosophy, will think we have reason to thank those who in this latter age have taken another course, and have trod out to us, though not an easier way to learned ignorance, yet a surer way to *profitable knowledge*. (Locke, 1975, chapter 12)

Locke's challenge to the authority of "learned ignorance" and his endorsement of "profitable knowledge" underscores the ideological nature of new Renaissance ideas about intelligence. In Locke's scheme those who create "general maxims" and "precarious principles" cannot produce natural world wealth, a well received idea in a culture whose focus on the material triggered significant socioeconomic transformations. Locke's notion of profitable knowledge reveals how intelligence, thought and knowledge began to be metaphors for new resources and commodity production. And, as we know, commodities must be assigned a demand value before they are produced, gathered, stored, measured, accounted for, and sold if profits are to be made. Most of these steps are nearly identical to how modern notions of intelligence are understood and assessed. During the past five hundred years, ideas and demonstrations of intelligence have taken various forms as a commodity.

Conceptually, "profitable knowledge" represents a consolidation of ideological elements binding ideas of intelligence with those about knowledge, increased revenues, welfare, economic advancement, and profit. Moreover, this consolidation triggered new ways of thinking about the nature of truth, value, and human social purpose. Margaret C. Jacob overviews its cultural effects:

> By 1700 scientific knowledge could offer uniform and universal knowledge about nature. . . . Yet precisely at that moment when these extraordinary conceptual tools came "on the market," the marketplace had dramatically expanded. After the mid-seventeenth century as Europeans traded, explored, conquered, or enslaved in new places amid new peoples, their mental universe became more complex. Non-Western peoples challenged ingrained assumptions about human nature or the universality of belief in a monotheistic deity. For the same elites who consumed science, commerce also brought unprecedented supplies of capital and encouraged applied science, which in turn promoted inventiveness. By 1780, first in Britain, capital and *ingenuity* [emphasis added] promoted industrial development, the application of machine technology to mining, transportation and manufacturing. After 1700 and largely before 1800 all Western peoples discovered more worlds, natural, geographic, technological, cultural, or simply human than had never been the case before or since. (Jacob, 1997, p. 60)

Jacob explains how the supply of venture capital for scientific and technological advances transformed commerce into an ideological language, a way of signifying meaning. In addition, the enterprising energy of Renaissance culture, with its remarkable production of new knowledge, required that new ideas of intelligence be formed in such a way as to be consistent with the message of new ideological content. Decidedly *human* notions of intelligence had to be aligned with the ideas about the autonomous individual, certainly more so than prior intelligence models, this in an age busy laying the groundwork for modern notions of social reality, individual authority, and the authority of reason. This new economy not only helped to construct a new ideology, it also supported a new knowledge system that challenged the bedrock of prior cultural thought. Traditionally divine or metaphysical models of intelligence were inconsistent with the basis of this new socioeconomic economy and its science. In essence, they were simply unable to advance the new enterprise of individuality, or to be recruited and recontextualized, to champion the emerging epistemological revolution. Before exploring how the economy of intelligence circulated during the Renaissance, I would like to briefly outline the conditions that enabled its creation, then to define its nature and explore the significant role that the "intelligencer" played in promoting the new economy. The term is a good example of how ideas of individualism, the production of capital, and new notions of intelligence coalesced ideologically during the Renaissance. The Renaissance economy of intelligence took form as ideological coalitions driven by the rise of market capitalism, the creation of new economic theories, and the evolution of new scientific methods. These coalitions took form as new knowledge clusters appropriated from physics, moral theology, optics, classical mechanics, calculus, and economics, with part of their effect being distinctions between "superior" and "inferior" kinds of intelligence. Moreover, the alliance between Renaissance art and new economic ideas, both praising the human and the individual, began to transform the ideological map of Western culture, creating different idea environments in which intelligence and genius were transposed into "profitable" human activities.

4 Renaissance Intellectual Trends

Historians have constructed various models of Renaissance intellectual culture by concentrating on ideas like autonomous individuality, secularism, naturalism, humanistic idealism, and the scientific method. What are missing in these works are demonstrations of how certain patterns, sustained by new ideas of nature, a new cosmological topography, and the production of experimental methods, essentially created a new science of "social utility" (McClellan and Dorn, 1999, p. 203) central to an economy of intelligence. Most Renaissance knowledge alliances, driven by notions of entrepreneurialism and social utility, reason, observation, and measurement, proclaimed a stability unavailable in prior religious systems. This ideology tooled an epistemology based upon new inquires into consciousness and the invention of a self-reflective, analytic subject whose measuring of the world achieved absolute truth. Arguably, this construct was the most significant production of Renaissance culture. Its alliance with empirical theory and the new science helped to develop new ways of thinking about human intelligence, creating methods that transformed elements of individuality into *objective* criteria. Within a century, these methods were institutionalized as social practices regulating new state controlled venues of power, authority, and rights.

This new epistemology transformed prior notions of celestial intelligence into the virtual flesh and blood of a human and *measurable* characteristic. And to do so, it subverted classical religious thought that had ideologically prevented humans from trusting their own minds to create certainty. *Human intelligence became the agent for this certitude.*

What makes Renaissance cultural ideology unique is how its emerging economy of intelligence produced new information and knowledge technologies and strategies. Although heralded as the age of individual "genius," the Renaissance signals the unprecedented cooperation between newly invented information networks, mostly material, but some virtual. Individuals and organizations that understood relationships between information and wealth carved new channels for capitalizing upon scientific and technological knowledge. By 1700, systematic scientific deconstructions of classical ideas of the universe, nature, and society were being performed on an international stage and in different languages that attracted audiences of the well educated as well as growing numbers of entrepreneurs and merchants. The Renaissance saw the emergence of a new economy and consumer class fascinated by the potential value of insight, innovation, and knowledge. One strategy to understand this process is to replace customary metaphors with an effort to explore the ideological significance of its material productions, concentrating on how certain inventions and practices nurtured an economy of intelligence that increased information production and dissemination: *an age that recognized the value of information, and capitalized upon it, did not ignore the potential material value of the intelligence that produced it.* In essence, the Renaissance not only invented a new form of being – the individual and his or her potential – it also assigned commercial and aesthetic value to information. The role different ideas of intelligence played in that culture cannot be understood without first knowing what part they played in the construction and success of a radically new ideology.

Trend 1: The First Culture of Individualism

The political dynamics of Renaissance culture helps to explain how new ideas of intelligence contributed to the emergence of Renaissance individualism. The Renaissance, like any historical era, was constituted by several unique transformations and contestations of competing authority systems. These changes came about, in part, through increases in academic disciplines, with each claiming its own authority to know the world in new and radical ways. A second cause was Rome's inability to answer the moral challenges posed by the rise of a mercantile culture. These two changes can, in turn, be attributed to the gradual socioeconomic, political, and scientific effects of Ockhamism, with its emphasis on empirical deductive methodologies, and the confluent disarray of the Papacy and Empire. In fact, tracing the sociopolitical dynamics of medieval and early Renaissance authority suggests that the cultural authority of past pillars of *Christianitas* began to be claimed by new institutions and arguments made by a class of highly regarded individuals. The Renaissance marks the first historical period in which a concentration of individuals, instead of institutions, claimed modes of truth to oppose Papal and local authority.

The roster of these new authoritative individuals constitutes a virtual *who's who* in the Renaissance: Bacon, Bayle, late Renaissance Protestant reformers, Copernicus, Dante, Rodiana, Melanchthon, Bruno, Erasmus, Elizabeth I, Ficino,

Galileo, Hobbes, da Vinci, Guillard, and Montaigne, many of whom centered their claims of truth on the dovetailing of reason with the idea of *self-evident* truths. Montaigne, in fact, went so far as to argue that to truly understand human nature he would need only to study one individual – himself. Not an easy task, given the protean nature of the self. Montaigne, moreover, may have been the first to tackle the problem of describing how human intelligence operates: "a spirited mind never stops within itself; it is always aspiring and going beyond its strength . . . its pursuits boundless" (Montaigne, 1968, p. 244). Although not very scientific, Montaigne constructs this intellectual drive in terms of an inherent nature, a quality echoed by Bacon in his *Novum Organum* when he suggests that "human understanding is unquiet; it cannot stop or rest, and still presses onward, but in vain. Therefore it is that we cannot conceive of any end or limit to the world, but always as of necessity it occurs to us that there is something beyond" (Bacon, 1960, Book 1, p. 48). Needless to say, reason, rational methods, and self-evident produced truths posed a significant threat to established religious power. This threat took the form of a simple question: why would individuals need the Church to establish truth when they could simply use their own innate intelligence to discover it, much in the same way that individualized copies of the Bible allowed readers to interpret it without the need for officially sanctioned institutional readings.

The idea of self-evident truth – critical to the new epistemology and economics of intelligence – arose from prior representations, primarily that of an "autonomous self-creator" evident in many religious and scientific discourses. The authority of the individual was part of a shift in philosophical interest in the sixteenth century, when the primary philosophical emphasis on the phenomenal world – as a reflection of divine truth – shifted to greater interest in specific epistemological questions. For instance, the paradox of how imperfect human beings can know divine perfection was raised repeatedly, as were questions about how humans could know the source of absolute truth. Recognition of this shift is critical to an understanding of how certain cultural modes of power operated within discursive alliances, particularly those that capitalized upon this new authority. Once knowledge became something that an individual could examine and verify in terms of "objective" methods, the idea of individuality authored and entered a new ideological system consisting of parallel ideas like consciousness, subjectivity, personal reflection, and, of course, intelligence, the driver of individuality. By the mid-seventeenth century intelligence became a means of differentiating and separating individuals while producing new social strata; the source of those differences was internal and unique, something to be explored and classified.

Assessing pre-Renaissance notions of the individual will help to establish a context for understanding why Renaissance versions of it represent such a radical

43

departure and why the construction of *human* intelligence played such a decisive role in the construction of modern individualism. Greek, Roman, and Medieval notions of personality and identity – grounded within a theocentric cosmology, the divinity of the human soul and reason, and the moral repudiation of the flesh – came under Renaissance attack with the advent of Augustinianism and nominalism. Together, these two ideas helped to organize a different epistemology in which the senses and interior human emotions became ways of knowing the world. According to Bouwsma, Augustinianism in particular "contributed to the disintegration of hierarchical conceptions in all domains of thought . . . to an emphasis on time, change, and history, and to a growing concern with action and social responsibility" (Bouwsma, 2000, p. 22). Moreover, Augustinianism had two important effects on pre-Renaissance representations of the self: although it reaffirmed that the self was a discrete faculty in a hierarchy of faculties, it also advanced

> a very different conception of the self: doubts of the value and power of reason and a blurring of the boundaries between the several supposedly distinguishable faculties arranged in order below it, language implying a view of the self as a mysterious and undifferentiated unity, its quality a reflection of another faculty previously recognized, the heart. (Ibid., p. 22)

These factors contributed to a significant invention: for the first time in Western culture a human being did not exist solely in terms of a cosmologically based hierarchy. In fact, this emerging non-hierarchical human, which we often associate with various hybrids of Romanticism, existentialism, and post-structuralism, had its origins in the Renaissance construction of the self.

One effect of this activity was the construction of new representations of how ideas of the body, the mind, the spirit, reason, and the soul were related. In this process, the spotlight was directed toward the human and human sensory knowledge, especially sight and hearing, with sight being the "noblest" of the senses that would later become the mascot metaphor for the Enlightenment. The spirit of such a transformation is evident in the *Novum Organum*, a text devoted to the "the kindling of light in the darkness of philosophy," the elevation of human creativity to near divine heights.

Historians have traced the sources of modern individualism to the age of Petrarch and Boccaccio, to the Florentine Medici era with its aesthetic, commercial, and political inventiveness, and to the scientific and literary achievements of the mid and late Renaissance. There is no reason to repeat these points, except to say that perhaps additional insight might be gained by exploring how its constitutive discursive elements, including intelligence, helped individualism to become the cornerstone concept of an emerging cultural orthodoxy. The scope of Renaissance individualism has quite a bandwidth. The bravado of Michelangelo's rushing into San Pietro's to carve his name upon the marble base of the Pietà because someone else was laying claim to it sharply contrasts with Cervantes's critique of the self-defeating imagination of extreme individualism in *The Ingenious Gentleman Don Quixote de la Mancha*. Although the word "ingenious" begins to be synonymous with intelligence in the seventeenth century, Cervantes is being ironic, using the cautionary metaphor to refer to excesses of unrealistic desires and inventions, an instance in a tradition that even in modern popular culture associates extreme genius with madness. This stereotype ultimately places social control over the presumed freedom given to the individual to produce.

Cultural historians often argue that the exuberance of Renaissance individualism was tempered by a fear of its extravagances. The archetype for this ambivalence was Prometheus, the thief who enlightens humanity by stealing divine intelligence. Although it violates a boundary, the theft is a gift of aspiration; it makes divine-like thought possible. This is Mirandola's message in his oration on human dignity: the intelligence of divine insight frees men to aspire to divinity. At the other extreme, the Promethean archetype is cautionary, its most demonic expressions those of irrational or insane desires. This theme is represented in Burton's *Anatomy of Melancholy*, Marlow's *Doctor Faustus*, and *Hamlet*, *Macbeth*, and *King Lear*, texts that dramatize the horror of misapplied intelligence and perverse ambition. In many of Shakespeare's tragedies, intelligence destroys intelligence, in that a character's mental superiority acquires vital information only to spin a plot of self-destruction. This pattern reveals that Renaissance culture was the first to associate superior intelligence with an evil we see later in such cautionary tales as *Frankenstein* and *Twenty Thousand Leagues Under the Sea*, or in hundreds of B movies or science fiction TV shows. These early stories warn us about thinkers, scientists, professors, and madmen whose superior intelligence glimpses another kind of intelligence, that of divine information, which produces something evil that then can only be righted by some natural or divine rebalancing or intercession.

These narratives ultimately reinscribe the basic message of Judeo-Christian culture, the story of the Fall, a story of violated boundaries in which the misappropriation of divine knowledge fathers death and time. Ron Howard's film *A Beautiful Mind* (2002) is a recent version of this narrative linking superior intelligence to insanity. Christopher Plummer's character, Dr Rosen, is the ultimate authority, a healer with a clearly ideological agenda. His is the unchallenged scientific authority that knows the difference between genius and delusion. His psychiatric effort and the film's point of view are far too busy reinscribing traditional ideological boundaries – particularly their validating of "objective" scientific knowledge – to see the significance of John Forbes Nash's delusions. Deluded as it may have been, Nash's schizophrenia deconstructs the psychological effects and politics of the Cold War, illuminating the insanity and paranoia of intelligence gathering methods, as well as the kind of world Cold War ideological tensions created. The methods he uses to construct his delusional narratives, his cutting of unrelated bits of popular media to fashion a coherent narrative composed of random fragments, is an ironic simulacrum, deconstruction and critique of the relationship between information and power during the Cold War. At his most psychotic moments, Nash creates a postmodern narrative that speaks the unspeakable, creating exaggerated stories that illuminate the madness engendered in the presumably sane world of espionage, mass atomic deaths, and fascistic intelligence agencies.

The dominance of the Promethean myth in Renaissance culture explains why Jacob Burckhardt argued that human beings became "spiritualized individuals." Burckhardt's classic but problematic argument assumes that the psychological is immune from the ideological, that it has no basis in either the creation or reflection of dominant modes of social power. His theory of why the Renaissance embraced individualism is based on the figure of the psychological exile, alienated by social instability, by a personal desire to produce private wealth, and by frequent threats of banishment. These factors, he argues, make exiles unique. He also argues that intolerable political and economic conditions spurred the development of exile colonies attracting those, like Florentine emigrants in Ferrara or the Lucchese in Venice, possessing unique ideas and personalities. A growing cosmopolitanism also allowed individuals to showcase their uniqueness. In the Italian Renaissance, individuality became a spiritual and material manifestation of some higher reality. Those mastering their cultures by becoming knowledgeable in many areas were identified as *l'uomo universale* because their intelligence and knowledge made them unique. The lure of social glory, admiration, and notoriety also contributed to productions of individuality, a common theme evident, for example, in Petrarch's *De vita solitaria* and "To Posterity." All this speaks to the fact that the emergence of individual "geniuses" was a primary cultural representation of Renaissance culture.

The spotlight placed on the individual and the unique in Renaissance culture also popularized activities related to self-discovery. Jules Michelet was the first to use the term "Renaissance" to describe the "discovery by man of himself and the world." One need only look to Dante's opening of the *Divine Comedy* ("in the middle of the journey of my life, in a dark wood, I found myself") as a primary indication of this Italian fascination with discovery. The popularity of self-discovery in art, science, and literature was an essential feature in the emergence of Renaissance humanism. It was a movement in which self-definition and self-discovery were important to those competing for positions within the existing framework of intellectual life and in such institutions as the courts, the universities, and the Church. Artistic forms of self-discovery and individual expression flourished because they were simply the primary media for self-definition. Boccaccio's *Biography of Petrarch* and Petrarch's autobiography exemplify these efforts, offering relevant models for the formation of ideological alliances made between the idea of humanism and various activities of self-discovery. Even the recovering of Greek culture was sustained by desires for self-discovery driven by humanistic ambitions. The popularity of self-discovery narratives and art also fueled interest in the natural world. Significant emphasis was placed on the visual in both the arts and sciences, with intelligence and observational methods, rather than religion, guiding the discovery of truth. Once truth was defined more as something a thinking individual perceived than as a divine force, ideas about intelligence became increasingly more useful for defining and mobilizing the production of self-discovered truths. Within a relatively short time, these assumptions took the historical stage as the source for truths that later became "self-evident" in many eighteenth-century political documents, including Jefferson's *Declaration of Independence*.

Trend 2: Humanism and the Individual

With its emphasis on self-discovery, individualism, realism, secularism, and science, humanism became a dominant force in Renaissance Europe, playing a significant role in producing the novel idea that intelligence was a unique human attribute as well as something that could be capitalized by converting knowledge into profit. Humanism began as a scholarly movement importing Byzantine collections of major Greek thinkers into Renaissance culture. This desire for a direct, non-mediated access to Greek thought, underwritten by the Medici family, guaranteed that scholars could access Greek versions of the "human," free from more officially authorized versions produced by Latin monks. Early archeologists excavating Greek and Roman art and ruins noted the humanity of Greek art. Whether recovered by scholars or archeologists, Greek cultural artifacts illuminated the power of human intelligence. For instance, scholars admired the intelligence manifested in the writings of exceptional minds. It took intelligence to decode and make sensible the meaning of Greek artifacts, and it took intelligence to deploy this new knowledge, placing it where its values could be most fully realized.

The excavation of Greek culture and the self-discovery it inspired led to wholesale imitations of Greek art and thought. In contrast to the flat and stylized iconography of the medieval period, many Renaissance artists followed Greek models by celebrating the natural lines of the human body, using their own self-expressiveness to imprint their private vision into their paintings, sculptures, architecture, and drawings. This interest in the human form served as the basis of Renaissance humanism, a movement that, in part, invented a dominant model of intelligence – its *divinely human* notion. It did so because its major tenet, the belief in human perfectability, held that humans possessed a divine-like intelligence, an idea evident in most of Ficino's work, as well as in Mirandola's *Dignity of Man*, Baldassare Castiglione's *Courtier*, Sir Thomas Elyot's *Governour*, and St Thomas More's *Utopia*. The following tenets of humanism underscore the popularity of a "noble" notion of intelligence: humans are capable of defining their own nature, and can fulfill nature's noblest potential; the human spirit is immortal; human society is better off living in an ideal commonwealth presided over by the ideal ruler; and the concept of an intellectual, asexual Platonic love is the highest form of pair bonding.

Humanism was a central force in the production of Renaissance individualism. Other ideas made similar contributions. For example, the gradual breakdown of the Church's authority inspired pride in local heritage and the affirmation of vernacular languages and dialectics. Moreover, the disintegration of the Holy Roman Empire created a vacuum of cultural standards, leaving the door open for the development of new standards centered upon the limits of "individual genius." Renaissance luminaries often speak to this new standard. In fact, when one speaks of Renaissance culture what come to mind are its inventors and artists, names or unique creations, rather than wars, social upheavals, or other typical historical signposts. Whether we are referring to the *Divine Comedy* or da Vinci or Newton, what become crystallized are representations of the intelligence that individuated a unique thinker, a consciousness celebrating its own grasp of complexity or an interior voice pursuing some "heroic" insight. And in some instances the consciousness that defined itself as an intelligence argued that it preceded existence itself. This is the case of the Cartesian *cogito* who "thinks" and, therefore, exists. Perhaps more than other idea, Descartes's proposition assigns a radical if not absolute privilege to human intelligence, a value that took many ideological trajectories over the next four hundred years.

Trend 3: Other Forces Shaping the Myth of Individualism

Other forces made individualism the ideological cornerstone of modernism. The expansion of the middle and merchant classes and increases in artisan and shopkeeper populations were economic manifestations of this new individualism, as well as those who, supported by early versions of venture capitalists, became *heroes* as their expeditions entered the New World and encountered presumably unlimited riches. All of these forces were, in part, either initiated or supported by the invention of new scientific methods and technologies, productions that tended to privilege intelligence and observational skills as tools for discovering the truth. Renaissance education produced students who represented the ideal of this authoritative individual, the self-educated whose infinite intellectual curiosity and wealth of knowledge could combine to produce a "genius."

Renaissance culture was fascinated with the relationships between vision, observation, dreams, and insight. Numerous texts explore how observations or lyrical dreams allow individuals to claim various kinds of universal power. What becomes clear is the dominance of the idea that the human imagination competes with, complements or replaces divine inspiration. Cases exist in which self-proclaimed "geniuses" argued that the air is no more than a stage full of images, or that their artistic challenge was to liberate a human form trapped inside a block of marble. In an era of profound individuality, no dream was impossible and the voyage motif took vagabonds to the moon (Ariosto), to the edges of the earth (Columbus), or to the unexplored and seemingly infinite caverns of the self, often represented as a new kind of terrestrial or sub-terrestrial space (Burton or Dante). In the Renaissance, the identity of "mankind" was transformed from that of a fallen spirit to that of a fabricator. This reorientation produced a maker, an artist, and a thinker who had the power to observe, dissect, analyze, measure, invent, and discover ideas of time, eternity, the human body, the earth, the distance between planets, and the human intellect. This reorientation, moreover, gave enormous significance to the source of those powers: human intelligence.

New kinds of information and production strategies are two other pieces, along with individualism, that explain why new ideas of intelligence were so critical to the success of the myth of individualism. Information production provided the means by which new productions of intelligence were materialized, circulated, commodified, and placed in public discourse. One of the distinguishing features of Renaissance culture was its invention of new modes of information production, in terms not only of the increase in those who could produce information, but also of how information was disseminated, the first being a matter of innovation, the second a matter of delivery technologies. The growing recognition that science could be a profession, for instance, not only encouraged more people to become publishing scientists, but also accompanied increased government and private support for scientific and technological endeavors. The Renaissance science of Descartes and Newton produced new alliances between emerging industries and scientists. Scientific societies, public schools, and literacy rates increased rapidly. Orthodox religion was left out of the new information loop because it could not compete; it could not provide the means for creating and delivering information to professional societies, journals, and guilds or to a new class of consumers interested in new ideas and technological innovations. No means existed for Church authority to have forecast this market-driven increase in information demand and production, since its principal information product was limited to scriptural discourse. Religious institutions simply could not keep up with the demands of a new reading public. Nor did universities that were largely church-controlled develop new centers of scientific knowledge. In fact, European universities were not the centers of scientific activity but centers of opposition to new ideas of nature. Scientists interested in nature had to develop independent venues far from the political reaches of the university. This opposition opened the door for private individuals and new organizations to support growing interests in scientific enterprise.

The invention of new modes of information production complemented new ways of inventing information. For instance, we cannot underestimate the role advances in print technology (cheaper production costs and greater market access to printed materials), ideas in economic theory, new commodity market practices, new institutionalizations of information (such as libraries and universities), and new forms of writing played in delivering "genius" to a growing consumer class. The mass production of books with large audience appeal and increased productions of original manuscripts and translations was supported by an abundance of investment capital and fervor requisite to the development of the print industry. For example, in 1533 John Leland became Henry VIII's "King Antiquary" and was given capital to search for classical manuscripts in convents, colleges, and monasteries, enlightenment that could turn a handsome profit.

As early as 1400, printing became a modern business, with book dealers and entrepreneurs commodifying information by creating new kinds of inventory (ready-to-sell manuscripts versus production-on-demand methods), fabricating new modern book distribution supply and distribution channels, and lowering information production costs by producing cheaper books. In some British cases, as with William Caxton (1422–91), Wynkyn de Worde, Richard Pynson, and Robert Copland, printers who were translators produced a wide range of literature to meet market demands. The market for information and culture was also indirectly assisted by a lack of copyright protection and growing toleration by censors.

The Renaissance also saw dramatic increases in the institutional mobilization of information. Modern universities increased their number and sizes, and public libraries increased the diversity and amount of their holdings. In addition, literature in those institutions began appealing to new classes of Latin and vernacu-

lar readers. In contrast to earlier epic or religious literature, Renaissance literature developed various self-expressive forms of first person narratives of belief.
Moreover, a strong tradition of rhetoric called the *ars dictaminis*, used in the production of textbooks and formularies, was used to train secretaries and future
notaries, who constituted an increasingly literate class of citizens. This method
assisted them in composing private and public documents, as well as speeches,
in both Latin and the vernacular.

The production and dissemination of cultural intelligence had other information production venues. By the sixteenth century, Western Europe had many
major publishing centers, including Frankfurt, Venice, Basel, Antwerp, London,
Lyons, and Prague. There were numerous international book fairs and scholarly
conferences dealing with the publication of various patristic and classical texts.
Book title catalogues had also been invented. Increases in literacy supported
more profitable book publications, evident by virtue of the fact that

> between the introduction of the printing press in the mid-fifteenth century and the
> end of the sixteenth, some 28,000 works appeared; in France alone close to a thou-
> sand titles were being published every year. . . . As better texts appeared, philolog-
> ical scholarship rapidly advanced and ancient writings were translated into the
> various vernaculars, further diffusing classical culture. (Goldthwaite, 1995, p. 15)

In addition, national governments began to realize the political value of print.
Standard law books and collections of statutes, for instance, were widely made
available to local judges. In addition, royal edicts and official opinions were now
being circulated among the lower classes.

The Renaissance also saw the standardization of printing techniques and new
sources that together created and popularized new kinds of literature. For
instance, instruction manuals and travel literature became popular because they
repeatedly demonstrated the human capacity to reduce the element of chance
in human affairs, often with an author speaking directly to his imaginary reader.
Books became more standardized, with the use of numbered pages, consistent
punctuation, running heads, indexes, standard page organizations, and other features providing the reader with a sense of spatial and textual order. Bacon knew
that books were intelligence delivery systems. There are several instances in the
Advancement of Learning that discuss how discourse allows for the aggregation
and trafficking of ideas that eventually formed cultural belief systems, especially
since books provide space for the production of individual and collective
intelligence.

Many institutional practices began to be standardized, the goal being to
protect what individuals produced. The concept of intellectual property rights,

guaranteed by patents and copyrights, emerged during the Renaissance, reflecting a growing awareness that human intelligence could be put to practical use and that as long as new discoveries went unnoticed their potential profit would remain unrealized. The first official patent record was issued to Filippo Brunelleschi by the Council of Florence in 1421 for his cargo ship design. The first patent law, by contrast, was established in Venice in 1474, its logic being the economy of intelligence, a means by which superior minds produced knowledge and "ingenious devices":

> we have among us men of great genius, apt to invent and discover ingenious devices; and in view of the grandeur and virtue of our City, more such men come to us every day from divers parts. Now if provision were made for the works and devices discovered by such persons, so that others who may see them could not build them and take the inventor's honor away, more men would then apply their genius, would discover, and would build devices of great utility and benefit to our commonwealth. (www.classes.lls.edu/fall2001/biotech/ppt/patent1.ppt)

The statute recognized the social utility of patents as a means to protect intellectual property, a virtual economic idea essential to developing and exploiting technological knowledge.

The invention of individualism, the creation of more opportunities for self-expression and knowledge production, and advanced methods of information dissemination, storage, and application all underscore the growing significance that new models of intelligence played in the development of the cultural intelligence of the Renaissance. In summary, intelligence began to be recognized as a means to create wealth and power, with individual genius an economic potential and social utility that could reward both the nation state and its innovative citizens. Renaissance ideas of intelligence also supported sixteenth-century scientific and philosophical ideas, especially those whose claim of certitude subverted traditional authority, and, in the process, reinforced the new epistemology of individualism. Before exploring Renaissance philosophy and science, I would like to suggest that the ideological success of the new Renaissance myth based on the *autonomous self-creator* came from interdisciplinary Renaissance discourse. Literary, scientific, and philosophical texts, essays, and treatises gained additional authority by having their central ideas supported by different disciplinary and metaphoric linkages. This happened at both single and multidisciplinary levels of idea production. For example, scientific and philosophical theories were often interrelated, with their concerns ideological in nature. Stephen Gaukroger (1995, p. 135) notes quite rightly that Descartes's "philosophical achievements are much more intimately linked to his interest in what subsequently have been considered 'scientific' questions than is commonly realized." We see the integration of many ideas at the multidisciplinary level, especially with the transdiscursive use of certain metaphors. For instance, there are texts, like the *New Atlantis*, that combine discussions of physics, particularly the nature of light, with inferences from economics and ideas about intelligence. Ideas in physics were often used to support market capitalism, a pattern evident in many of Bacon's writings, which also used intelligence descriptors to construct models that combined insight (optical and cognitive) with value (economics). Metaphors of "brightness," "illumination," "insight," "mysteriousness," "fullness," and "emptiness" helped to provide ideological support for individualism, with metaphors of light and economics suggesting that since it is a true rarity, "superior" intelligence is extremely valuable, as are highly intelligent ideas.

Renaissance thought, evident in its science, art, literature, and philosophy, was frequently centered on various examples of individuals inventing themselves. Renaissance self-construction consisted of deploying self-organizing and self-regulatory methods, evident in the autobiography, the portrait, and a "discourse" on "method," in which a self invents itself and achieves certitude by knowing that it is a doubting consciousness. Moreover, four philosophic frameworks ground the majority of Renaissance efforts to achieve truth and certitude:

- investigations of metaphysical and abstract systems, with ideas of the material world based on them;
- the development and institutionalization of Christian philosophy derived from grafting Greek and Near Eastern thought onto the roots of the Christian religion;
- empirical knowledge of the material world validating abstract systems;
- epistemological conflicts between reason and faith remaining largely unresolved given the impact of radical tendencies in scholastic thought, particularly Ockhamism.

These tenets circulated throughout the fourteenth and fifteenth centuries at a time when medieval thought was focused on static models of reality that would eventually be challenged by new economic theories and political activities, the tension exacerbated by a growing incompatibility between the ideology of emerging market capitalism and medieval Christian Platonism. These tensions ultimately expanded the range of philosophical content and altered traditional conceptual boundaries, especially science systems. The emergence of universities, the development of new social classes, and the creation of new cultural institutions created new cultural goals and competitions, as well as catalyzing consumer-class interest in new ideas and knowledge. The primary challenge to traditional theology and Christian philosophy came from natural philosophy and natural theology.

Together, these two philosophical areas created new notions of the human and external nature, the goal to transcend traditional epistemological impasses caused by differences in Greek, Latin, and Arabic thought. This shift is made explicit in what happened in fifteenth-century Venice and Florence, two of the most commercially successful cities in Europe. Italian philosophers and scientists discovered a way out of the moral impasse of medieval scholasticism, an argument derived from Aristotelian science, which argued that human intelligence was darkened due to a corrupted and fallen human nature. They turned to the liberal arts to argue that human consciousness and the creation of a knowledgeable individual increased the potential for human moral integrity, aesthetic sensibilities, and creativity. Contrary to what we might think, humanism was instrumental in the birth of modern science. The following chapter explores how different philosophers used theories of intelligence to help to invent Renaissance individualism, humanism, and the new science. Renaissance philosophical discourse shows that intelligence was a critical element in the invention of individualism.

5 Renaissance Philosophy and Fabrications of Intelligence: From Montaigne to Hobbes

The name Montaigne and the concept of humanistic individualism are synonymous. The French essayist may have been the first Western thinker to construct a moral philosophy focused primarily upon the individual. For Montaigne every individual represents the entire scope of the human condition, and, therefore, it is incumbent upon individuals to discover truth through a process of a highly disciplined self-study:

> The world always looks straight ahead: as for me, I turn my gaze inward, I fix it there and keep it busy. Everyone looks in front of him: as for me, I look inside of me; I have no business but with myself; I continually observe myself, I take stock of myself, I taste myself. Others always go elsewhere . . . as for me, I roll about in myself. (Montaigne, 1968, pp. 219–20)

In addition to validating observation as a tool of inquiry, anticipating its scientific role, and to constructing self-discovery in largely economic terms – as a "business" or an "enterprise," or in taking "stock" – Montaigne constructs his "self" as both a philosophical and a scientific entity: "I study myself more than any other subject. That is my metaphysics, that is my physics" (Ibid., p. 821). And in two essays, "On the Education of Children" and "Of Pedantry," Montaigne argues that the individual is an exemplar of what is most natural to man. The point to be made is that Montaigne's concept of an interior self gains authority by representing an all-inclusive, easily appropriative metaphor, a self-regulating entity whose nature consists of divine, natural, scientific, philosophical, economic, and legal qualities, a tradition we see carried over to the majority of Renaissance philosophers, including Descartes.

Montaigne assigns intelligence several roles, his goal being to advance the ideological potential of this new interior construct. In one instance he asks: "The intelligence that has been given us for our greatest good, shall we use it for our ruin, combating the plan of nature and the universal order of all things, which says that each man shall use his tools and means for their comfort?" (Ibid., pp. 33–4). And in his *Essays 1* he argues that the intelligent are those who seek out knowledge and truth, whereas the unintelligent are those who obediently follow their beliefs:

> they follow the appearance of first impressions, and have some color of reason on their side to impute our walking on in the old beaten path to simplicity and stupidity, meaning us who have not informed ourselves by study. The higher and nobler souls, more solid and clear-sighted, make up another set of true believers, who by a long and religious investigation of truth, have obtained a clear and more penetrating light into the Scriptures. (Ibid., p. 32)

In these two references, intelligence is a "gift" from an undefined source – not anything divine – but something "given." Intelligence can also be misused or be destructive when it violates the "universal order of all things" that dictates that human industry and technology be employed on behalf of that system ("their comfort" referring back to the "things" included in the concept of "the universal order of all things"). The second quote suggests that intelligence is an open-ended pursuit of knowledge, in contrast to thinking in terms of habitual patterns, "the old beaten path to simplicity and stupidity." In both cases, intelligence is represented as a force that supports universal order while protecting against the sterility of habitual thought. In this way, intelligence functions as a regulatory entity serving "universal order." Finally, Montaigne situates intelligence and individualism in an interdependent relationship, with intelligence supporting the development of a self-reflective individual who, in turn, uses his intelligence to continually discover his center, these expeditions into the human interior being consistent with the dynamics of universal laws.

While Montaigne links intelligence to individual consciousness, George Berkeley mystifies its spiritual nature. In his *Philosophical Commentaries*, he argues that the mind is an unknowable spiritual substance that perceives and wills ideas. Since the spiritual substance is unknowable, there can be no question of distinguishing any mental faculty like the will, the understanding, or intelligence. All are manifestations of a spiritual entity that wills and perceives. In his *Principles of Human Knowledge* Berkeley states: "Besides all that endless variety of ideas or objects of knowledge, there is likewise something which knows or perceives them, and exercises divers operations, as willing, imaging, remembering them. This perceiving, active being is what I call mind, spirit soul or my self" (I, p. 12). In Berkeley's view, if the self is part of the divine mind, then intelligence must be a spirit. He explains his notion of the mind by presenting an extended metaphor:

As colours in a dark room become real with the introduction of light, so the material world becomes real in the life and agency of Spirit. It must exist in terms of a sentient life and percipient intelligence, in order to rise into any degree of reality that human beings can at least be all concerned with, either speculatively or practically. (Ibid., p. 221)

He argues that existence is dependent upon mind: "For as to what is said of the absolute existence of unthinking things, without any relation to their being perceived, that is to me perfectly unintelligible. Their *esse* is *percipi*; nor is it possible they should have any existence out of the minds, or thinking things which perceive them" (Ibid., p. 259). Berkeley complicates the philosophical notion of Renaissance intelligence, making it part of what literally recognizes the existence of all things, one of several variants of the sixteenth-century divine–human model.

Although Leibniz's notions of intelligence are similar, they deserve attention because of their construction. In some instances, Leibniz mirrors Greek metaphysical theory when he refers to God as the prime intelligence, but also deploys extended metaphors to modernize notions of intelligence, relating them in various ways to the human mind, to machines, and to mathematics. For instance, in a letter in the *Leibniz–Clarke Correspondence* (Alexander, 1956, p. 126), Leibniz states that "I don't think I can be rightly blamed for saying that God is *intelligentia supramundana*. Will they say, that he is *intelligentia mundana*; that is, the soul of the world? I hope not." Here Leibniz is reflecting traditional thought, as he does in *A Specimen on Dynamics* when he refers to Aristotle's attaching "intelligences to the rotating spheres" (Leibniz, 1989, p. 91), or when he writes to Johann Bernoulli that "intelligences like ours, created in a special sense in the image of God, are governed by laws far different from those by which those lacking intelligence are governed" (ibid., p. 171). This last quote demonstrates how certain philosophical and natural law ideas were recruited during the Renaissance to support the beginning of new institutions, especially those beginning to deal with individuals Leibniz euphemistically describes as "lacking intelligence."

Leibniz's point illuminates another aspect of the historical ideology of intelligence, particularly the significance of certain correlations between ideas of intelligence and their institutionalization forms embodied in their numerous classifications, scales, and hierarchies. During the Renaissance mentally disabled people could be represented in several ways. For instance, those Leibniz believed were governed by "laws" different from divine forces either thought to be satanic, prophetic, or innocents unstained by sinful human characteristics. "Simple minds" were often kept as court jesters or fools, with Shakespeare frequently giving them prophetic insight (*King Lear*, I. iv). The astronomer Brahe had an "imbecile" as a close companion, treating his utterings as divine revelations. Alchemists, naturalists, and herbalists wrote about and created remedies for mental disability. Church parish records reveal that those with learning disabilities were "idiots," while the mentally ill were "mad." Families with insane children knew that public opinion would have them pay for their relatives' upkeep in such places as Bedlam or Bethlem hospitals, and the origin of private lunatic asylums may have begun with the practice of using servant lodgings as care centers.

A review of Renaissance medical literature and institutional practices indicates the pervasiveness of the idea that intelligent individuals or classes were closer to God, while the unintelligent reflect the mundane or evil, as is the case with Caliban in *The Tempest*. The unintelligent were generally thought of as having little insight, as suggested in Leibniz's point that "the difference between intelligent substances and substances that have no intelligence at all is just as great as the difference between a mirror and someone who sees" (Leibniz, 1989, p. 66). This quote also corresponds to his opinion that "Substances are either simple or composite. Simple substances or monads are either intelligent or without reason. Intelligent monads are called spirits and are either uncreated or created. A created intelligent monad is either angelic or human and is also called a soul" (ibid., p. 199).

Most of the Leibniz's ideas about intelligence are orthodox: God is a divine intelligence, intelligences are angel-like guiding forces, human intelligence is a reflection of God, and, most importantly for my ideological interest in intelligence, different natural laws separate the intelligent from the unintelligent. They underlie Robert Adam's (1994, p. 212) argument that intelligence, particularly the intellect, played a central part in Leibniz's metaphysics:

> Since Leibniz attributes to the intellect the ability to construct corporeal aggregates taking form as phenomena, it becomes obvious that the intellect's part in our perception of corporeal phenomena is particularly important and includes both mathematics and physics. Among the features of phenomena that we perceive primarily by the intellect are forces. . . . He regards the presence of body as constituted by a "force" of acting and resisting, which we perceive, not by imagination, but by the intellect.

However, despite Leibniz's generally traditional representations of intelligence, there are other instances in which his metaphoric divine–human model of intelligence proves ideologically significant, constituting a departure from traditional philosophical thought. For instance, in *A New System of Nature*, he argues that

We must not indiscriminately confuse minds or rational souls . . . for they are of a higher order, and have incomparably greater perfection than the forms thrust into matter . . . minds being like little gods in comparison with them, made in the image of God, and having in them some ray of the light of divinity. That is why God governs minds like a prince governs his subjects, and even like a father cares for his children, whereas he disposes of other substances like an engineer handles his machines. Thus minds have particular laws, which place them above the upheavals [revolutions] in matter, [through the very order which God has put in them]; and we can say that everything else is made only for them and that these tumultuous motions themselves are adjusted for the happiness of the good and the punishment of the wicked. (Leibniz, 1989, p. 140)

A similar point is made in the *Discourse on Metaphysics* (1686). While referring to the "skill of the Great Worker," Leibniz states:

I recognize and praise the skill of a worker not only by showing his designs in making the parts of his machine, but also by explaining the instruments he used in making each part, especially when these instruments are simple and cleverly contrived. *And God is a skillful enough artisan* to produce a machine which is a thousand times more *ingenious* than that of our body, while using only some very simple fluids explicitly concocted in such a way that only the ordinary laws of nature are required to arrange them in the right way to produce so admirable an effect; but it is also true that this would not happen at all unless God were the author of nature. (Leibniz, 1989, p. 54)

He amplifies the above points later in the *Discourse* by suggesting that by conjoining morality with metaphysics:

we must not only acknowledge God as the principal and cause of all substances and all beings, but also as the leader of all persons or intelligent substances and as the absolute monarch of the most perfect city or republic, which is the universe composed of all minds together. God himself being the most perfect of all minds and the greatest of all beings. For certainly minds are the most perfect beings and best express divinity. And since the whole nature, end, virtue, and function of substance is merely to express God and the universe . . . there is no reason to doubt that the substances which express the universe with the knowledge of what they are doing and which are capable of knowing great truths, God and the universe, express it incomparably better than do those natures, which are either brutish and incapable of knowing truths or completely destitute of sensation and knowledge. And the difference between intelligent substances and substances that have no intelligence at all is just as great as the difference between a mirror and someone who sees. (Ibid., p. 66)

In his essay *On Nature Itself* (1698) he maintains that

> there is no such thing as the soul of the universe. I also agree these wonders [of nature] which present themselves daily, and about which we customarily say . . . that the work of nature is the work of intelligence, should not be ascribed to certain created intelligences endowed with wisdom and power [*virtus*] only in proportion to the task at hand, but rather that the whole of nature is . . . the *workmanship* of God, indeed, so much so that any natural machine you may choose consists of a completely infinite number of organs . . . and therefore requires the infinite wisdom and power of the author and ruler. (Leibniz, 1989, p. 156)

What makes these citations ideologically different from pre-existing ideas of intelligence is that like ideas advanced by Hobbes, Bacon, and Locke they locate intelligence in new spaces that have significant political and socioeconomic implications. In essence, Leibnizian notions of intelligence are consistent with the overall Renaissance pattern of producing ideas combining human and divine qualities. His notions of intelligence have ideological significance because they reduce fixed notions of authority and supernatural "law" to a process, from agency to activity if you will. The result proves mutually beneficial to both old authority and the new epistemology, preserving the idea of absolute from challenges posed by Renaissance scientific thought, while, at the same time, rivals gain power by acquiring authority traditionally associated with the divine. This complicated alliance assures a mutual ideological survival for three competing Renaissance domains of power: the monarchy, the Church, and the new claims of science. With the use of highly figurative language, Leibniz locates two different models of authority – the divine and the natural – within the same ideological parameters.

More importantly, Leibniz's notions of intelligence help the larger Renaissance effort of constructing new models of social order and behavior. These constructions underscore, in part, what makes Renaissance productions of intelligence original. For although they in content may imitate or even subvert prior notions, Renaissance ideas of intelligence have as much to do with inventing and ordering new political and knowledge systems as they do with establishing the scientific basis of intelligence. This dual purpose – of a blossoming science that also helps to create and maintain sociopolitical hierarchies – is what makes Renaissance contributions to the social history of intelligence uniquely modern. Like other Renaissance minds, Leibniz modernizes intelligence by humanizing it, refashioning it ideologically to be consistent with new ideas in science and technology, coupled with new theories of nature and mathematics. In essence, Leibniz appropriates older notions of divine intelligence in order to construct the ideology of Renaissance thought.

This effect is evident when Leibniz humanizes divine intelligence. He does so by defining human minds as "little gods" with a "ray" of divine light pervading them. In what essentially constitutes a feedback loop, God reproduces little versions of himself within the space of individual minds and then receives his "rays" back from them. Leibniz appropriates the ideological power of the genealogical to argue that human minds are "ruled" by God in the same way that princes govern their subjects or a father cares for his children. The argument uses a divine model to justify a political paternalism evident in the following analogy: God is to humankind as a father is to his children or a prince is to his subjects. This argument is also historical, reflecting a sixteenth-century European political and socioeconomic conflict in which challenges were being made to the papal authority of the "Holy Father" on the basis that European monarchies were substitute "fathers," or, in some cases, "princes," their figurative male offspring.

Leibniz's view of intelligence also assigns authority to new scientific ideas and technological advances. He places his combined divine–human intelligence at the core of a new social, economic, and political order by describing God as an "engineer" who easily controls "his machines" (Leibniz, 1989, p. 140). Moreover, he argues that God's production skills are evident in both his designs and the "instruments" (ibid., p. 54)" used to create them, a point indicative of the importance instrumentation was beginning to play in the burgeoning authority of Renaissance science. With his point that "God is a skillful enough artisan to produce a machine" (ibid.), Leibniz echoes the emerging challenge that Cartesian thought posed to traditional Church authority. And when he argues that the "work of nature is the work of intelligence," that "the whole of nature is . . . the *workmanship* of God," Leibniz reflects the new authority of natural philosophy. Lastly, he explains how intelligence is related to the "new mathematical sciences," arguing that "it is true that the mathematical sciences would not be demonstrative and would consist only in simple induction or observation . . . if something higher, something that intelligence alone can provide, did not come to the aid of imagination and senses" (ibid., p. 188).

Leibniz's representations of intelligence are complicated because of their apparent inconsistency. For instance, when Leibniz discusses metaphysics, intelligence is divine. However, when he deals with science, technology, mathematics, and politics, intelligence is a human–divine hybrid. These differences speak to ideological obligations, particularly to the way the Renaissance myth of individualism was being formed, the myth essentially a knowledge system requiring little support from traditional metaphysics. Why? Because emphasis on individualism, discovery, invention, observation, nature, and wealth production needed a human – not divine – foregrounding. Leibniz's writings, as with other sixteenth- and seventeenth-century texts, can be characterized in precisely these terms, as a contributing source in a new modern discourse in which the human was not simply invented but given specific qualities that could be systemized.

René Descartes (1596–1650) undoubtedly occupies a central role in the history of intelligence because he defined human beings as *thinking* beings – his famous *I think, therefore I exist* is arguably the ultimate ontological proof (being as a state of thinking). The importance that ideas of intelligence play in Cartesianism becomes clear when we treat Descartes as an early cognitive philosopher interested in establishing an internal basis of truth: the doubting subject, augmented by a *method*, achieves a unique certainty by integrating mathematics and fixed systematic processes. The constellation of Descartes's thought was guided by two fundamental ideas: internally consistent rules can demystify all phenomena; and an orderly consciousness is consistent with the self-regulatory order of the universe. Although they appear in several contexts, Descartes's ideas about intelligence have two qualities: intelligence has an instrumental role in producing knowledge and validating truth; and intelligence partially determines the uniqueness of an individual's identity. Moreover, intelligence determines, in part, who we are and why we are different from each other. These are indeed important characteristics in an age searching for strategies to translate abstract ideas about individualism into actual behaviors, social codes, and institutional practices. The value Descartes assigns to intelligence becomes evident when placed against the larger backdrop of his primary philosophical goal – the development and application of an analytic method that consistently produces certainty. This goal explains why Descartes's overall philosophical efforts might be best described as an epistemological enterprise, driven by a mathematical method blending the logic of a closed system of internally valid propositions with systematic observations of external phenomena.

The ideological role mathematics plays in Cartesianism is often overlooked, despite the fact that the majority of its validity rests on the implicit certitude assigned to mathematics as a cultural mode of power. This is the story of Cartesianism, the politicization of mathematics, its collaboration with science eventually forging the uncontested social authority that we today automatically grant statistics and psychometrics. As we shall see shortly, the social application of mathematical theory "officially" began when French Enlightenment *philosophes* invented and instituted "political arithmetic." Mathematics also proved invaluable in Descartes's hunt for *scientia*, a genuine, systematic, and comprehensible knowledge of reality based upon a set of reliable universal principles. For instance, his mathematicization of physics helped to invent modern science, leading the way by integrating algebra, calculus, and geometry in a methodology to tackle long-term problems in classical mechanics. Descartes became a model for Renaissance scientists and philosophers willing to jettison the medieval

practice of attributing qualitative connections to perceived causes in favor of sub-
suming particular events, forms, or phenomena under rules of abstract mathematical laws. Readers of Descartes cannot help but be amazed at his thirty-year
effort to apply mathematics to the study of metaphysics, theories of nature,
mechanics, physiology, ethics, and even psychology. His is the work of an epis-
temologist using ideas of intelligence and the doubting subject as tools for inventing universal yet self-produced certainty.

Like those of many other Renaissance thinkers, Descartes's philosophical
enterprise integrates several ideas. For instance, the universe is made knowable
by a subjective consciousness. What makes this autonomous self philosophically
original is that Descartes assigns it primacy over phenomena observed. His thinking subject is the *cogito* who uses consistent rules to avoid the irrationality of
emotional thought, the basis of classical myth and religious systems. Descartes's
goal is to minimize the intervention of religio-mythic agency in analytic thought
so that the thinking subject can explore the world in terms of a rational method.
Intelligence fits into this project by *being the capacity and faculty to make the universe rational*. This claim marks a significant moment in the history of intelligence
because it adds a rational component and criteria to the emerging humanization
of intelligence.

The purpose of locating Descartes within the economy of intelligence is to
show that Descartes was far more interested in formulating an epistemology
of certitude for the new myth of individualism than in developing the entrepreneurial science fostered by British natural philosophers. Despite his focus,
Descartes's work contributed to the emergence of wealth creation and market
capitalism in the mid and late Renaissance by establishing the authority of individualism as a philosophical, scientific, and economic force.

The role intelligence plays in Cartesianism can be traced through two of his
most important works. The first, the *Rules for the Direction of the Mind* or *Rules
for the Direction of Thinking* (*Regulae ad directionem ingenii*, 1628), immediately
alerts us to problem of translations. The traditional translated title lacks the accuracy of the current one – *Rules for the Direction of Our Native Intelligence* – offered
in the latest Cambridge version. The choice of *Native Intelligence* is consistent with
Descartes's argument that the innate powers of the mind achieve truth far more
effectively than methods used by traditional thinkers, theologians, and Christian
philosophers. Moreover, this new translation underscores the idea of the proper
guidance provided by the *ingenium* – the "native intelligence" or innate authority of mind. Since the Latin term has the same root as the word *genus* (race, stock,
birth, descent) and *generare* (to procreate), it connotes an inborn, natural, and
transferable human attribute. The Latin word *ingenii* is derived from the word
ingenium, referring to an innately natural disposition or mode of thinking, as in

feci ego meum ingenium or *vigor ingenii*. Past translations using "mind" or "thinking" in their titles ignore Descartes's thesis that demonstrative rules, produced by intelligence, regulate the behavior and applications derived from natural (native) intelligence.

This shift in meaning is critical in understanding the ideological history of intelligence because it signals the transition from divine or divine–human models of intelligence to *strictly human and natural constructions of intelligence*. Although Descartes repeatedly situates intelligence within human beings throughout his writings, he does on occasion refer to prior "celestial" intelligences. But even in these instances, he remains first and foremost a new scientist, unable to make a judgment without evidence: "I do not on that account infer that there are intelligent creatures in the stars or elsewhere, but I do not see either that there is any argument to prove that there are not. I always leave questions of this kind undecided, rather than deny or assert anything about them" (Descartes, 1991, p. 59).

The *Rules for the Direction of Our Native Intelligence* deserves closer scrutiny because it is a central text in the history of intelligence in so far as Descartes links a hierarchical model of intelligence – scalable levels of intelligence – to the presumably unquestionable authority of mathematics. Instead of defining intelligence in traditional divine or metaphysical terms, Descartes's treatise advances the new idea that knowledge arises from a "certain and evident cognition" and a mental awareness of self-evident truths. Descartes's desire for certitude is established in rule one, its goal being to coach the mind into forming valid judgments. Rule two makes rule one possible by establishing the value of mathematics:

> Of all the sciences so far discovered, arithmetic and geometry alone are . . . free from any taint of falsity or uncertainty . . . these considerations make it obvious why arithmetic and geometry prove to be much more certain than other disciplines: they alone are concerned with an object so pure and simple that they make no assumptions that experience might render them uncertain. (Ibid., pp. 1–2)

Rule three defines Descartes's epistemological target: "we ought to investigate what we can clearly and evidently intuit or deduce with certainty, and not what other people have thought or what we ourselves conjecture. For knowledge can be attained in no other way" (ibid., p. 2). There is also the hint here of his now famous axiom: "Thus everyone can mentally intuit that he exists, that he is thinking, that a triangle is bounded by just three lines, and a sphere by a single surface, and the like" (ibid., p. 3).

The ideological effect of the first three rules is to bring knowledge, mathematics, certainty, and autonomous individualism together in one conceptual family, promoting the idea that mathematics and self-evident or rational rules can produce absolute certainty. In this model, authority is an epistemological rather than transcendent construct, derived not from celestial source, but from the autonomous subject. In turn, this methodical practice prevents individuals from engaging in the inconsistencies of prior knowledge systems or from being misled by transient phenomena. The alliance Descartes forges between consciousness and certitude represents an important moment in the evolution of Western philosophical thought and cultural history. To have the social power and institutional scope they currently possesses, modern ideas of intelligence had to be constructed on the basis that human consciousness could envision and produce certainty. The idea of self-evident truths in Cartesianism becomes one of many influences laying the groundwork for the politicization of the scientific concept in French and American revolutionary literature a century later. Without the assurance of absolute certitude inherent in mathematics and Descartes's method, the commonplace practice of mathematically measuring and scaling intelligence begun in earnest in the early twentieth century would have proved impossible.

Descartes employs rule four to prove how native intelligence and the capacity for self-evident observations produce truth. He asserts that "a method" is needed "if we are to investigate the truth of things." He then suggests that the way intelligence operates is critical to his method: "if our intellect were not already able to perform them [operations like deductions], it would not comprehend any of the rules of the method" (ibid., p. 4). Tautology aside, Descartes links his method to the economic, much like Locke and his idea of *profitable knowledge*, by insisting that "so useful is this method that without it the pursuit of learning would . . . be more harmful than profitable." His representation of *mental* profit is given credibility when he asserts that "great minds of the past were to some extent aware of it [his method], guided to it even by nature alone." This is an important point: nature, not any transcendent agency, is now the beacon guiding the mind to the safe harbors of certainty. Descartes also constructs representations of profitability, intelligence, and methodology in terms of garden imagery, asserting that "the human mind has within it a sort of spark of the divine in which the first seeds of useful ways of thinking are sown." There are instances in which "seeds . . . however neglected and stifled by studies which impede them, often bear fruit of their own accord" (ibid., p. 4). Metaphorically, the mind can produce profitable ideas or metaphoric "seeds" that "bear fruit of their own accord." This hint of highly productive economic autonomy – "their own accord" – provides the individual mind with the authority of production.

If earlier rules metaphorically associate intelligence and the Cartesian method with productivity, rule six argues that certitude can only be achieved by following a "proper" order or arrangement of facts. Descartes defines his method as "the ordering and arranging of . . . objects. . . . We shall be following this method exactly if we first reduce complicated and obscure propositions step by step to simpler ones" (ibid., p. 6). The primacy of this "ordering" and "arranging" of "objects" is then associated with consciousness in rule seven: "to make our knowledge complete, every single thing relating to our understanding must be surveyed in a continuous and wholly uninterrupted sweep of thought, and be included in a sufficient and well-ordered enumeration" (ibid., p. 7). This may arguably be the first example in Western thought of ideological power assigned to the practice of autonomous self-ordering, qualities that traditionally were associated with a transcendent agency. There is little doubt as to the eventual institutional value assigned to this "proper" sequencing and arrangement of knowledge in industrial and modern culture. For instance, it appears in academic, legal, governmental, and penal population management systems, or as the basic mechanism for mass production, or as intelligence test criteria, or in the scientific method, whether demonstrated in a lab analysis of deadly pesticides or in the authoring of a software program.

Rule ten states that

> to acquire discernment we should exercise our native intelligence by investigating what others have already discovered, and methodically survey even the most insignificant products of human skills, especially those which display or presuppose order . . . since not all great minds have such a natural disposition to puzzle things out by their own exertions. (Ibid., p. 11)

Descartes outlines the *proper* practice:

> we must not take up the more difficult and arduous issues immediately, but must first tackle the simplest and least exalted arts, and especially those in which order prevails – such as weaving and carpet-making, or the more feminine arts of embroidery, in which threads are interwoven in an infinitely varied pattern. Number-games and any games involving arithmetic, and the like, belong here. It is surprising how much all of these activities exercise our native intelligence, provided of course we discover them for ourselves and not from others. (Ibid.)

Besides constructing an impersonal authority based on notions of "proper order" and ideas about the kind of intelligence related to self-autonomy, Descartes shows that intelligence is never static, but can always be augmented:

> If, after intuiting a number of simple propositions, we deduce something else from them, it is useful to run through them in a continuous and complete train of

thought, to reflect on their relations to one another, and to form a distinct and, as far as possible, simultaneous conception of several of them. For in this way our knowledge becomes much more certain, and our intellectual capacity is enormously increased. (Ibid.)

The *Rules for the Direction of Our Native Intelligence* articulates the earliest version of the scientific method and lays the foundation for what will eventually form dominant ideological strands in modern Western culture. Descartes's essay places human intelligence at the center of a newly invented system of certitude using various figural-based constructions of knowledge, mathematics, nature, consciousness, measurement, and order to produce and validate self-autonomous individuality. In his own way, Descartes produces an abstract ordering system that during the Enlightenment takes form as a social epistemology shaping the configuration of Western political, social, and economic institutions.

The radical nature of the Cartesian system is evident in his *Discourse on Method* (1637). Arguably the *Discourse* is as much a philosophical autobiography as it is a scientific treatise, a not altogether surprising combination given the ideological relationships forming between the new Renaissance myth of individualism and the nature of the new scientific method, a practice placing authority in the hands of the individual scientist. It makes good sense that Descartes would combine three types of writing, the literary, scientific, and philosophical, especially since Renaissance literature, art, and science all shared the common goal of creating and validating the act of self-production. Descartes comments on himself frequently. For example, he confesses at the onset: "I have never presumed my mind to be in any way more perfect than that of the ordinary man; indeed I have often wished to have as quick a wit, or as sharp and distinct an imagination, or as ample or prompt a memory as some others" (ibid., p. 20). Descartes's choice of words indicates how Renaissance notions of intelligence were poised for ideological appropriation, with qualities of being quick, sharp, and prompt being associated with speed, effective readiness (weapons maintained and readied for maximum advantage), abundance, sufficiency, and precision. These are all given positive values, with speed, preparation, sufficiency, and precision eventually functioning as the base criteria for modern intelligence tests, as well as highly valued components or elements of effective economic processes or industrial production methods. For the past three hundred years, these values have often been transposed so that their production aspects were attributed to the objects produced. A case in point: the speed, sufficiency, and precision of how a BMW is produced become the exact values that sell the car; production value and commercial value become identical. This equation of production with object value is basic to the logic and grammar of capitalism.

Descartes surveys his early life by explaining why he liked mathematics: "because of the certainty and self-evidence of its reasonings" and his surprise of discovering "that nothing more exalted had been built upon such firm and solid foundations" (ibid., p. 23). He then relates that after school he spent

> the rest of my youth travelling . . . testing myself in the situations which fortune offered, and at all times reflecting upon whatever came my way so as to derive some profit from it . . . much more truth could be found in reasonings which a man makes concerning matters that concern him than in those which some scholar makes in his study about speculative matters. . . . And it was always my most earnest desire to learn to distinguish the true from the false in order to see clearly into my own actions and proceed with confidence in this life. (Ibid., p. 24)

While the first part of the *Discourse* argues that certitude is possible with the integration of mathematics, truth, and profit, part two deals with the "principal rules of the methods which the author has sought" (ibid., p. 20). What follows is Descartes's famous scene of being shut up "alone in a stove-heated room where I was completely free to converse with myself about my own thoughts." His isolation prompts the observation that underscores the essence of Renaissance achievement, the production of a creative and autonomous individual: "there is not usually so much perfection in works composed of several parts and produced by various different craftsmen as in the works of one man" (ibid., p. 25). Descartes offers several examples of those who prove his point: "Peoples who have grown from a half-savage to a civilized state, and have made their laws only in so far as they were forced to by the inconvenience of crimes and quarrels" (ibid.), and "those who from the beginning of their society have observed the basic laws laid down by some wise law-giver. Similarly, it is quite certain that the constitution of the true religion, whose articles have been made by God alone, must be incomparably better ordered than all the others" (ibid., p. 26). Descartes then transfers these examples of individual perfection to a science essentially grounded upon the individual, particularly his or her "natural powers" or intelligence and elementary "reasoning":

> Hence . . . conclusion of sorts . . . I came to think that the sciences contained in books, at least those involving merely probable arguments and having no demonstrative basis, being built up and developed little by little from the opinions of many different persons, do not get so close to the truth as do the simple reasonings of a man of good sense, using his natural powers, can carry out in dealing with whatever objects he may come across. (Ibid.)

Descartes reinforces his point by stating that "My plan had never gone beyond trying to reform my own thoughts and construct them upon a foundation which is all my own" (ibid., p. 27).

Once Descartes situates an intelligent individual at the center of his new science, he then lays the foundation of his "method," which consists of the following rules:

> never say anything as true if you did not have evident knowledge of its truth . . . divide each of the difficulties under examination into as many needed parts as possible . . . proceed with your analysis in an orderly manner, beginning with the simplest and most easily known objects, ascending, step by step, to the knowledge of the most complex, and by providing order to objects that have no natural order of precedence and make complete enumerations, comprehensive reviews, and leave nothing out. (Ibid., pp. 25–7)

Shortly after listing these steps, Descartes returns to the most famous part of his *Discourse*:

> I noticed that while I was endeavoring in this way to think that everything was false, it was necessary that I, who was thinking this, was something. And observing that this truth "I am thinking, therefore I exist" was so firm and sure that all the most extravagant suppositions of the sceptics were incapable of shaking it, I decided that I could accept it without scruple as the first principal of the philosophy I was seeking. (Ibid., p. 36)

Descartes's point ultimately privileges the "I" as an *a priori* construct, this self that precedes and predetermines the ontological. Ultimately, this privileging assigns exclusive authority to the "I" centered within the individual in the same way a center point is related to the circumference of a circle. This new model of truth production places an unprecedented importance on intelligence as the source enabling Descartes's "I" to be a certainty producer. From this point on, post-seventeenth-century ideas of intelligence had to be constructed from within the epistemological dynamics of the Cartesian system.

In several places, Descartes uses his method to argue that even the notion of perfection is subject to the "I":

> since I knew of some perfections that I did not possess, I was not the only being which existed . . . but there had of necessity to be some other, more perfect being on which I depended and from which I had acquired all that I possessed . . . to know the nature of God, as far as my own nature was capable of knowing it, I had only

to consider, for each thing of which I found in myself some idea, whether or not it was a perfection to possess it. (Ibid., p. 37)

And when he discusses intelligence – as a mental quality or celestial guide – Descartes develops a unique human–divine combination model in which intelligence is a perfection regardless of what form it takes:

> But since I already recognized very clearly from my own case that the intellectual nature is distinct from the corporeal, and as I observed that all composition is evidence of dependence, and that dependence is manifestly a defect, I concluded that it could not be a perfection in God to be composed of these two natures, and consequently that he was not composed of them. But if there were any bodies in the world, or any intelligences or other natures that were not wholly perfect, their being must depend on God's power in such a manner that they could not subsist for a single moment without him. (Ibid., pp. 37–8)

The *Discourse* concludes with a comparison of differences between animals and humans that further illuminates the ideological potential of the dominant Renaissance model of intelligence. Descartes notes "that although many animals show more skill than we do in some of their actions . . . the same animals show none at all in many others." He further reasons that these skills do

> not prove that they have any intelligence, for if it did then they would have more intelligence than any of us and would excel us in everything. It proves rather that they have no intelligence at all, and that it is nature which acts in them according to the disposition of their organs. In the same way a clock, consisting only of wheels and springs, can count the hours and measure time more accurately than we can with all our wisdom. (Ibid., p. 45)

This passage makes three points: skill complexities are not intelligence indicators, animals have no intelligence, and nature alone programs animal behavior. The more revealing implication, however, underscores Descartes's interest in machines, especially in terms of how their mathematics-like qualities (precision, exactness, consistency, efficiency, and predictability) produce accuracy. The complexity of Descartes's view of intelligence is indicative of the ideological ferment of Renaissance culture, particularly as various contests between old authority and the new power of individualism reflected appropriations of intelligence ideologically consistent with each view. The major conflict between claims for divine authority and individual expression underscores the essential context for Renaissance philosophy.

By 1500, the Papacy recognized its need to enter into numerous debates about material and immaterial truth and individual and universal authority, the effort based upon Rome's need to defend its own interests and power. One outcome of Papal entrenchment was the propagation of deterministic notions of intelligence, especially when "natural" philosophy began to be taken seriously. As more neo-Platonist arguments came into service to counteract the rise of naturalistic philosophy, a new emphasis was placed on the ontological nature of human experience and on operational systems of thought evident, for instance, in Descartes's *Discours de la méthode*. Existing metaphysical notions of truth began being subjected to an analysis characterized by such logical methods as categories, propositions, syllogisms, inference, demonstration, topics, and fallacies, as well as by a new epistemology centered on "natural" human faculties.

Other Italian philosophers contributed to the growing ideological potential for new ideas about intelligence. For instance, in his *Disputa de l'ase*, Anselm Turmeda asserted that the nobility of humankind could be proved by virtue of the fact that divine intelligence is continuously incarnated in human form. Similar ideas were presented in Antonio de Ferrariis's *Epsitola de nobilitate* (1488) and Giovanni Pico della Mirandola's *Oratio* (1486), works that advanced the new myth of individualism. Likewise, Marsilio Ficino believed that intelligence and a healthy body went hand in hand, his main idea being that while reason provides humankind with a godlike power, our intelligence offers us an unlimited capacity to provide for our health and ourselves. His *Three Books on Life* (1480) offer advice on becoming an intellectual and improving one's health. In Book I, *De vita sana*, Ficino defines black bile as the physical cause of both melancholic madness and genius, with Saturn affecting intellectuals more than other planets. His astrology is tied to the belief that heavenly bodies, guides, are animated with impersonal intelligences, which, in turn, are made manifest in humankind. He asserts that nine guides help those who travel from the hardships of life to the high temples of the Muses. One set of guides resides in the soul, where there is "a fierce and firm will, *sharpness* of intelligence, and a tenacious memory" (Ficino, 1989, p. 109). This is perhaps one of the first instances in which a non-spiritual adjective is used to describe intelligence. What was once a divine or celestial intelligence is replaced by a purely technological quality – a *sharpness* – that cuts and dissects in order to produce a clarity of focus and insight. This indirect reference to optics, time, and metal working shows an early ideological appropriation of scientific and technological metaphors. Ficino argues that intellectuals are often negligent: "only the priests of the Muses, only the hunters after the highest good and truth are so negligent and so unfortunate, that they seem wholly to neglect the instrument with which they are able to measure and grasp the whole world." The implication is that intelligence is a means of both measuring knowledge and owning it. In an early example of a natural view of intelligence, Ficino traces the flow of the intelligent spirit through the body:

> After being generated by the heat of the heart out of the more subtle blood, it flies to the brain; and there the soul uses it continually for the exercise of the interior as well as the exterior senses. This is why the blood subserves the spirit; the spirit, the senses; and finally, the senses, reason. (Ibid., p. 111)

Ficino resorts to the divine ancestry of intelligence in his naturalization of it by stating that "the spirits generated from this ascend (of vital power) to the citadels of the brain and of Pallas, in these [citadels] the animal force, that is the power of sense and motion, dominates" (ibid., p. 112).

Ficino offers medical advice for the intelligent: they should "avoid phlegm and black bile. . . . For just as they are inactive in the rest of the body, so they are busy in the brain and the mind. . . . Phlegm dulls and suffocates the intelligence, while melancholy, if it is too abundant and vehement, vexes the mind" (ibid., p. 113). He also theorizes that melancholics are usually very intelligent. Alluding to Aristotle and Plato, he surmises that "most intelligent people are prone to excitability and madness. Democritus too says that no one can ever be intellectually outstanding except those who are deeply excited by some sort of madness." Those who "excel everyone in intelligence . . . seem to be not human, but divine" (ibid., p. 117). Ficino specifies the exact reason why black bile makes people intelligent:

> When black bile is intensely concentrated, placed under high pressure, hotter and brighter, vigorous in motion, and pouring forth continually from a solid and stable humor, they can support an action for a very long time – when supported by such compliance, our intelligence explores eagerly and perseveres in the investigation longer. Whatever it is tracking, it easily finds it, perceives it clearly, soundly judges it and retains the judgement long. (Ibid., p. 121)

Lastly, intelligence can be strengthened by the drinking of theriac, a medicinal form of antidote taken from vipers. In addition aloe, various herbs, rose water, amber, and wine are recommended to increase one's intelligence (ibid., pp. 139–41). Ficino's contribution to the history of intelligence is certainly obvious. Although he refers to the divine and celestial aspects of intelligence, more often than not he places intelligence within the boundary of the human, more precisely the human body, which in various ways "makes" intelligence. His range of metaphoric representations of intelligence is noteworthy, with intelligence ranging in nature from a concentrated liquid to a high pressure, or from something hot and bright and quick and vigorous in motion to something solid and stable. In essence, these qualities assign to intelligence the capacity to explore, track, discover, perceive clearly, interpret, and retain. In Ficino's scheme, intelligence is natural and therefore machine-like and controllable. Using observation and scientific methods, individuals can diagnose and treat the lack of intelligence with certain herbs. Ficino is the first thinker to argue that intelligence can be manipulated with pharmacological aids, and in so doing locates a now purely human intelligence to an equally human construction – the world of science.

Other Renaissance philosophers produced new ideas about human intelligence. For instance, in his *Pensées* Blaise Pascal (1623–62) weaves his ideas of intelligence through such topics as human knowledge, morals, skepticism, and a new sense of humanity. He proclaims early in the *Pensées* that "All man's dignity lies in thought. But what is thought? Mere folly! Thought, then, is something admirable, incomparable by its very nature. Strange defects would be needed to render thought contemptible; those it has are such as render it ridiculous. How noble by nature! How base by defects . . . man is obviously made for thought . . . the order of thought is to begin with self, and go on to its Author and its destiny (Pascal, 1995, pp. 158, 159). He also argues that "the more intelligent we are, the more readily we recognize individuality personality in others" (ibid., p. 149). Pascal was also one of the first to model human nature on mathematical models. For instance, in *Man's Disproportion* Pascal uses geometry as metaphor for human nature. *Fragment 43* asserts: "Let us know our limits. We are something, but we are not all, such existence as we have deprives us of the knowledge of first principles whose source is Nothing; and the pettiness of our existence hides from our sight the Infinite" (ibid., p. 19) and that "Our intelligence stands in the order of Intelligibles just where our body does in the vast realm of Nature" (ibid., p. 25). In a section entitled "Geometry – Finesse or Mathematics – Penetration, Intuition," Pascal argues that there are two kinds of intellect:

> the one, which reaches swiftly and deeply the conclusions of the premises, and that is the penetrative (accurate) mind; the other, which embraces a great number of principles without mixing them, and that is the mathematical mind. The first is strong and straight, the other is broad. Now it is possible to be the one without the other, for the mind may be strong and narrow, or, equally, broad and feeble. (Ibid., pp. 499–500)

Baruch Spinoza (1632–77) integrates divine and human models of intelligence in his writings primarily because the Jewish humanist believed that God and nature were essentially identical. For instance, he argues that humans can "attain well-being through knowledge . . . of God. . . . I do not say that we must know

Him just as He is . . . for it is sufficient for us to know Him to some extent in order to be united with Him. . . . . That this intelligence, which is the knowledge of God, is not the consequence of something else, but immediate" (Runes, 1951, p. 299). He also asserts in his *Critique of Traditional Religion* that "the intellect is the better part of us," that the "true intellect can never come to perish," and that human freedom is a "a firm existence, which our intellect acquires through immediate union with God" (Curley, 1985, p. 68). Elsewhere he argues that since "knowledge is the first and principal cause of all these passions, it will be clearly manifest that if we use our Intelligence and Speculation aright, it should be possible for us ever to fall a prey to one of these passions which we ought to reject. I say our Intelligence, because I do not think that Speculation alone is competent to free us from all these" (Runes, 1951, p. 111). Spinoza is also one of the first Renaissance philosophers to link the power of intelligence to the power of rationality: "Wherefore of a man, who is led by reason, the ultimate aim or highest desire, whereby he seeks to govern all his fellows, is that whereby he is brought to the adequate conception of himself and of all things within the scope of his intelligence" (ibid., p. 245). This example indicates how intelligence creates both the rational and self-identity. Finally, Spinoza is one of the first thinkers to create different types of intelligence: there is actual, divine, infinite, practical, intuitive, and pure intelligence. And like Descartes, he uses the Latin term *ingenium* (*verstand/vernuft*) to refer to a native intelligence.

In his *The Search after Truth* Nicolas Malebranche (1638–1715) asserts that "what will be said about it [the mind] could be said as well about pure intelligence and *a fortiori* about what we have here called pure understanding that the mind" (Malebranche, 1997, p. 198). Like Spinoza, Malebranche believes that "the only purely intelligible substance is God's . . . we shall be unintelligible to each other until we see each other in God, and until He presents us with the perfectly intelligible idea He has of our being contained in His being" (ibid., p. 218). And in a nod to the notion of celestial divine guides, he states that "if a man knew the number of angels, and that for each angel there were ten archangels, and that for each archangel there were ten thrones, and so on with the same ten-to-one proportion up to the last order of Intelligences, his mind could know at will the number of all these blessed spirits" (ibid., p. 254).

These ideas of intelligence from well known Italian, Spanish, German, Dutch, French, and Swiss thinkers demonstrate how the two Renaissance models of intelligence operated, and they also prepare the way for a radically different view of intelligence offered by Thomas Hobbes (1588–1679). In essence, Hobbes may arguably be the first philosopher to bring the ideological potential of intelligence to consciousness. For Hobbes, intelligence functions politically because all human attributes are essentially political and material, this argument being part of his larger theory that human nature produces social reality. His major work, *Leviathan*, argues for a new political philosophy and new modes of social organization, specifically those based upon the new methods derived from physical and human sciences. This call for change meant that prior modes of political analysis, those based on ethics, hermeneutics, and religion, had to be replaced by scientific methods, with Hobbes's argument being more vocal and direct than those made by Descartes and Bacon. Since *Leviathan* presents the notion that society functions as a self-organizing system, it has prompted some modern thinkers, like Dyson (1998), to argue that Hobbes's Leviathan is a self-organizing system possessing a life and intelligence of its own. I shall not argue that Hobbes was a proto-architect of postmodern cyberspace, his treatise a demonstration of a collective and transcendent organism like Teilhard de Chardin's Noosphere. However, I will argue that Hobbes understood the relationship between human psychology and social systems and how intelligence functions socially. This makes him a unique figure in the history of intelligence.

Intelligence, for Hobbes, is primarily a material and physical phenomenon, since humans are corporeal objects governed by physical and material laws. In essence, thought is no more or no less than the internalization of external stimuli. In his causal scheme, sensations produce feelings that in turn produce decisions and actions. Moreover, since human beings are inherently selfish, they seek to maximize pleasure and minimize pain. From these basic ideas, Hobbes argues for natural law, monarchies ruled by the consent of the governed, and the need for a "social contract" to control the natural state wherein individuals are engaged in continuous battle for dominance and gain. And since the goal of any society is to increase individual happiness, laws must exist to insure that the selfish do not dominate the many. Hence, the purpose of social authority is to enforce the social contract.

So where does the idea of intelligence fit into Hobbes's radical politic? For Hobbes, intelligence is strictly an internal human attribute as well as an equalizer, a tool that humankind uses to overcome threats posed by other human beings and nature. This point is made throughout *Leviathan*: the intellect helps humans to defend against nature. Second, language complexity is a barometer to intelligence: it distinguishes animal and human intelligence. Hobbes places intelligence at the center of what constitutes the human: "the cause of understanding . . . sendeth forth an intelligible species, that is, an intelligent being seen; which, coming into the understanding, makes us understand" (Hobbes, 1962, p. 3). Later, in chapter 8, he observes that "by virtues intellectual, are always understood such abilities of the mind, as men praise, value and desire should be in themselves; and go commonly under the name of a good wit; though the same word wit, be used also, to distinguish one certain ability from the rest" (ibid., p.

56). Intelligence is clearly a virtue and an advantage in Hobbes's scheme. He distinguishes two types of intelligence. There are acquired wit and natural wit, with the latter representing intellectual skills acquired by experience ("without method, culture, or instruction") rather than social instruction. Natural wit consists of two parts:

> celerity of imagining, that is, swift succession of one thought to another; and steady direction to some approved end. On the contrary a slow imagination, maketh that defect, or fault of the mind, which is commonly called dullness, stupidity, and sometimes by other names that signify slowness of motion, or difficulty to be moved. And this difference of quickness, is caused by the difference of men's passions. (Ibid., p. 57)

Hobbes's point here makes the speed of mental activity a criterion, an indicator separating speed from dullness. The reason for this position stems from his assumption that motion was the most elementary of all facts. Variations in motion explain how nature, society, and the human mind function. He adds that "the causes of this difference of wits are in the passions . . . principally, the more or less desire of power, of riches, of knowledge, and of honor. All of which may be reduced to the first, that is, desire of power. For riches, knowledge and honor, are but several sorts of power" (ibid., pp. 59–60). Lastly, Hobbes assumes that intelligence differs very little among people, with variations being a matter of motivational differences driven by a passion for power.

Unlike most Renaissance philosophers, Hobbes applies biology, psychology, and the scientific method to an understanding of how human nature determines the human condition. "Natural wit" driven by the desire for power is a significant and unique Hobbesian construct, providing the ground for the development of radically new models of intelligence for the next four hundred years. Many modern assumptions about intelligence – its genetic basis, its being a mark of individual power or something measured in terms of abstract quickness – can be traced to Hobbes's *Leviathan*. Finally, Hobbes's thinking underscores a Renaissance trend in which the claims of science began to rival the authority that prior philosophical discourse had in determining ideas about the nature and source of intelligence.

6 Smart Renaissance Science

New ideas found their greatest reception in Renaissance science, playing the primary role of legitimizing the new science. Renaissance science came into being with certain ideological ambitions. Perhaps as important as the science it produced, the Renaissance developed a unique *culture* of science, a radically new way of knowing human beings, the world, and the universe. I would like to argue that new ideas of intelligence played a significant role in the construction of Renaissance science, embedded primarily in its economic aspects, as well as in some of its major discoveries, several being precursors to our contemporary notions of intelligence. I present a brief overview of Renaissance science before exploring the relationship between ideas of intelligence and the incarnation of scientific societies, the role of the "intelligencer," and specific scientific contributions made by Vesalius, Boyle, Cardano, Galileo, Bacon, and Leibniz.

At the core of Renaissance science lies its construction of a historically different type of truth, no longer a matter of faith or belief subject to the ineffable but predictable knowledge derived from empirical observation and systematic procedures. The age of gauges and rules was subversive, with experimentation, calculations, documentation, and instrumentation (microscopes, telescopes, and other optical devices) challenging the classical idea that interest in an object should be proportionate to its size. Other instruments, such as time measurement devices, thermometers, barometers, air pumps, and lab apparatus, had equal effect, with novice labs becoming official venues for experimentation and employment. New tools and processes created other scientific venues, such as observatories and botanical and zoological gardens. Advances in medicine created anatomical theaters of blood-stained slabs in which the Renaissance fascination with the human directed scalpels toward new interiors and complex systems. The era also saw the invention of Napier's logarithms, statistics (mortality tables), theories of probabilities, geometric ideas determining scales of magnitude, the study of higher plane curves, volumes, and areas, infinitesimals, and differential and integral calculus. Part II of this volume shows that Renaissance contributions to the history of mathematics and its related technologies, like calculation machines, may have played the most significant role in the eventual enculturation of science, particularly in developing institutional procedures for measuring and evaluating an individual's intelligence. The privilege given to measurement as a means of achieving truth transferred to the value of the objects measured. This is certainly true in the case of intelligence tests; measurement not only produces a scale that determines a value, but, importantly, its practice attests to the authority of the hierarchies created.

In this chapter I would like to show how the abstract concept of intelligence was transferred into a science and technology that targeted classical theories of mechanics, astronomy, biology, chemistry, acoustics, magnetism, political science, and physics. These challenges required a new kind of intelligence to subvert these ancient theories – *an intelligence that literally becomes flesh.*

The optimism fueling this new inquiry, its tools, and its discoveries stands in sharp contrast to the epistemological crisis they generated, especially the anxiety resulting from challenges to traditional facts, to how classical knowledge was produced, and to the social power agencies associated with and privileged by such conventional thought. Moreover, the acceleration of scientific discoveries challenged the medieval cosmographies of earth-bound chaos and the evil of concentric circles, geocentricity, and divine ascension, replacing them with ideas that the earth was something to study, that human beings were creators of order, and that free will could overcome the power of fate. The fact that *exotic* "New World" cultural behaviors could not be explained within the extant parameters of Aristotelian and Christian thought catalyzed and proved the necessity for developing more adequate knowledge systems. Europeans experienced all these stories and technologies, and many of them became apprehensive. As scientists probed the universe, and once hidden phenomena became visible, the older order's capacity to explain human history and nature was being challenged. In essence, prior models of the universe no longer held. Instead of consisting of heavenly gates and gods populating divine spheres, the universe was vast, dark, and infinitely downward.

In this climate of challenge and doubt, Renaissance scientists, like their philosopher counterparts, pursued the challenge of creating universal certitude, an abstract system that could continually achieve absolute truth despite variations in the phenomenal world. The production of this system was not entirely free of problems. The combining of reason (reified as a human attribute) with a self-validating method, together with the invention of the natural sciences, created an essentialist rationalism. This is a system of thought in which the identification of attributes like consistency, order, or pattern formations – the practice of determining their mere presence – proved more valuable than any critique of their validity or nature. It seemingly never dawned on Renaissance advocates of the method to be skeptical of their own enterprise: that order, logic, and consistency – elements of certitude "discovered" in their method – were what had already been defined as the dominant characteristics of nature itself. Although this mirror imaging of method and phenomenon may prove to be the only means of achieving ultimate truth, it was nevertheless a construct with obvious ideological significance, especially in the history of intelligence.

As part of its construction, this rationalist knowledge system appropriated other circulating ideas, including those about the nature of *human* intelligence, a key factor in the argument that the source of certitude was human rather than divine. Part of the explanation of why intelligence became and continues to be the most valued human faculty lies in the fact that it was not only associated with the dominant philosophy of modern Western culture, but more importantly defined as a source of rational thought itself. The space separating intelligence and rationality is ideologically negligent. And once it was paired up with empirical analyses, rationality became the ideological rival to existing religion-based knowledge systems. In essence, new thinkers wondered how humans could reason, observe, analyze, and achieve absolute certitude if there wasn't an internal human mechanism enabling such activities. Given this question and premise, it was then consistent to assume that those with the highest degree or amount of intelligence would be the most inventive and rational, except in those cases in which excesses of intelligence caused madness. This popular notion didn't come into cultural prominence until the Romantic revolt against rationality, the notion being part of the basis of Romanticism's anti-reason ideology. This explains why there were no cautionary examples of Victor Frankensteins exhuming bodies from foggy Renaissance graveyards.

By the mid-seventeenth century, reason not only became the means by which the regularity and perfection of nature could be understood and even deified, as is the case with Isaac Newton, but also became a rallying point for an epistemologically driven social revolution. In Book I of the *Novum Organum*, Francis Bacon explains why the revolution was long overdue:

> The subtlety of nature greatly exceeds that of sense and understanding; so that those fine meditations, speculations and fabrications of mankind are unsound, but there is no one to stand by and point it out. And just as the sciences we now have are useless for making discoveries of practical use, so the present logic is useless for the discovery of the sciences. (Bacon, 1960, X, p. xi)

Rupert Hall amplifies Bacon's social point by arguing epistemologically that

> in attacking the conventional science of the sixteenth century it was possible to outflank the higher-order generalizations altogether by showing that the facts deduced from them were simply not true. . . . The weakness of conventional science was also its strength; the whole authority of the magnificent interlocking system of thought bore down upon an assault at any one point. . . . Logically to doubt Aristotle on one issue was to doubt him on all, and consequently some problems of the scientific revolution, which may now seem to involve no more than the substitution of one kind of explanation for another, were pregnant with consequence since they implied the annihilation of extant learning. (Hall, 1962, p. 35)

The success of this revolution can be attributed to two factors: to Bacon's and Hobbes's notion of a "practical use" science; and to various institutionalizations of that practicality taking form as scientific societies, libraries, publishers, links with industry, laboratories, and to a lesser extent universities. New ideas of intelligence followed this trend toward practicality, finding places within certain privileged individuals and careers that helped to assure that science would become a dominant myth in the seventeenth century.

Perhaps the best illustration of the Renaissance conversion of science into a social practice, into a common myth with socioeconomic implications, comes with Bacon's famous allegorical community, which appeared in the *New Atlantis* (1627). His notion of the "House of Saloman" is the equivalent of a national organizational business schema, with "Merchants of Light" harvesting valuable scientific and technological ideas from other lands, "Depredators" researching books for new scientific facts, "Mystery Men" collecting mechanical art experiments, "Pioneers" testing new experiments, "Compilers" tabulating their results, "Dowery Men" implementing their potential practical benefits, "Lamps" directing new experiments, "Inoculators" who test them and, lastly, "Interpreters of nature" translating scientific observations into social axioms. Given this scheme, it is easy to argue that Renaissance science was as much a catalysis for the period's economy of intelligence as the rise of market capitalism, the two working in concert. Science not only challenged existing thought, but its new methods were consistent with the myth of individualism and new economic processes. Moreover, proof of the growing ideological power of Renaissance science is evident in the increase in new institutional programs, as well as social programs and school curricula that linked the identification of intelligence with material productions and wealth. The equating of intelligence to wealth had the effect of positioning individual intelligence within a new social hegemony as a mark of class superiority. Interestingly, modern films about intelligent people, those like *Little Man Tate* or *Good Will Hunting*, present characters whose *genius* is nurtured by well meaning representatives of the upper class. As we shall see, the equation of intelligence with class was used in the nineteenth and twentieth centuries to justify euge'nic practices based on class delineation.

In his exploration of the relationship between English science, religion, and capitalism James R. Jacob argues that although the economic views of major seventeenth-century natural philosophers were not inherently capitalistic, they nevertheless possessed "their own distinctive economy ideology in which science, especially Baconian science, played a key role." Jacob argues rightly that

> beginning in the seventeenth century with Bacon himself, a hitherto undetected tradition of moral and political discourse emerged to address basic questions regarding the creation and distribution of wealth and the role of the state in relation to private property. This unexplored tradition, running like a thread throughout the seventeenth-century, took a critical turn in response to what its mid-century exponents regarded as the then-current excesses of utopianism, Harringtonianism, and Hobbism. As the result, we shall see how a small circle of Oxford natural philosophers who were among the principal founders of the Royal Society charted their own distinctive course in addressing fundamental economic and political issues, just as we already know they did in religious matters. (Jacob, 1998, pp. 20–1)

The primary seventeenth-century agenda for the new "natural" philosopher was to increase common knowledge about nature, which, in turn, often initiated social, religious, and political reform. The guiding premise was that science could play a dynamic role in this reform, with a growing knowledge of nature that "would make all men more pious by revealing God through the study of nature; it would make better leaders by instructing them in God's providential rule over the universe and instilling in them the virtues of reason and moderation . . . Finally science would increase prosperity" (ibid., p. 21). Throughout his writings, Bacon argues that the distribution of wealth among the many would help to stabilize the sociopolitical world, his thesis being that significant increases in knowledge and greater human control over nature were *gifts* of a providential agency.

Although Bacon may have been the first to argue that science was an antidote to diseases of unemployment and poverty, others held somewhat similar views, those like Gabriel Plattes (the title of his main work, *A Discovery of Infinite Treasure* (1638), being a rather telling one), Samuel Hartlib, Ralph Austen, and Walter Blith. This group held the radical position that the state could confiscate individual property if lands were not being used to maximize the economic benefits drawn from scientific insight. According to Plattes the solution to human avarice is "not only to apply science to agriculture but to metamorphize that monster [covetousness] really into good husbandry and godly providence . . . which . . . is the surest way for the well ordering of the universe." Plattes also shared the common idea that a scientifically guided industry and labor force could be a source for moral reformation, the argument that "industry" – as a way of working and as an economic force – could help to maintain a viable balance between virtue and wealth. The more optimistic believed that "industry" might even reconcile them. Hobbes also moralized and politicized economics, advocating state control over the property of its subjects when individual wealth threatens the stability of the Commonwealth.

There were others who advanced collaborations between science, economics, and political state stability. The members of the Oxford Experimental Philosophy Club – Matthew and Christopher Wren, John Wilkins, Robert Boyle, William Petty and Robert Hooke – offered their own unique solutions to the relations between wealth and commonwealth stability, the rights of the sovereign and an individual's right to profit, most of their attention being centered on the conflict between sufficiency and unlimited wealth. For many, the solution came from religion and its establishing of a comfortable subsistence. Religion was also able "to civilize men, and make them more inquisitive in learning, and more diligent in practicing their several professions . . . the flourishing of arts and science hath so stirred up the sparks of men's natural nobility and made them of such active and industrious spirits, as to free themselves in a great measure from slavery" (Jacob, 1998). Jacob continues his quoting of Wilkins: history shows that "the flourishing of arts and sciences will spur men to greater and greater industry, whose outcome will be wealth distributed to provide a sufficiency proportioned to social station. And the engine driving the whole process is true religion" (ibid., p. 35). Robert Boyle adds another aspect to the appropriation of morality and religion to economic stability by arguing that the political economy hangs upon the production of more human intelligence: "It is because of man's intelligence," he alone being endowed with the gift of reason, that he is "bound to return thanks and praises to his Maker, not only for himself but for the whole creation. Man's curiosity is part of his greedy nature, hence it leads to the discovery of nature" (ibid., p. 36). Boyle notes in *Some Considerations about the Reconcileableness of Reason and Religion* that the innate tendency of human intelligence is to consider the mind to be the measure of truth and reality. This tendency, however, becomes destructive when trying to find out what is true of nature. The intelligence that invents new knowledge may also guarantee good citizenship. Hobbes, along with other natural philosophers, believed that "the advancement of learning should alter and improve men's behavior toward one another and toward the state, that the increase, spread and application of knowledge should make men not only wiser and richer but also better, at least more obedient subjects" (Jacob, 1998, p. 38). This thinking may have had its source in the Cartesian belief that science could aid humankind in gaining power over nature, and, in the process, society could achieve a higher level of moral as well as material culture.

The prologue to the charter of the Royal Society (1662) asserts that religious and scientific education promotes morality. Wren, a well known member, argued that industry can be "informed and made productive by science." It is industry in this sense that will make for both political order and a good society in which "wealth and poverty," as he says, "are diffused in just proportion to everyone's industry, that is, to everyone's desserts" (Jacob, 1998, p. 40). Here and elsewhere, members argued that a science-driven private industry would be the best assurance for a self-regulated morally grounded economy in which production is maximized and the resulting wealth justly distributed. In 1664, Thomas Mun's *England's Treasure by Forraign Trade* dealt with the question of how England could increase its national wealth and power. His solution was simple: hard work, minimizing imports, maximizing exports, and the encouragement of minimal local consumption of domestic goods. His dedication explores the values inherent in Protestant morality, sobriety and disciplined industry. Jacob also quotes Houghton's idea that "prodigality and luxury [seventeenth-century consumerism] were at worst morally neutral and at best economically beneficial because they stimulated production and ultimately increased wealth and profits" (Jacob, 1998, p. 40).

For most members of the Royal Society there was a direct connection between superior intelligence and scientific information made available to entrepreneurs who could increase their wealth and profit. Given this equation, and as Jacob notes, "virtue would take care of itself" (ibid., p. 42). Jacob concludes his survey by arguing that English natural philosophers "were advocates of economic growth and prosperity. All men, they hoped, would become industrious producers of wealth" (ibid., p. 43). I should like to add that whether such support was or wasn't inherently capitalistic in nature is less important than staying mindful that what underlay these various arguments about the moralization of a stable political economy was the production of new knowledge. Bacon called it the "advancement of learning": it had an exact method, an exact goal, an "industriousness" for the capacity and zeal for work, and it required the creation, identification, and deployment of intelligence.

Comments about the nature and value of national scientific societies are additionally revealing, especially showing connections made between information, intelligence, and business. For example, Seth Ward's 1652 letter suggests that:

> our first business is to gather together such things as are already discovered and to make a booke with a generall index of them, then to have a collection of those which are still inquirenda and according to our opportunityes to make inquisitive

> experiments, the end is that out of sufficient number of sure experiments, the way
> of nature in workeing may be discovered [how nature works . . . why work?] . . .
> we have conceived it requisite to examine all the bookes of our public library . . .
> and to make a catalogue or index of the matters . . . so that greate numbers of
> books may be serviceable and a man may at once see where he may find whatever
> is there concerning the argument he is upon, and this is our present business.
> (Robinson, 1949, pp. 69–70)

Thomas Sprat's *History of the Royal Society* confirms Ward's point and outlines
the aims of the membership:

> Their purpose is, in short, to make faithful *Records*, of all the Works of *Nature*, or
> *Art*, which can come within their reach: that so the present Age, and posterity, may
> be able to put a mark on the Errors, which have been strengthened by long pre-
> scription, to restore the Truths, that have lain neglected; to push on those, which
> are already known, to more various uses: and to make the way more passable, to
> what remains unreveal'd. This is the compass of their Design. (Sprat, 1959, pp.
> 61–2)

Robert Hooke argued that all the observations and experiments fostered by the
Royal Society would lead to great advances in natural knowledge, often referring
to those advances in terms of a "treasure." Sprat explains how the Royal Society
functioned as a library as well as a place for doing science. Sir Robert Moray
makes the similar point that "The business & designe of the Royal Society" is
"To improve the knowledge of Naturall things and all usefull Arts . . . by Experiment" and "To attempt the recovering of such allowable arts and inventions as
are lost" (Hunter, 1995, p. 172). Even Wren's preamble to the Royal Society links
intelligence, empire, and enterprise:

> And whereas we are informed that a competent number of persons of eminent
> learning, ingenuity, and honour . . . meet weekly . . . to confer about the hidden
> causes of thing, with a design to establish certain and correct uncertain theories
> . . . and by their labour in the disquisition of nature to prove themselves real bene-
> factors to mankind. . . . We have determined to grant our Royal favor, patronage
> and all due encouragement to this illustrious assembly, and so beneficial and laud-
> able an enterprise. . . . We have long and fully resolved . . . to extend not only the
> boundaries of Empire but also of the very arts and sciences. (Ibid., pp. 104–5)

The Society was historically the first to implement the ideals of science on a
grand social scale. Its archives, journals, academic linkages, celebrities, experiments, labs, discoveries, and famous meetings made the Royal Society a power-

ful institution that ultimately invented another kind of intelligence: "We have given . . . that they . . . enjoy mutual *intelligence* and knowledge with . . . strangers and foreigners . . . without any molestation, interruption, or distur-bance . . . provided [this be] in matters or things philosophical, mathematical and mechanical" (ibid., p. 105). This new intelligence, a metaphor for valuable and privileged information, the information of future national security agencies, is produced by the intelligence of human aptitude. This is an important moment in the history of intelligence because it unites the source and production of intel-ligence, privileging those whose superiority or ingenuity resulted in the produc-tion of valuable and frequently commercial knowledge. The Renaissance economy was also the first to develop the capitalization of both kinds of intelligence.

7

Profitable Knowledge and Intelligence Becomes a Career

In an age that invented the individual and the entrepreneurial, it is quite consistent that those who had or recognized superior intelligence should also have a title, a means of recognizing intelligence and converting it into various forms of capital. Francis Bacon may arguably have been one of the first to conceive of what we today call "knowledge or intelligence management" or "intellectual capital," taking an abstract human quality, like intelligence, and applying it to another abstract structure, like an organization or corporate culture. Bacon invented the term *intelligencer*, defining it as a "Merchant of Light," as it appears in *New Atlantis* (1628), and it became a source of Locke's later version, his idea of "profitable knowledge."

In the modern history of science, the term intelligencer refers to a person in the business of gathering, promoting, advancing, and disseminating scientific discoveries and technological inventions for profit. What originally was part of what a scientist such as Leibniz did eventually became a mini-industry, a niche market for specialists, especially given the tremendous proliferation of scientific knowledge during the seventeenth century. The popular term for these workers, "philosophical merchants," referred to individuals who traded information, those knowledge merchants who made healthy profits by serving the scientific community and reinforcing the growing dominance of the new natural or scientific philosophy. A representative list of these early intelligencers includes Henry Oldenburg, the first secretary of the Royal Society, Nicolas Claude Fabri De Peirsec, Marin Mersenne, and Samuel Hartlib, who together created significant correspondence and information networks, linkages providing them with access to current scientific and technological knowledge.

Intelligencers were frequently multilingual, worked as diplomats, and were keen information consumers, promoting scientific journals, establishing scientific academic communities, and knowing the profit potential for any given theory or claim. Their publicized efforts often resulted in new collaborations and networks drawn among leading scientists, technologists, and, even a century later, a whole new class of wealthy individuals known as industrialists. In less than two centuries, intelligence and industry, two metaphors for insight and discipline, became the abstract catalysis for the production of a new sociopolitical system and class structure.

Intelligencers were adept at making scientists reveal the content of their work. Many of them worked to insure the commercialization of such scientific knowledge by working as editors and sectaries of new publications and organizations. In today's corporate-speak parlance, intelligencers were late Renaissance "information gate-keepers," consultants who played a significant role in shaping the scientific myth of modern Western culture. Socially, employment as an intelligencer was considered a form of privilege because the production and exchange of intelligence capital was often described as being noble. This myth of the noble use of intelligence to generate profit (meaning both state improvement and money making) arose from the growing ideology that the production of intelligence, together with scientific discoveries and technological innovations, could promote the common good, and at rates and values far greater than the individual profit gained by such class improvement. But even more important to a social history of intelligence is the fact that the intelligencer marks the first time in Western history when ideological cooperations were formed between capitalism, science, moral religion, technology, and a political economy guaranteeing that utilitarian interest would insure state and private stability. Moreover, in this climate of expanding political capital, intelligence was not only referred to as a superior producer of potentially valuable knowledge, a genius, but also became a metaphor, perhaps even a metonymy, for knowledge itself. Hence it took the intelligent to produce intelligence, a gifted lot of special individuals who produced information advantage, the *intelligence* that gave governments, politicians, industrialists, and entrepreneurs leverage, ascendancy, and superiority over any competitor. Finally, such a market for information profit created an entirely different way of understanding the purposes of learning and the various institutions and practices responsible for producing, assessing, and regulating the production of intelligence.

The Renaissance commodification of knowledge anticipates critical issues of postmodernism. For instance, in his book *The Postmodern Condition*, Jean-François Lyotard discusses postmodern knowledge much in the way Bacon, Locke, and members of the Royal Society did during the Renaissance:

> The relationships of the suppliers and users of knowledge to the knowledge they supply and use is now tending, and will increasingly tend, to assume the form already taken by the relationship of commodity producers and consumers to the

> commodities they produce and consume – that is, the form of value. Knowledge
> is and will be produced in order to be sold, it is and will be consumed in order to
> be valorized in a new production: in both cases, the goal is exchange. (Lyotard,
> 1984, pp. 4–5)

The Renaissance was the first era to begin converting knowledge into a commodity, to make it valuable in a developing exchange economy. This capitalization of information required an ideological control mechanism, a way to produce, monitor, and measure the kinds of knowledge proving most valuable. I believe that modern notions of intelligence, stemming from the human model, functioned precisely as such a mechanism, creating an ideational structure to control the production or exclusion of certain kinds of information.

Raymond Williams once noted that natural philosophy was the source of the idea that the advancement of learning should alter and improve human behavior and that the expansion, dissemination, and deployment of knowledge make human beings not only wiser and richer but moral, a concept Williams and other Marxists have frequently deconstructed.

8 Intelligence and Dominant Renaissance Scientists

Renaissance ideas about intelligence circulated within scientific discourse, especially within the fields of astronomy, chemistry, physics, and mathematics. The idea of intelligence proved valuable to certain Renaissance scientists, its scope of application from the human body to celestial bodies, and from divine intelligence to personal intelligence. For example, Andreas Vesalius's (1514–64) *De Humani Corporis Fabrica* (1543) is guided by the new human model of intelligence. By focusing on the natural and physical nature of the body, he ignores the tradition of studying the human only in so far as its mirrors a universal divine and perfect intelligence. Other early anatomists, such as da Carpi, Dryander, Estienne, Canano of Ferrara, and Massa, followed suit, preferring the physical to the metaphysical, the measuring of nature to the verification of official yet untested *a priori* universals. Copernicus and Kepler followed a similar trajectory, their measurements of elliptical planetary motion being more a matter of physical principles and mechanics than supernatural intelligence. Neither astronomer had a theoretical need to argue for a prime mover or to describe intelligence as a planetary force. This reasoning is consistent with their efforts to replace the Ptolemaic model with a heliostatic one.

Robert Boyle (1627–91) argued that a mechanical intelligence guides the universe. His writings show the mechanistic influence of Descartes and Gassendi and the social vision of Bacon as he argues that when God created intelligent beings, he deliberately limited their understanding in order to reserve absolute knowledge to the afterlife. Boyle's proof of the intelligence of design came in his famous Strasbourg analogy. The clock modeled the universe; its regular motions were a set of rules nature obeyed and natural philosophers could discover. By arguing that a divine craftsman made the clock, Boyle simultaneously avoided theological controversy while also promoting the value of science. His mechanistic view of intelligence appears in such works as "A Requisite Digression" and "About the Excellency and Grounds of the Mechanical Hypothesis." In the former he discusses natural phenomena, especially the "first productions of the world," and insists that the world could not have been created without the "need of a powerful and intelligent Being" or "an intelligent agent" (Stewart, 1979, pp. 173–4). For proof, he refers to the writer manipulating a quill and the Strasbourg clock, insisting that their complexity of motion and machinery owes itself to the "skill of an intelligent and ingenious contriver." Prior to this he argues that "opus naturae est opus intelligentiae" (ibid., p. 161) and that "it is far from being unlikely that such skilful contrivances [the complexity of body functions] should be made by any being not intelligent, that they require a more than ordinary intelligence to comprehend how skilfully they are made" (ibid., p. 168). This latter point, referring to the complexity of the human body, represents an early construction of modern intelligence; it equates divine intelligence with individuals intelligent enough to understand the nature of divine creation. This argument – and its ideological significance – gains authority simply by equating intelligent human beings with divinity, the kind of pop culture linkage Einstein enjoyed. Boyle clearly breaks with tradition in his "About the Excellency and Grounds of the Mechanical Hypothesis" when he argues that "those very Aristotelians that believe the celestial bodies to be moved by intelligences have no recourse to any peculiar agency of theirs to account for eclipses" (ibid., p. 140). Perhaps most importantly, Boyle is the first to place as much emphasis on intelligibility as on the nature of intelligence, his interest being what human capacity made it possible to understand natural phenomena.

The emergence of modern science and the name Galileo are often mentioned in the same breath. His place in the history of intelligence is unique because it combines a significant departure from traditional notions of intelligence with a new association of intelligence with mathematics, as well as an existential drama of personal intelligence. Galileo's conflict with Church authority represented a clash of authority between institutional power and individual insight. Galileo is the first instance in Western culture in which an individual's intelligence becomes the subject of popular culture, taking narrative shape as a hero whose individual power of intelligence and insight opposes the blindness of state power. Although Galileo made significant contributions to science, it is his individual and defiant intelligence that history remembers, his a voice saying: "Why should I believe blindly and stupidly when I am told to believe, and subject the freedom of my intellect to someone else who is just as liable as I am to error" (Galileo, 1962, volume 6, p. 341).

Galileo challenged conventional notions of intelligence by arguing that intelligence was human and political in nature, that it was to be understood in terms of freedom and nature, rather than as something ineffable. Here Galileo breaks from the celestial intelligence idea of heavenly bodies offered by earlier Renaissance thinkers, like Pietro Pomponazzi, who were still under the sway of Aristotelian thought. A similar celestial model is presented in Donne's "Valediction: Forbidding Mourning": "Let man's soul be a sphere, and then, in this, / The Intelligence that moves, devotion is." In his *Dialogue on the Great World Systems*, Galileo argues that "Nature made human reason skillful enough to understand . . . some parts of her secrets" (Galileo, 1953, volume 2, p. 289) and in a June 16, 1612 letter suggests that he was comforted by the fact that

> the spots and my other discoveries are not things that will pass away with time as did the novae of 1572 and 1604 or the comets, whose disappearance from the skies do so much to claim those whose minds were in such anguish during their presence. The spots, by contrast, will torment them ceaselessly, because they refuse to vanish, and it is only fitting that nature should thus punish the ingratitude of men who have maltreated her for so long by foolishly shutting their eyes before the very light she provided for their edification. (Galileo, 1962, volume 11, pp. 326–7)

Although he links human intelligence to nature, Galileo less frequently makes connections between "divine wisdom" and human insight, on occasion deploying both the divine – human and strictly human model of intelligence. However, his is not a traditional divinity; instead of being detached, it interacts with human beings, sharing insight and knowledge. For instance, in his *Dialogue*, there are

> extensively or a multitude of intelligibles which are infinite . . . and intensively, inasmuch as that term imports perfectly some propositions, I say that human wisdom understands some propositions as perfectly and is as absolutely certain thereof, as Nature herself; and such are the pure mathematical sciences, to wit, Geometry and Arithmetic. In these Divine Wisdom knows infinitely more propositions, because it knows them all; but I believe that the knowledge of those few comprehended by human understanding equals the Divine, as to objective certainty, for it arrives to comprehend the necessity of it, than which there can be no greater certainty. (Galileo, 1953, p. 114)

He extends this argument by stating that

> The Divine Wisdom by the simple apprehension of its essence comprehends without temporal ratiocination, all these infinite properties which are also, in effect, virtually compromised in the definitions of all things, and, to conclude, being infinite, are perhaps but one alone in their nature gradual motion, the Divine Mind, like light, penetrates in an instant, which is the same as to say has them always all present. (Ibid., p. 115)

In these examples, Galileo links divine and human intelligence in a radical and novel way, suggesting that both can comprehend infinite propositions and properties in terms of an "objective certitude" because of an aptitude for "pure mathematical sciences." This association is radical because classical analogies of divinity and mathematics – those made especially by pre-Socratic and Pythogorean philosophers – assigned truth to transcendental entities rather than to anything human, natural, or temporal. But more importantly, Galileo's identification of intelligence with mathematics may be the first historical instance in which the ideological content of modern ideas of intelligence was established, creating a correlation between an abstract human attribute and the means of objectifying it within various mathematical categories, hierarchies, and topographies. I preface the next chapter's exploration of the ideology of Enlightenment mathematics by briefly exploring how Galileo's construction of mathematics was appropriated and politicized by new seventeenth- and eighteenth-century state institutions.

In *Le Mecaniche*, Galileo indicates that the essence of mathematics is to substitute quantitative for qualitative concepts. Galileo charts this substitution across a wide mathematical spectrum, his primary accomplishment being the transference of the deductive order of geometry into the study of physics and classical mechanics. His second accomplishment was to explore concrete situation analysis to discover general patterns. Galileo's idealized sense of mathematics came from his reading of Archimedes' formal proof, which allowed the Italian to apply the postulation of ideal conditions in geometry to physics. Throughout his work, Galileo breaks from tradition by favoring experiential insights over *a priori* absolutes, a strategy that along with Descartes's method signals the dawn of modern science. The primary tool responsible for the new science was the telescope because it put Galileo into direct contact with what he would then theorize about, theorizing on the basis of the observation of heavenly bodies rather than some imaginative religion-based drawing made up of hundreds of concentric circles with nymphs and angels holding up stars or illustrations made of geometric symmetrical designs. His cosmology was radical because it was based upon experiential science and several of his efforts subverted classical theories of celestial or transcendental intelligence. For instance, his discover of lunar craters challenged the notion of the perfection of celestial or intelligent bodies and his evidence to support the Copernican theory – the existence of sunspots – proved that the heavens were imperfect. His own inventiveness – the creation of a new model of the universe, the detailing of differences in the speeds of free falling bodies, the creation of a geometry-based science of motion, his transformation of the very nature of mechanical analysis, and his analytic system, which replaced simple physical causality with the power and value of rationality – drew attention to his personal intelligence as well as to the rationality and mathematics that seemingly made it possible. Galileo literally brought intelligence into the world of scientific research, intelligence of insight and intelligence as a metaphor of the knowledge insight creates, using reason and observation as the primary tools for his "genius," with observational data utilized and integrated in the body of science. In short, Galileo brought technology and mathematical reasoning into the measurement of an observable and predictable reality, using his individual human intelligence to challenge and displace prior notions of divine intelligence. His method produced absolute certitude, indicating that divine, natural, and human intelligence were engaged in the production of practical scientific knowledge.

What is one to make of a prayer concluding arguably one of the least read but most influential books in Western culture, Bacon's *Novum Organum*? "Therefore do thou, O Father, who gavest the visible light as the first fruits of creation, and didst breathe into the face of man the intellectual light as the crown and consummation thereof, guard and protect this work, which coming from thy goodness returneth to thy glory." The reference to a divine – human model of intelligence is surprising coming, as it does, from the first commodifier of intelligence, from "an exponent of the "Maker's knowledge tradition: a tradition which postulates an intimate relationship between objects of cognition and objects of construction, and regards knowing as a kind of making or as a capacity to make" (Perez-Ramos, 1988, p. 88). The Baconian plan for creating commodity intelligence – producing the insight behind profitable knowledge – is rather straightforward: the pursuit of simple natural qualities reduces the complexity. This method, in turn, creates simple laws that unleash innovation, power over nature, and wealth. For Bacon, the social benefits of the scientific enterprise have been squandered by "idols of the mind" whose fixation with dogma making and despair of knowledge has created "the deepest fallacies of the human mind. For they do not deceive in particulars . . . but by a corrupt and ill-ordered predisposition of mind, which it were perverts and infects all the anticipations of the intellect" (Bacon, 1861, volume 9, pp. 97–8).

As a remedy, Bacon wrote *The New Atlantis*, his utopian allegory of a world where scientific entrepreneurialism, imperialism, and market capitalism construct an ideal society and quality of life. Its narrator calls his tale a "natural history" of the customs, rituals, and culture of the island Bensalem. Its society is governed by the appropriation and commercialization of intelligence, the conversion of brilliance into information that turns into money. The dominant ritual is straightforward: every twelve years ships with three representatives are charged with gathering "the knowledge of the affairs and state of those countries to which they are designated, and especially of the sciences, arts, manufactures, and inventions of all the world." This "intelligence" then finds its way back to Bensalem in the form of "books, instruments and patterns in every kind" (ibid., volume 3, p. 146). These procurers are "merchants of light," a term that not only combines commerce and intelligence but engenders the Renaissance *economy of intelligence*. Bacon's "merchants of light" engage in the acquisition and production of knowledge, help to invent dissemination technologies, and actively promote market capitalism. In Bacon's story inventors are given a special social status; they are remembered. There are galleries on the island housing statues of "all principal inventors" of the past. Moreover, whenever an "invention of value" is produced a statue of its inventor is erected. The innovator is then given a "liberal and honourable reward" (ibid., pp. 165–6). Ideally, Bensalem is a commercial culture marked by its Christian charity, its amassing of great knowledge, and its civility.

Intelligence operates in two ways in Bacon's discourse: it is the means by which valuable information is produced, taking the material form of what the intelligent make. Intelligence, for Bacon, is the means by which humankind can expose the mysteries of Nature so that phenomena like heat, force, energy, color, and motion can ultimately be controlled and manipulated. This intelligence of insight, control, and manipulation takes material form in the production of tools, machines, and technical achievement. For Bacon, intelligence is neither an abstract essence nor an external phenomenon; its true value is in its demonstration, a material production whose value and measurements refer back indirectly to the kind, level, or amount of intelligence implicit in the object produced. This notion of intelligence becomes as important as Galileo's, the two being the dominant strands that form the ideological mosaic of modern ideas about intelligence, particularly the modern idea of its *demonstration through an instrument that measures and classifies in order to normalize.*

Although intelligence takes several Baconian forms, each nevertheless is discussed in terms of either an overt or an implied commodity value. For example, in *The Advancement of Learning*, he describes the deconstruction of Nature and its resulting intelligence in terms of a payment, particularly a "bill" collecting: "there will hardly be any main proficiencies in the disclosing of nature, except there be some allowance for expenses about experiments . . . and therefore as secretaries and spials of princes and states bring in bills for intelligence, so you must allow the spials and intelligencers of nature to bring in their bill" (ibid., volume 2, p. 76). Bacon also sees new collaborations of academic intelligence in terms of advancement: "For as the proficiencies of learning consisteth much in orders and institutions of universities in the same states and kingdoms so it would be yet more advanced, if there were more intelligence mutual between the universities of Europe than now there is" (ibid., p. 78). His commercialization of intelligence also makes the study of knowledge less an inquiry into the rules of its formulation and more a matter of understanding things, particularly the body, the mind, and Nature:

> knowledge concerning the sympathies and concordances between the mind and body . . . this knowledge hath two branches: for as all leagues and amities consist of mutual Intelligence and mutual Office, so this league of mind and body hath these two parts; how the one discloseth the other, and how the one worketh upon the other; discovery and impression. (Ibid., p. 102)

Bacon draws attention to the ideological nature of intelligence and knowledge by claiming that "it follows that the improvement of man's intelligence and the improvement of his lot are one and the same thing" (ibid., volume 3, p. 612). In the preface to his unfinished *Instauratio*, he assumes that those who seek knowledge do so "for the benefit and use of life, and that they perfect and govern it in charity" (ibid., volume 8, p. 36). This same idea appears in his *Valerius Terminus of the Interpretation of Nature* (Bacon, 1861, volume 6, pp. 33–4), in *The Advancement of Learning* (ibid., pp. 134–5), and in the *Novum Organum* (ibid., volume 8, pp. 162–3). Bacon's making of intelligence, knowledge, and learning critical elements in his new myth of progress sets the stage for Condorcet, Turgot, Comte, and Spencer to agree that there is a historical law that tends toward the perfection and happiness of the human race. Moreover, this perfection is directly tied to the growth and development of human intelligence and scientific knowledge. Bacon's agenda ultimately anticipates the utilitarian spirit of nineteenth- and twentieth-century industrial culture.

This part of the book has focused on how Renaissance ideas of intelligence, particularly in its humanized version, were appropriated by Renaissance scientific discourse for support of its new methods and rational-empiricist biases. It has also shown how the new science and the new political economy cooperated in forming Renaissance culture. Exploring the correspondence between this new economy, new ideas of intelligence, and new technologies of self-production is critical to a broader understanding of the ideological history of smart.

Summary of Part I

Part I of this book began with Greek theories of intelligence and ends with Renaissance scientists. In it we have seen intelligence function as one might use a tool. This is an interesting metaphor given the significance of an era that used a host of conceptual tools to help to revolutionize traditional marketplaces and, in the process, invent a new economy of applied intelligence. This new economy, and the invention of the individual and new scientific methods and technologies, rank as the chief ideological productions of the Renaissance, manifested, as they were, in the most important of culture-making sites. Two new conceptualizations of intelligence emerged, which not only helped to support those productions in their ideological formations, but also would set the stage and standards by which we understand modern intelligence. Whether purely human or human by way of divine synthesis, human intelligence became a metaphoric device (discursively) as well as a literal tool (institutionally) for making ideas of humanism, individuality, science, technology, and market capitalism the cause for eighteenth-century Europeans to awaken to a "new sense of life."

Renaissance notions of intelligence were, in part, responsible for Enlightenment culture having "an expansive sense of power over nature and themselves: the treadmill of human existence seemed to be yielding at last to the application of critical intelligence" (Gay, 1977, p. 3). When it could be seen as mastering the world with its tools and observational measurements, intelligence not only began to be associated with certainty and uncontestable truth but became real; intelligence became as much an empirical thing as the very material inventions or insights it created. The majority of this ideological thinking came from the enculturation of Isaac Newton, what many academic writers have called social Newtonianism or the application of Newtonian methods to social institutional behaviors. Part II explores how Enlightenment appropriations of Newtonianism, particularly in France, took form in social mathematics, a methodology ultimately responsible for modern ideas and clinical practices of intelligence. In essence, one need not be surprised that France began measuring intelligence, or its use of mathematics to scale, chart, and objectify the presumed rational interior of the human mind. As mathematics was used to map the globe or create market capitalism, so was it now employed to chart and materialize the heretofore invisible potential of a individual who was ironically free to be subordinate to modern state, legal, and medical policies.

Part II

Bright Lights, Fallen Apples, and Clinical Gazes: Intelligence and the Enlightenment

The monarchs mean to strengthen their own position by debasing their subjects with all the vices of dissoluteness, and they dispose them to endure slavery at the hands of stronger nations. The nations mean to dissolve themselves, and their remnants flee for safety to the wilderness. . . . That which did all this was mind, for men did it with intelligence; it was not fate.

Vico, *The New Science*, 1744

One cannot escape the feeling that these mathematical formulas have an independent existence and an *intelligence* of their own, that they are wiser that we are.

Hertz Heinrich, *Men of Mathematics*, 1937

9 Intelligence and the Enlightenment

· The modernization of ideas of intelligence – those responsible for how we commonly understand intelligence – can be traced primarily to various sociopolitical and mathematical ideas coming out of the Renaissance and finding greater alignment in the eighteenth century. The power of those influences on contemporary ideas of intelligence is obvious, evident, for example, in Herrnstein and Murray's *The Bell Curve* (1994), whose results rest solely upon these intersections, especially the automatic certainty given statistics, social theory, race theory, and symbolic system certitude. Neither author ever puts into question the key assumption that representations of racial differences (in the form of race classifications, numbers, graphs, or scales) can effectively model or substitute for the "objective" phenomenon studied. Moreover, neither defends his statistically grounded work from poststructural critiques of mathematics, those offered by Rotman, Aronowitz, Wittgenstein, Lakatos, Popper, Harré, Dowling, Restivo, and Ernest, who have challenged conventional assumptions about the certainty of mathematics and model theory. And despite the fact that Herrnstein and Murray's arguments were based upon traditional statistics, their critics fell into an old trap by paying far more attention to the book's content and arguing with its conclusions. They did not explore how its claims were ideologically grounded. Critics swallowed the hermeneutical hook, as it were, ignoring the value of Foucault's "archeological" approach to argue from within the ideological circle protecting Herrnstein and Murray's "logic." An archeological interest would have shown how their claims were tied more to a system of assumptions than to an actual science of the phenomenon examined. On one level *The Bell Curve* revalidated meritocratic individualism, and, on the other, the scientific, it was simply bad science, woefully inadequate in testing its assumptions. If voodoo economics exists so can voodoo science.

Foucault's *Order of Things* (1994) helps to explain the role of political and mathematical intersections formed during the later history of intelligence. In fact, these alignments relate specifically to four Enlightenment events: the social application of Newtonian science (Newtonianism), the invention of the "human sciences," governmental use of social mathematics, and revisions of Renaissance notions of intelligence. It is no news that these ideas and their practices produced a new cultural order, a world of new political theories, state practices, and notions of a continuously controllable and "politicized" individual. These elements form the infrastructure of modern social reality. They revolutionized Western culture by *normalizing* social behavior and intelligence, creating practices for accessing, evaluating, and judging an individual's character, his social compliance aptitude, her intentions, his intellectual potential, and even her "moral intelligence." These ideas arose with eighteenth-century philosophers who appropriated Newtonian mathematics in order to develop and methodize the "human sciences" and "human nature," two new typographies that measured the human *interior* in the same way external phenomena were measured and charted. As key components of this new secular-scientific-social myth, ideas of intelligence were drawn into ideological service by being connected with social and legal concepts related to the "political individual." In several important instances, these ideas were made *synonymous* with *reason* itself, the premier Enlightenment construct assigning to the human an ability to continue Renaissance-initiated efforts to produce and profit from absolute certainty. This is, for example, what Condillac meant when he constructed an interior landscape based purely on a mental calculus intelligence:

> of all the operations described here, there is one that crowns the understanding
> . . . and that is reason. Whatever our idea of it, everyone agrees that only reason
> is a wise guide in public life, and it alone makes progress in search of truth. So we
> must conclude that reason is just a knowledge of how to control the operations
> of the mind . . . reason results from the operations of the well-controlled mind.
> (Condillac, 1970, volume 2, pp. 11, 480–1)

In this instance a metaphor, *reason*, combined with another, *intelligence* or understanding, is assigned the status of absolute truth, then defined as the product of a "well-controlled" mind (the agency that the also controls the social world), before finally being redefined as the fundamental element of human nature. New ideas of intelligence were called into ideological duty once the "rational human" was constructed, evident, for instance, when Buffon argues that "animals have only one mode for acquiring pleasure, the exercise of their sensations to gratify their desires. We also possess this faculty: but we are endowed with another source of pleasure, the exercise of mind, the appetite of which is the desire for knowledge" (Buffon and Le Clerc, 1862, volume 1, p. 295).

The Enlightenment created ideological mosaics consisting of new theories of the *human*, new ideas about intelligence, new beliefs in individual rights, and new social uses for science, technology, and mathematics. It is little wonder that tracing the trajectory of these mosaics to their contemporary influences is so difficult. Or that the majority of clinical procedures based on now *standardized* ideas of intelligence are practiced daily in courtrooms, schools, offices, and clinics, with little knowledge of the genealogical, historical, and ideological implications of those practices. This phenomenon of practice without historical or politically knowledge – what amounts to ideological compliance – may speak to the bio-epistemological, to how biological processes and brain function together to shape the knowability of the world, or to how the brain processes divergent, anomalous, or inconsistent information. Theoretically, executive brain functions may ultimately be responsible for neural and biological homeostasis, shaping certain incoming data into a kind of default file or prescribed social behavior, which in turn produces external forms of social homeostasis. The brain that continually produces social order ultimately guarantees its own continuity, consistent with the aims of natural selection and DNA replication. This theory may explain why clinicians administer intelligence tests knowing little about the sociopolitical forces served by their efforts or knowing nothing about the ideological history privileging such a seemingly innocent, worthwhile, and unchallengeable "therapeutic intervention."

The relationship between figures of "enlightenment" and intelligence can be traced to three dominant metaphors reflecting the ideological dynamics of Enlightenment representations of intelligence. The first is ubiquitous *enlightenings* or the politically liberating lights ignited originally by Renaissance humanizations of intelligence. These mental illuminations did not occur in a cultural vacuum; they were, as the argument goes, the presumable byproduct of the mind's ability to reason and conceptualize its own ultimate freedom. In fact, the two terms – enlightenment and intelligence – began to be used interchangeably during the eighteenth century. The writings of several social and theoretical philosophers underscore the Enlightenment politicization of the *intelligent* individual, the subject whose degree of autonomy and freedom is directly proportionate to his level of ignorance. On the political side of the Enlightenment, freedom was contingent upon one's intelligence.

The second metaphor extends the first, linking mental enlightenment to the privileging of a special kind of *insight*, of a superior knowledge related to the methodological thinking manifested in calculations and scientific ideas. This knowledge, manifested in the methods it produced, was eventually transformed into social concepts grounding many modern institutional practices. Voltaire linked the idea of innate superior intelligence to the supreme scientist of his age:

"if true genius consists of having been endowed by heaven with powerful genius, and of using it to enlighten oneself and others, then a man like M. Newton (we scarcely find one like him in ten centuries) is truly the great man" (*Lettres philosophiques*, 1773, volume 1, p. 153). Buffon, in his *Histoire Naturelle*, often makes a similar point, arguing that a scientist who sees both vast and minute phenomena from a single perspective can claim to be a genius.

The third connects abstract enlightenment to the concrete world of new specialists whose power resides in their intelligence to observe, diagnose, and cure. This was the new power of the clinician and supervisor, their steady *gaze* healing sick bodies, sick minds, sick workers, and sick citizens, those whose *containment* and assessment would help to insure social and economic stability. This is the eyesight that sees with certitude; its methods are a guarantee that the physical body and the body politic could be stabilized by surveillance and scientific observation.

These metaphors also supported other evolving Enlightenment ideas of intelligence. For instance, the dominant modern belief that intelligence is an *objectified* human attribute is rooted in eighteenth-century thought. This idea forms the basis of the modern history of intelligence: if Renaissance thought transformed metaphysical intelligence into something human, empirical, and potentially commercial, the intelligencers, if you will, then the Enlightenment promoted and refined that effort by making *scientific* and *institutionalizing* this transformation. These were the actions of philosophers and policy-makers who used science, mathematics, and sociopolitical theory to argue a century later that its objectivity made intelligence measurable. The idea of measuring a human "interior" can be traced to Enlightenment methods of representation, to the abstraction of signs from the material world and their organization into new truth formations that *virtualized* the conceptual, making it equally, if not more, real than the real. In essence, this new epistemology *ideates* something; it arranges things that then take on abstract forms seemingly more real than its referent. The Enlightenment may historically have been the first era that ideologized representations, placing importance on the capacity to make descriptions replace "real" entities unavailable for observation and immediate experience. In the process a new cultural inventory of signs and constructs was constructed, those like the human sciences, the human, new class systems and hegemonies, new state practices, Habermas's "public sphere," Foucault's "subject," and even habitual modes of thinking in terms of modernity. In essence, Enlightenment ideas of intelligence became modern when their earlier humanization became *political, virtual, critical,* and *productive* in terms of commodity, capital, and social regulation policy. They became modern when their meanings reflected a universal human attribute engendered in institutional practices based upon "natural" law theory, the idea of inalienable human rights and the value of rational thought. By virtue of their significance, these ideas led to a belief in *critical* intelligence, what Peter Gay (1977) identifies quite rightly as the collective belief in the power of rational humans to shape their destiny.

The modernization of intelligence, as an *internalized* human attribute, also paralleled the institutionalization of the *politicized individual or subject*. This byproduct, perhaps more than others, would eventually help to produce the self-monitoring individual or the monitoring of those unable to self-monitor, those whose intelligence would be measured and classified largely in terms of the socioeconomic demands of the forever self-monitoring state pursuing its own homeostasis. Later, we explore this chain of ideological implications when we look at the state rationale behind its request that Binet formulate a mental test at the turn of the twentieth century.

The trend of politicizing human attributes drew heavy ideological support from mathematical, scientific, and social theory collaborations. The byproduct was a significant increase in the creation and use of social, legal, medical, and institutional strategies valorizing self-awareness and self-diagnostic practices. The idea that citizens could help to effect state stability by observing, assessing, and regulating themselves through self-monitoring practices or through professional medical practices arose from both Newtonian influences and the invention of an unprecedented form of representational space – the literal yet metaphoric virtualization of the subject. Foucault explores this space in terms of a knowledge system that produces the conditions, the status, and the imaginary or seemingly "real" social world needed to create and control the subject. By definition, individuals exist as a construct proportionate to their desire to invent themselves as "legitimate" subjects, with the state authoring the terms of legitimacy. Consequently, in the modern era, one's life is spent seeking and monitoring various sanctioned legitimizations, whether they are familial, social, educational, religious, or economic in nature, those authored by "ideological state apparatuses" (Althusser, 2001, pp. 127–86).

Ideas of intelligence also contributed to the invention of the *self-monitoring* subject. Certain self-measurement practices established ways of constructing truth that ultimately shaped future conceptualizations of intelligence. Modern notions of intelligence, including those implicit in many clinical practices, would simply be non-existent if those practices could not be validated by a representational or symbolic assessment tool, usually a document, test, or score representing and objectifying an invisible internal attribute. Intelligence tests have traditionally *evaluated* "underachieving" students, "troubled" children, thousands of army recruits, hundreds of thousands of immigrants, institutionalized patients, "low functioning" sterilized individuals, convicts headed to death chambers, and even new "Silicon Valley" employees; in sum, millions and millions of people made into subjects by being subject to various social classifications. As I shall indicate, even the most innovative of contemporary ideas about intelligence have a legacy, a history born in social regulatory practices forged in the political and scientific mills of seventeenth- and eighteenth-century thought.

Although it produced ideas like natural rights, the free individual, and a rational universe, and although it used scientific methods ultimately as social control mechanisms, Enlightenment thought nevertheless produced a problematic intelligence. On the one hand this intelligence rated the *rational* individual so as to create new knowledge with commercial value, yet, on the other, it deployed a set of mathematically grounded practices that valorized certain knowledge and marginalized other. Interesting enough, clinical and scientific practices would evolve that employed various classification techniques, including, among other things, the identification of individuals who either advanced or threatened social stability. This practice became routine once France sponsored the creation of the 1905 Binet–Simon Scale to determine the potential mental and moral impairment of lower-class children. It is also apparent nineteen years later, when the US Supreme Court upheld the decision to sterilize those of "low" intelligence (*Buck* v. *Bell* 274 US 200, 47 S Ct 584, 71 LEd 1000 (1927)).

Part II of this book explores three metaphors – those of *enlightenment*, *insight*, and the *gaze* – to better understand Enlightenment contributions to the history of intelligence. I begin in chapter 10 with a sketch of the ubiquity of metaphoric *enlightenment* before moving in chapter 11 to an exploration of the *insights* derived from Newtonianism and social mathematics. Chapter 12 explores the invention of the clinical *gaze* as a precursor to modern psychological practices related to intelligence. These chapters lay the groundwork for tracing the social history of smart in nineteenth-, twentieth-, and twenty-first-century culture.

10 Illuminating Enlightenment Intelligence

Metaphors of enlightenment circulate freely through eighteenth-century discourse, creating national and individual identifies, defining highly valued careers, advancing women's rights, shaping educational and economic policy, and establishing key Enlightenment beliefs. Traditional ideas of light were given an entirely new historical status during the eighteenth century, with those reflecting the power of self-created knowledge replacing those of abstract metaphysical insight. These metaphors of light functioned ideologically by being symbolically associated with the mind and the emerging political system, with ideas like reason, liberty, individual natural rights, and personal happiness forming ideological alliances. Berkeley, for instance, spoke of "that ocean of light, which has broke in and made his way, in spite of slavery and superstition," while Alexander Pope praised new integrations of science and philosophy, declaring "Nature and Nature's laws lay hid in night / God said, let Newton be! And all was light" (Im Hof, 1994, p. 4). Foucault (1975, p. xiii) places this "light" in post-structural perspective, suggesting that eighteenth century "light . . . was the element of ideality – the unassignable place of origin where things were adequate to their essence." Tracing the itinerary of this new light of "ideality as essence" is essential to understanding the birth and ideological behaviors of modern ideas of intelligence.

First off, metaphors of illumination took form as the new light of national identities. While England inflated its national ego, basking in the brilliance of Newtonian light, the French celebrated political liberation as intellectual illumination (*lumiéres*). This light radiated the "understanding, knowledge and perspicuity" needed "to lead man to the perfection of knowledge and human wisdom" (Im Hof, 1994, p. 4). Germany, likewise, rallied nationally around terms, like *"aufklärung"* and *"erleuchten"* (to illuminate), that removed "veils and screens that obstruct . . . sight, making way for light to enter . . . hearts and minds to illuminate the former and warm the latter and hence make its way into those realms of truth and order where man's destiny and happiness hold sway" (ibid., p. 5). The Italians, by contrast, were more earthbound, assuming that "legislation, trade, public reputation and security" depended "on the enlightenment of nations" (ibid., p. 6). Other European countries, the Dutch and Scandinavians among them, used illumination metaphors to model new political utopias and to create new ways of constructing knowledge, new "light" based squarely in reason. This new force could do many things; in fact, it could penetrate "every sphere of human activity," including "political economy, politics, the civil and military constitution, religion, morals, public education, the sciences, arts and crafts and husbandry" (ibid., p. 7). In short, the power of reason placed *light* at the heart of the En*light*enment.

Metaphors of light circulated throughout many influential philosophical, political, and scientific texts sharing similar themes. For instance, they often expressed a growing belief in progress achieved through various investments in human intelligence. A variety of French, British, and German texts celebrated human potential, with writers interspersing metaphors of bright lights with those of an "invisible hand" benefiting human existence. Turgot, the economist, argues about the historical advances of the human mind (Meek, 1973), insisting that the more enlightened the individual mind the greater the opportunity for even greater perfection. Diderot speaks of "enlightenment" in terms of progress achieved through a "science" of man. In a October 12, 1760 letter to Sophie Volland (*Correspondence*, volume 3, in Lough and Proust, 1976, p. 120) he claims that "the centers of shadow have never been fewer and smaller than they are today; philosophy marches forward with giant steps, and light accompanies and follows it." And, in the *Encyclopédie* he urges that the tools of natural science be used to forge a social science based upon "Man" or human study: the human being "is the single place from which we must begin. . . . Man is, and must be, the center of all things . . . man . . . the thinking or contemplating being. . . . It is the presence of man which makes the existence of beings meaningful" (ibid., p. 56). Voltaire likewise links metaphoric enlightenment to France's political destiny. In a letter to Bernard Louis Chauvelin on April 2, 1764 (ibid., p. 231), Voltaire asserts that "Everything I see scatters the seeds of revolution which will definitely come. . . . Enlightenment has gradually spread so widely that it will burst into full light at the first right opportunity, and then there'll be a fine uproar."

Writers in support of women's rights appropriated metaphors of light and accomplished their initiative by ensuring that the light of superior intelligence shone upon Enlightenment women. Institutional changes reflect the effects of this new light. For instance, by becoming more secular, marriage provided women with new property and inheritance rights. This one change became the sun that illuminated the dawn of modern women's rights, providing them with a new legal status from which they could use and capitalize upon various legal mechanisms. Peter Gay notes that "the *philosophes* were at home with intelligent women – one thinks of Diderot's Sophie Volland, Voltaire's Madame du Chatelet, and the cultivated Parisian ladies who played hostess to *philosophes* for all over the world – and they made attempts to treat them as equals, as well as an item on the agenda of reform" (Gay, 1977, p. 33). In the *Encyclopédie*, Diderot argues that women are more intelligent than men (*Essai sur les femmes*), and Mary Wollstonecraft in *A Vindication of the Rights of Woman* (1792) argues that enlightenment proves that women are "moral beings," that they should have a chance to become intelligent, and should "let love for man be only a part of that glowing flame of universal law, which, after encircling humanity, mounts in a grateful incense to God."

Metaphors of enlightenment also gave traditional careers a new spin. Popular essayists, for instance, glorified the intelligence and knowledge of the "new" merchant. Defoe, for instance, identifies "the true-bred merchant" in terms of a "universal scholar" who "understands languages without books, Geography without maps," and therefore is "qualified for all sorts of employment in the State" (Sutherland, 1956, pp. 46–7). Addison too suggests in *The Spectator* that "There are not more useful Members in a Commonwealth than Merchants. They knit Mankind together in a mutual Intercourse . . . they knot Mankind together in a mutual intercourse of good Offices, distribute the Gifts of Nature, find Work for the Poor, add Wealth to the Rich, and Magnificence to the Great" (Bond, 1965, p. 296). Tributes to the commercial spirit, whether from Turgot, Defoe, Addison, Smith, Stuart, Say, Sismondi, Ricardo, or Adam Smith, forged an economics grounded in social utility. Many influential writers of the eighteenth century tied corresponding advances in knowledge and revenue to the bright lights of intelligence.

Well lit advances in human progress, as the reasoning went, were predicated upon the freedom given intelligence to produce new knowledge. And what best could nurture material progress other than a superior education? In the Enlightenment, *intelligence became a matter of class*, with superior intelligence linked to one's level of education and social status, the two coexisting in relatively the same socioeconomic class ranking. In fact, most of the eighteenth-century curriculum was divided along class lines, with the caliber of curriculum differing significantly between private and public schools. Despite calls for better public education, children were seen as a source of cheap labor. Even Voltaire objected to the education of laborers' children, those who could be exploited on rural farms and in large factories. The availability of cheap labor kept even the most liberal of Enlightenment thinkers from arguing too strongly for advancing the intelligence of lower-class citizens.

Eighteenth-century writers also used metaphors of light to describe brilliant minds and help to produce what was fundamentally an ideological revolution. In some cases the two functioned collaboratively, with the idea of intelligence being a catalyst for political liberation. Kant, for instance, defines the era in terms of a critical intelligence. In his 1784 essay *"Was ist Auflärung"* or "What is Enlightenment," Kant politicizes a historically unique Enlightenment construct, the idea of a "critical intelligence," or *sapere aude*, a daring to know, an *individualized* knowing, that presumably triumphs over the enslaving conditions of prior knowledge systems. For Kant, enlightenment occurs when individuals use their intelligence to overcome a self-incurred immaturity, the product of depending upon others for truth. The bright lights of this enlightenment illuminate those courageous enough to use their own critical intelligence (Wood, 2001, p. 135). In short, Kant makes intelligence a condition of freedom, weaving reason and intelligence into a synonymous cloth, while defining freedom as courageous cognition. Elsewhere Kant speaks to the popularity of the term Enlightenment: "People talk a great deal about Enlightenment and ask for more light. My God! What good is all this light if people either have no eyes or if those who do have eyes, resolutely keep them shut (in *Idee zu einer allgemeinen Geschichte in weltbürgerlicher Absicht*, 1784; Gay, 1977, p. 106). For Kant, the exercise of reason produces enlightenment, and intelligence plays a primary role in both inventing and capitalizing upon reason. In his *Critique of Pure Reason*, Kant defines intelligence as the means by which individuals know themselves (Kant, 1781, p. 167), as the fundamental means by which a liberated person exists as a unique individual (ibid., p. 169). He argues that intelligence, or the "higher faculties of cognition," consists of three components: reason, understanding, and judgment. Elsewhere Kant argues that the very nature of logic correlates to the structure of the mind and that imitative and creative intelligence differ on the basis that the highest intelligence opposes the imitative: "Genius is a talent for producing that for which no definite rule can be given, and not an aptitude in the way of cleverness for what can be learned according to some rule; and that consequently *originality* must be its primary property" (Kant, 1790).

Kant's idea that intelligence creates reason, which in turn produces liberation, was a consensus concept operating throughout Enlightenment discourses. For instance, William Roscoe's *Life of Lorenzo de' Medici* (1795) argues that freedom expands and strengthens the intellect. Liberation was associated with "critical intelligence" because it helped to create profits: "the age of Enlightenment was an age of academies. . . . In the academies and outside of them, in factories and workshops and coffeehouses, intelligence, liberated from the bonds of tradition, often heedless of aesthetic scruples or religious restraints, devoted itself to practical results; it kept in touch with scientists and contributed to technological refinements" (Gay, 1977, p. 10).

Critical intelligence also played a role in the development of eighteenth-century commerce. For instance, the relationship between reason, freedom, and commerce is evident in Voltaire's argument that "where there is no liberty of conscience, there is seldom liberty of trade, the same tyranny encroaching upon the commerce as upon Religion" (Voltaire, 1952, p. 43). Lastly, critical intelligence allowed Enlightenment Europeans to experience "an expansive sense of power over nature and themselves: the pitiless cycle of epidemics, famines, risky life and early death, devastating war and uneasy peace – the treadmill of human exis-tence – seemed to be yielding at last to the application of critical intelligence" (Gay, 1977, p. 3). Other writers and artists used different metaphoric versions of *light* for different reasons. Commenting on his *Enlightenment* (1792) engraving, Daniel Chodowiecki noted that "perhaps because the phenomenon itself is still a novelty, the supreme achievement of reason has not yet been accorded a gen-erally acknowledged allegorical emblem other than the rising sun" (Im Hof, 1994, p. 3). In his "Essay on the Principles of Population" (1798), Thomas Malthus defined Enlightenment revolutionary forces in terms of

> the great and unlooked for discoveries that have taken place of late years in natural philosophy, the increasing diffusion of general knowledge from the extension of the art of printing, the ardent and unshackled spirit of inquiry that prevails throughout the lettered and even unlettered world, the new and extraordinary lights that have been thrown on political subjects which dazzle and astonish the understanding. (Gay, 1977, p. 5)

The idea of critical intelligence occupied a central place in the development of Enlightenment ideology. In fact, the Enlightenment can be understood as various applications of critical intelligence largely resident in metaphors of vision. Critical intelligence literally produces "*in*-sight," a practice underscoring the important point that the "domination, the hegemony, of a visual paradigm in our cultural history," beginning with Greek culture, "has been dominated by an ocularcentric paradigm, a vision-generated, vision-centered interpretation of knowledge, truth, and reality" (Levin, 1993, p. 2). With Enlightenment culture, however, the ocularcentric paradigm became a "seeing inward," its effect being the production of knowledge generated by the interiority of an individual har-vesting his or her "in-sight." This in-sight was also critical in developing what Foucault defines as the gaze, a term explored in chapter 12.

The notion of critical intelligence took other forms. For instance, there was the light of "genius," a concept of significant interest to the Abbé de Condillac:

> Although we commonly use the word "genius" to mean the highest point of per-
> fection to which the human mind can aspire, nothing varies more than our appli-
> cations of this word, for each of us uses it according to his own way of thinking
> and the compass of his mind. To be regarded as a genius by the common run of
> men, all one has to be is inventive. This quality is no doubt essential but it must be
> combined with a right-thinking mind that consistently avoids error and that puts
> the truth in the most appropriate light for making it understandable. (Condillac,
> 1970, p. 136)

He qualifies this idea:

> To follow this notion precisely, we must not expect to find true geniuses. We are
> not naturally created fallible. Philosophers bestowed with this title know how to
> invent. We cannot even withhold the advantages of genius from them when they
> are discussing matters that they make new through their discoveries. . . . We appro-
> priate everything we discuss better than others do. Thus, if they scarcely lead us
> beyond ideas that are already understood, they are merely better than average
> minds, at most men of talent. If they go astray, they are false minds. If they go
> from error to error, interlinking them and creating systems, they are visionaries.
> (Ibid., p. 138)

Metaphors of enlightenment were busy in eighteenth-century discourse,
helping to represent everything from the very nature of the times to the nature
of individual genius, with the idea of critical intelligence forming the basis for
how individuals could reason and produce new knowledge with commercial and
political value. Whether they were metaphors of ubiquitous *enlightenings* or
metaphors of *insight*, figures of illumination and vision worked hand-in-hand discursively with the advance of knowledge, a progress that would have literally
been impossible without the critical intelligence making such light visible. And
Newton cast the brightest light in the Enlightenment.

Enlightenment *Insight*: Fallen Apples, Social Mathematics, and a New Intelligence

An archeological tracing of modern ideas of intelligence indicates that Newtonian mathematics played a critical role in formulating the human or social sciences that grew to depend on measuring human nature. A brief overview of Newtonian influences illuminates how Enlightenment *social mathematics* ultimately laid the groundwork for constructing modern ideas and clinical practices related to intelligence.

The Gravity of Newton's Ubiquitous Apple

Newtonianism is the institutionalization of scientific ideas that helped to create a new social ideology during the eighteenth century. Its power came from its range and scale of applicability. Dobbs and Jacob (1995, p. 76) describe this power in terms of the "totality of its explanatory power," in which "atoms, small bodies, the earth, the sun, and the planets fit together in one conceptual whole." Much of what this book is attempting to make vocal hinges on understanding that Newtonianism provided much of the ideological material to modernize ideas of intelligence. Newtonianism provided the logic, the intellectual content, for equating divine intelligence to human intelligence and divine creation to the production of knowledge, wealth, divine truth, and scientific certitude.

Newton's *Opticks* and *Papers and Letters on Natural Philosophy*, for instance, frequently refer to the relationship between gifts of human insight and divine intelligence. D'Alembert, the French popularizer of Newton's "method," makes a similar claim when he argues that "the discovery and application of a new method of philosophizing, the kind of enthusiasm which accompanies discoveries, a certain exaltation of ideas which the spectacle of the universe produces in us; all the causes have brought about a lively fermentation of minds" (Cassirer et al., 1951, pp. 46–7).

There was intoxication because the methods demonstrated in Newton's *Mathematical Principles of Natural Philosophy* (1687) articulated Enlightenment science. These methods were based on four principles:

1 Mathematical models are true representations of how the universe operates.
2 The universe, like mathematics, behaves rationally and predictably.
3 The universe is mechanistic.
4 The physical phenomena of the universe cannot be explained by revealed religion or theology.

These axioms generated volumes of empirical knowledge about the physical world. Scores of new calculations and observations not only increased "critical intelligence," but, more importantly, created new strategies for systemizing and ordering knowledge, for putting acceptable knowledge in its proper place. The power of Newtonianism also came from its creation of a new body of *malleable* knowledge capable of easy conversion into organized scientific, economic, and social systems. For example, this new pattern appears in the biological work of Hooke, Swammerdam, Buffon, van Leeuwenhoek, and Linnaeus, especially in the last's *Systema Naturae* (1767). The power of this book came from its arrangement and cataloguing of presumably "all" information into a single "Linnean" classification system consisting of species, genera, families, orders, classes, phyla, and kingdoms. More importantly, this is arguably the first text to define the ontological status of *being human* in terms of a *Homo sapiens*. For arguably the first time in Western history a creature's intelligence is its primary distinguishing attribute.

Newtonianism spread into other fields. For instance, while Boyle, Cavendish, Priestly, and Lavoisier used Newtonian methods to modernize chemistry, Von Guericke and Franklin made important advances in electricity. Even the non-scientific used Newtonian science to champion assorted causes. Richard Bentley, for example, used a series of lectureships to show how the "new science" refuted popular claims for atheism. Bentley argued that Newton's "proof" demonstrated unequivocally that the universe could not have been produced mechanically.

Although Newtonianism developed from specific tenets and scientific practices, it evolved into a system that had "little to do with the actual man and his thinking." In fact, "his religious and metaphysical vision slipped out of the thought, values, mechanical practices, [and] even the religiosity that we label the culture of Newtonianism" (Cassirer et al., 1951, p. 64). Newtonianism became part of a pervasive ideology, much in the same way that current information technology metaphors structure contemporary thought: its popularizers brought the Enlightenment out of the drawing rooms of the elite and to the middling classes, proclaiming science the key to human progress. Through mechanics in particular, Martin said, "we have here opened to our minds the wondrous laboratory of nature, and the stupendous processes therein carrying on, unheeded and unthought of by the vulgar." Even earthquakes, volcanoes, and comets, although dangerous and destructive, were no longer "secrets in the school of natural philosophy." In addition, it was claimed, every mechanic and manual trade could be improved by Newton's science. Now applied science promised self-improvement, profit and status. (Ibid., p. 89)

The institutionalization of Newtonian thought was accelerated by advances in the content and delivery of eighteenth-century education, with two things explaining the popularity of Newtonian curriculum, one a matter of applicability, the other a matter of profit. Peter Earle explains the value of this new education:

Many people and especially middle-class people were . . . losing faith in the educational value of the classics, for reasons summed up by Frances Brokesby in 1701: "Many things in learning the grammar are imposed that are toilsome and needless, several things that may be useful are not taught in due season . . . further, that the learning which is acquired at grammar schools is of little or no use to such as are set to ordinary trades, and consequently that time might have been better spent in attaining some useful knowledge, nay much more profitably in learning to write a good hand, arithmetic, and other things of this nature." (Earle, 1989, p. 66)

Christ's Hospital School boasted that it "gave scholars the 'opportunity of instructing themselves in writing and arithmetic,' the more immediate and necessary qualifications for their preferment in the world" (ibid., p. 67). This boasting underscores how changes in British education during the early Enlightenment can be attributed to "the spread of specialist writing and mathematical schools" (ibid.). In addition, the *Principia*'s systematic explanations of how nature worked became the subject of new books and curricula written expressly for and by engineers and for teachers committed to technological advances.

This trend in Newtonian education was supported by Jansenists and Oratorians, given their emphasis on developing math and science curriculum. Dissenting schools, as they were called, began preparing students for business employment modeled upon Newtonian principles. And those looking for pedagogical support for this new education turned to Locke, whose *Some Thoughts Concerning Education* (1693) argued for Newtonian methods, insisting that children should be taught by rote methods and practices (sections 66–78) and that

113

they, like the universe, are rational (section 81). Finally, the period saw Newtonian methods shape education policy not only in England but also on the European mainland, with La Chalotais's *Essai d'education nationale* (1766) representing the first significant effort at implementing and nationalizing a state educational system. This effort was supported by both Montesquieu and Helvétius, the former arguing that the first law of education should be the preparation of citizens (Gay, 1977, p. 512), the latter suggesting in his *De l'espirit* that there was a connection between the forming of a person and the form of a government. Finally, popular education made its way to the marketplace, where children could buy such new books as *The Philosophy of Tops and Balls*, published by Tom Telescope, and many diaries, some of which gained popularity because they were written by children. The Telescope text claims that "in the Dutch Republic of the 1790s a boy of affluent parents routinely attended scientific lectures and read books about science and natural religion." Finally, it was the dissenting academies that opened education to new fields in science education. Instead of seeking traditional institutions, many upcoming business families with industrial interests in the late eighteenth century opted to send their adolescent boys to academies in which medical and scientific education was considered among the best. Rather than using ancient grammars, these students used mechanical instruments and devices, the very tools Newton used at Cambridge.

Receptivity to Newtonianism was also aided by an emerging political dynamic, a new ideology centered on the individual and supported by a new class of individuals investing in the economic potentials of the new science. Newton's method became political once its rational system was seen as a means to stabilize the body politic. The title of Desaguliers's poem "The Newtonian System of the World, the Best Model of Government" (1728) could not be more to my point. The trend started in England in the 1690s with a variety of church and state officials committed to maintaining a hard fought social order. A good many of these clerics, landed aristocrats, and government agents did not want to relive the chaos of the English Civil War and the Glorious Revolution. John Toland, for instance, appropriated Newtonian science to create political arguments to oppose any perceived radicalism. He, in fact, used Newton to argue for a materialist explanation of human affairs, historical changes, and government. Newton's principles were also used to create contractual theories of government, appearing in the writings of Newtonians like Halley, Keill, Cates, and Desaguliers.

The public side of Newtonian politics also had a private side. According to Robert Markley, Newtonianism fostered

the creation of a subject who is empowered by the possession of scientific knowledge and who is both the recipient of and a conduit for the practical aspects of this

114

knowledge. If mathematics registers the dynamics by which absolute values are interposed into the material realm, then . . . this process of interposition takes the form of the individual's internalizing of mathematical law – of the metaphysics of order – to become the kind of subject who can exist in a harmonious relationship to a revalued nature . . . this subject naturalizes the disciplinary technologies of self-policing . . . and makes that individual subject to the forms of power that this knowledge [scientific] promotes. (Markley, 1993, pp. 208–9)

Markley's idea unites Newtonianism, the internalization of mathematics as an epistemological system, and efforts at institutionally driven forms of self-policing, the three becoming a power ideological force. The significance of this collaboration is addressed below.

Newtonianism also affected the availability of investment capital. Research shows that middle- and upper-class investors were intent on commodifying new technologies and scientific knowledge, converting their symbolic value into practical value. Jacob notes that far from the purely mathematical world of French Newtonianism or its proof of a Great Architect of the Universe, there was also the everyday world of machines, industry, and work. It was particularly in this world of applied mechanics that Newton arguably had his greatest impact (Jacob, 1997, p. 110).

Dobbs and Jacob (1995, p. 111) present a comprehensive view of the educational, socioeconomic, and ideological impact of social Newtonianism:

Principia's explanation of the mechanics of local motion took form in new books and curricula written by engineers and teachers extolling the virtues of technological innovation. In the Royal Society of London, but especially in numerous provincial scientific and philosophical societies, this mechanical learning formed the centerpiece of discussions, demonstrations and lectures. Into this setting of not only formal but just as important, informal institutions for applied scientific learning came eighteenth-century entrepreneurs, engineers, government agents, even skilled artisans, faced with economic and technological choices and receptive to new knowledge systems that promised new solutions. The route out of the *Principia* (1687) to the coal mines of Derbyshire or the canals of the Midlands was mapped by Newtonian explicators who made the application of mechanics as natural as the very harmony and order of Newton's grand mathematical system. They operated within the forum of civil society, a vast interlocking network of private voluntary associations, public lectures, and informal study groups to be found in almost every provincial city and town. The mathematical and mechanical practitioners often combined their skills with traditional values and attitudes, but most often was the certainty that the *Principia* offered learning about the heavens and about everyday motions accessible to anyone who could master a handbook.

The key phrase – "knowledge systems that promised new solutions" – underscores the socioeconomic potential of Newtonianism. How else can we explain s'Gravesande, Desaguliers, Galiani, and Boerhaave and their use of empirical methods and mathematic applications to solve scientific, electrical, medical, and technological problems? Scientists and philosophers turned to Newton for tools to create scientific explanation of human systems, a trend that especially attracted the French. Thinking that mechanical laws could illuminate nature's secrets, many Enlightenment minds believed that morality and ethics could also be explained in terms of principles derived from mechanics and geometry. Theologians and religious writers argued that the metaphor of a predictable machine, whether a watch, the human body, hydraulic systems, or gears, proved divine symmetrical design. Given these assumptions it was easy to contend, as William Paley often did, that nature was essentially a set of mechanisms designed and operated by a divine engineer. Finally, the ubiquity of Newtonianism can be traced in terms of scope, spreading from the heavens to the earth and anchoring Western science by using mathematical means to achieve religious, metaphysical, philosophical, and socioeconomic stability.

Foucault and Newtonianism

Newtonianism's greatest influence came with its use in the socialization of *methodical* rationalism, a power that produced knowledge systems that ultimately validated new forms of state power and economic practices. This power interests Michel Foucault in his *Order of Things* (1994), a text centered on the exploration of epistemological relationships between this new social rationalism and the science of social mathematics. This is the new science of "arithmétique politique," which used numbers and theorems to measure and authenticate sociopolitical, economic, and legal state policies. It was also the first science of the body politic.

These practices occupy much of Foucault's interest in the classical period, an era he claims was the age *not* of *inherent* reason but of a manufactured, synthetic, and emergent reason, a byproduct of certain discursive and social practices. Foucault contends that the age of complex epistemological mechanics was preoccupied with a general science of *order* exemplified by its invention of knowledge structures like the "table" or "grid," configurations with obvious political and ideological functions. For instance, Benedict Anderson notes in his study of the nation state that Enlightenment maps allowed "colonists to think about their holdings in terms of a totalizing classificatory grid. . . . It was bounded, determinate, and therefore – in principle – countable" (O'Meara et al., 2000, p. 51).

These abstractions functioned as closed and *only* internally consistent *objective* constructs, structures that encoded, ordered, analyzed, and rendered binary identities and differences. Gone was the earlier epistemology of similitude, the way of seeing that Cervantes thematizes in *Don Quixote*. In that world, words and things are related: things have signatures, and objects have external characteristics marking their essential quality and signifying their relationship identities. Quixote, the dreamer, reasons within an analogical epistemology that unifies phenomena. We laugh at Quixote because he sews a world together that in many ways is no longer recognizable.

By contrast, the classical episteme consists of three topologies and practices: *taxinomia* or classification, *genetic analysis* or linear orderings, and *mathesis* or the science of equalities. The three produced a unique Enlightenment knowledge system based on the premise that order creates or reflects reality when the "real" elements of a system are properly organized. Condillac is one of many voices arguing for the universality of this system: "In nature's lessons we see a system whose parts are all perfectly well ordered" (Condillac, 1970, p. 383). Moreover, Enlightenment order was an internally self-ordering and self-validating concept, being what "is given in things as their inner law, the hidden network that determines the way they confront one another" (Foucault, 1994, p. xx).

Foucault contends that reason and rationality were the *products*, not the *causes*, of new methods of knowing. As Jones and Porter (1994, p. 1) observe, for Foucault "the rise of rationality should be read as the legitimizing of power rather than as a challenge to it." This idea, in part, explains how ideas of intelligence were modernized and why the later creation of intelligent measurement tests – given their source – was inherently ideological. Think of the entire modernization of intelligence in terms of a closed-loop feedback system: reason and rationality produce criteria fundamental to that modernization, and those criteria measure an individual's ability to reason. In more simple terms, we can read IQ testing metaphorically, with reason listening for its own echoes, the assumption being that reason is not equally distributed within individuals. The louder or quieter the echo, the more or less intelligent the test taker. Moreover, tools like classification, ordering, hierarchical schemas, and analogical analysis were *not* what reason produced; they were the means by which reason eventually became a privileged ideological concept, a convenient metaphoric buzzword reflecting a way of knowing, ordering, and controlling the world. This was the emerging world of *critical intelligence*.

For Foucault, rationality is the outcome of ordering practices, and is not an inherent human quality. This point is fundamental to understanding my argument that intelligence too can be understood as a cultural invention with a social history, rather than being a "scientifically proven" or objective human attribute.

And even if it were the latter, that would not negate all the ideological traffic associated with intelligence. The seemingly coincidental rise of rationality and the popularity of the idea that intelligence is a central human attribute is, in fact, not very coincidental. The two attributes historically complemented each other, with both arising from an identical knowledge system that has guided the truth trajectory of Western thought since the late seventeenth century.

Whether we believe intelligence really exists as a physical phenomenon or not, our current collective experience of it has a history. Ideas of intelligence do not exist in a cultural vacuum. Ideas of intelligence have an ideological history, its modern ideations having emerged in accord with the structural formations and components of eighteenth-century knowledge systems. How did this occur?

Foucault argues that classical approaches to grammar, natural history, and wealth analysis changed imperceptibly in the eighteenth century. What was different was the degree, location, significance, and representational status accorded the visible, replacing analytic methods grounding prior modes of inquiry. For instance, because Renaissance analysis focused on an object's external characteristics, natural beings were seen as occupying a space in natural history given their external forms and behaviors. This epistemology of similitude fell to the pressure of dramatic epistemological changes, namely the popularity of Newtonian methods. Previous methods of external description eventually gave way to a new focus on internal and organic structures. This pattern even extended to new uses of language. Prior emphasis on the transparency of language (hence similitude) changed to a systemization of its interior architecture and inflectional dynamics. Most importantly, the construction of interior abstract systems ultimately devalued the kind of knowledge produced by finding shared similarities.

According to Foucault a major epistemological shift occurred during the Enlightenment, when newly invented explanatory systems positioned themselves apart from and even *a priori* to representation. These systems relied on similar tools. The most dominant were *mathesis* and *taxinomia*, strategies operating within "the project of a general science of order; a theory of signs analyzing representation; [and] the arrangement of identities and differences into ordered tables" (Foucault, 1994, pp. 71–2). The two operated in accord with the Classical *episteme* or sets of formational rules and created two kinds of practices: the "utilization of the symbols of possible operations upon identities and differences" and "an analysis of the marks progressively imprinted in the mind by the resemblances between things and the retrospective action of the imagination" (ibid., p. 73). The space of these practices was defined by a new "region of signs," a symbol topography and inventory that extended but never transgressed the boundaries of empirical representations:

What makes the totality of the Classical *episteme* possible is primarily the relation to a knowledge of order. When dealing with the ordering of simple natures, one has recourse to *mathesis*, of which the universal method is algebra. When dealing with the ordering of complex natures . . . one has to constitute a *taxinomia*, and to do that one has to establish a system of signs. These signs are to the order of composite natures what algebra is to the order of simple natures. But in so far as empirical representations must be analyzable into simple natures, it is clear that the *taxinomia* relates wholly to the *mathesis*; on the other hand, since the perception of proofs is only one particular case of representation in general, one can equally well say that *mathesis* is only one particular case of *taxinomia*. Similarly, the signs established by thought itself constitute, as it were, an algebra of complex representations; and algebra, inversely is a method of providing simple natures with signs and of operating upon those signs. (Ibid., p. 72)

As a science of tabular classification expressing static and universal order, *taxinomia*

implies a certain continuum of things (a non-discontinuity, a plentitude of being) and a certain power of the imagination that renders apparent what is not, but makes possible, by this very fact, the revelation of that continuity. The possibility of a science of empirical orders requires, therefore, an analysis of knowledge – an analysis that must show how the hidden . . . continuity of being can be reconstituted by means of the temporal connection provided by discontinuous representations. (Ibid., pp. 72–3)

By contrast, *mathesis* is "a science of equalities, and, therefore of attributions and judgments; it is the science of truth. *Taxinomia* . . . treats of identities and difference; it is the science of articulations and classifications; it is the knowledge of beings . . . it establishes the table of visible differences . . . it defines, then, the general law of beings, and at the same time the conditions under which it is possible to know them." But, more importantly, *mathesis* becomes a way of living: it constitutes "an ontology, and it is in this form that it has dominated the formal disciplines right up to our day" (ibid., p. 74). The influence of *mathesis* and *taxinomia* cannot be understated, the two creating modern sciences that "carry within themselves the project of an exhaustive ordering of the world; they are always directed, too, towards the discovery of simple elements and their progressive combination; and at their centre they form a table on which knowledge is displayed in a system contemporary within itself" (ibid., pp. 74–5). To prove the validity of Foucault's point all one need do is read closely from Condorcet's *The Nature and Purpose of Public Instruction* (1791): "Among these applications of social mathematics to the operation of the human mind, there should also be included the technical or even mechanical means of executing intellectual operations: such as the art of arranging historical, chronological, or scientific materials in tables or registers, or that of forming or deciphering codes, such as arithmetical machines" (Baker, 1976, p. 194).

Mathesis and *taxinomia* have more than a casual application to this study. Foucault's emphasis on revolutions in knowledge paradigms provides a framework for understanding how forgotten ideas and knowledge systems underlie the majority of theories and clinical practices related to intelligence. For instance, Foucault's analysis suggests that Newtonian based mathematics invented an ideological use for mathematics. He demonstrates how mathematics, statistics, categorization, classification, and evaluation – all abstract systems of order – were appropriated to support and stabilize a new political order. More importantly, his analysis challenges the typically unchallenged authority given reason, the most crucial component in any Western theory of human intelligence. In short, there is simply no intelligence without reason and vice versa.

Foucault challenges the epistemological mechanics of this tautological relationship. Modern theories of intelligence operate under the guiding assumption that intelligence is defined and measured by demonstrations of rational thought, of logical and verbal reasoning, mathematical skills (numerical computations and the solving of geometrical and algebraic problems), memory, and, in some cases, general knowledge. Simply put, the degree of a person's intelligence is determined by his or her capacity to reason. This notion is problematic because, as in Foucault's analysis of reason, intelligence may be as much a construct as it is a natural phenomenon; that is, more the product of a knowledge system than a proven innate human attribute. Intelligence, like reason, may also be the *product* of the Classical *episteme*, more likely part of a formal but forgotten systemization of knowledge that eventually became a supportive element in an ideology, rather than simply being the cause for assessing its objective nature or performance.

Foucault's critique also challenges the modern idea that mathematics *discovers* abstract and natural truth. This challenge has its history as well as a cadre of supporters. For instance, in his *Origins of Geometry* Husserl argued that geometry has more to do with human "idealizations" than with "real" natural shapes. Likewise, Foucault's critique of the originary, the "pure" truth idealization *discovered* by mathematics, unearths the epistemological content of eighteenth-century thought, particularly its claim of discovering *original* truths through a knowledge system constituted by purely arbitrary structural configurations.

Several of Foucault's ideas also explain why a cultural studies approach to the history of intelligence is preferable to other methods, particularly those lacking epistemological self-reflection. Traditional historical scholarship dealing with the history, nature, and dynamics of intelligence has generally not addressed the implications of Foucault's critique of the Classical *episteme*. This would require scholars to subject their arguments, ideas, concepts, and practices to issues related to the problematic nature of representation. In essence, no modern idea or theory of intelligence has been thoroughly deconstructed, with most scholarship and clinicians having failed to inquire into the near automatic validity given representation as the basis for their methods. Moreover, scholars have generally ignored *scientific* formations of intelligence and their ideological content. Nor have they generally compared the origin of conventional ideas of intelligence with the rules, mechanisms, or methods ordering the epistemological constructions of certain eras engaged heavily in creating new ideas of intelligence.

Foucault's interest in modalities of order affords the opportunity to see how Newtonianism became a sociopolitical force that, in turn, inspired the Enlightenment invention of social mathematics, a tool providing mathematical "proof" of the existence of intelligence. Knowing the history of this invention is critical to my archeological efforts. This tracing requires an understanding of those "rules of formation . . . never formulated in their own right, but . . . found only in widely differing theories, concepts, and objects of study." It also requires an interrogation of "the basis or archeological system common to a whole series of scientific representations or products dispersed throughout natural history, economics and philosophy of the Classical period" (Foucault, 1994, pp. xi–xii). Without this level of interrogation, ideas of intelligence will remain scientific facts that obscure their ideological and metaphoric nature.

Social Mathematics

> Philosophy [i.e. natural philosophy, or science] is written in that vast book which stands forever open before our eyes, I mean the universe; but it cannot be read until we have learnt the language and become familiar with the characters in which it is written. It is written in mathematical language, and the letters are triangles, circles and other geometrical figures, without which means it is humanly impossible to comprehend a single word. (Galileo, *Il saggiatore*)

The history of social mathematics enjoys a cast of interesting players, and as the historical offspring of political arithmetic, it constitutes a "systematic study of social numbers," evolving from an interest in the "calculation of insurance or annuity rates" into "the promotion of sound, well-informed state policy" (Potter, 1986, p. 18). Foucault demonstrates that mathematics became a method of organizing knowledge that migrated into political policy discourse, where it authorized and sanctioned new governmental, institutional, and medical practices. The effect of this process is historically obvious: state sanctioning of mass IQ tests in the twentieth century, as well as legal or medical reasons for administering current IQ evaluations, is tied to a legacy of social mathematics and the assumption that mathematical constructs *represent* the real. A number of important movements in the history of social mathematics are worth noting. For example, the evolution of mathematics, the continuous Renaissance emphasis on measurement, and the application of statistics to institutional practices all had a role in the development of social mathematics, with each deserving an overview.

The history of mathematics generally includes the invention of geometry (geometric conceptions), algebraic equations to determine interrelations of magnitude, logarithms, statistics and theories of probabilities, the study of higher plane curves, volume and areas, infinitesimals, differential and integral calculus, and the invention of calculation machines. Pythagorean and Platonic thought created the persisting tradition that mathematical objects are eternal and independent of flux because they reflect higher realities, yet they can explain the dynamics of material reality. In general, the history of Western mathematics is marked by increases in the use of practical measurement in geometry, physics, calculus, mechanical engineering, and most industrial and consumer technologies. By the sixteenth century, arithmetic and geometry entered the world of daily activities like accounting, paying taxes, trading, surveying, constructing, and engineering. This world of everyday mathematics cut its own path, its preference for material accuracy and ease of repetitive procedures being different from its past of theory and abstract inquiry.

Two factors were responsible for this shift toward practical mathematics. The first is that in an "age of reason and mathematics . . . nothing was more natural than to apply reason and mathematics to pressing public questions" (Gay, 1977, p. 345). The Newtonian celestial assumption – that the universe was a machine with a finite set of laws – went parochial when mathematics and rational systems were applied to investigations into politics, history, economics, and human character. Second,

> from the seventeenth century onward, mathematics, like other activities in European culture, became increasingly specialized. As a result, mathematicians increasingly worked with materials created within their own community. Each new generation worked with the manufactured objects – symbols and notational systems – of the previous generation. The continuity of this process marked the professionalization of mathematics. This helps explain why Western mathematics . . . becomes more and more removed from everyday empirical observation. (Restivo, 1992, p. 8)

Its transformation into a new kind of profession, along with its migration into the social world of new state politics, provided mathematics with a new and comprehensive authority. "On a simple level . . . mathematics came to signify not only the measurements of positions and apparent (observed) angular speeds, and the rather straightforward application of plane and spherical trigonometry to the solutions of problems of the celestial sphere"; its Newtonian laws also were applied to an

> increasing quantification of qualities ranging from temperature to speeds. The ideal was to express general laws of nature as mathematical relations . . . such laws expressed number-relations or geometrical properties, and they were formalized in ratios or proportions . . . [and since] such mathematical laws use physically observable quantities (volume, weight, position, angle, distance, time, impact, and so on), they can to a large degree be tested by further observations and direct experiment . . . or the test may be the verification or nonverification of a prediction . . . or the accurate retrodiction of past observations. Obviously, some kind of numerical data must provide the basis for applying or testing such general or specific mathematical laws. In all of this there is and there need be no concern for physical causes. (Cohen, 1978, p. 33)

The growing popularity of statistics represents another important Enlightenment social trend. Like other material applications of mathematics, statistics functioned as an epistemology, its focus less on numbers and theory, and more on shaping and managing state operations. Given the everyday preference for accurate and repetitive procedures, together with a growing loss of interest in mathematical theory and calculus, it becomes clearer that Enlightenment mathematics was generally more focused on applications of mathematical ideas or processes than on pure or abstract theory.

The Italian derivative of the modern word *statistics* refers to the state or a statesman, one concerned with reasoning about the state, as in *"ragione di stato"* (Pearson, 1978, p. 2). Interest in understanding potentially cyclical state dynamics began in seventeenth-century England with the work of John Graunt and William Petty, the founder of the school of "political arithmetic," a term Diderot later uses in his *Encyclopédie*. Both men affirmed Baconian views of government. And much in the way that future human sciences would describe human behavior in terms of various number schemes, Petty and Graunt believed that numbers and calculations could be applied to a country's citizenry.

What came out of their work, given advances made by Halley, DeMoivre, Bernoulli, Euler, Poisson, and Laplace, was the new calculus of *probability*. This branch of mathematics deals with random variables, classification of variables, distributions and density functions, conditional cumulative distribution, expectation value or averages, properties of averages, median, range, percentiles, distribution spreads, and conditional probability, functions that would later become evident in the production, use, and evaluation of mental tests. In fact, to retrace the evolutionary path leading to modern theories of intelligence we need to understand the evolution of social mathematics or statistics as a social science, Quetelet's effort to determine the numerical regularities of society, the formulation of statistical laws, and Galton's work on variation dynamics.

There were other forces behind new found uses of Enlightenment social mathematics, particularly those combining mathematics and the invention of the "moral" or "human" sciences. For instance, in his *Mathematical Elements of Natural Philosophy*, Willem s'Gravesande praised Newton's mathematics for its applicability, asserting that the foundations of Western science should be mathematically grounded, with particular value given to numbers, theorems, and laws because of their ability to construct models of stability. In essence, many Newtonians believed that almost everything could be understood and represented by numbers or patterns, including human sociopolitical and economic behaviors. Hume thinks that "the great advantage of the mathematical sciences above the moral consists in this, that the ideas of the former, being sensible, are always clear and determinate, the smallest distinction between them is immediately perceptible, and the same terms are still expressive of the same ideas, without ambiguity or variation" (Hume, 1748, section 7, part 1).

The call to apply mathematics to the human sciences came from several quarters. For instance, demands for precision in social and economic practice began in the seventeenth century. According to Sir William Petty, Bacon's *Advancement of Learning* made a

> judicious parallel in many particulars, between the Body Natural and Body Politic, and between the arts of preserving both in health and strength; and as its anatomy is the best foundation of one, so also of the other, and that to practice upon the politic, without knowing the symmetry, fabric, and proportion of it, is as casual as the practice of old women and empirics. (Woolf, 1961, p. 155)

Hume's *Enquiry Concerning Human Understanding* argues for a general theory of human nature, while his *Treatise of Human Nature* defines itself as "an Attempt to introduce the experimental Method Reasoning into Moral Subjects." The *Treatise* invites readers to consider the attraction of using objectified knowledge for human ends, since it is "evident that all the sciences have a relation, greater or less, to human nature" (Hume, 1898, pp. xix – xxiii).

The fusion of mathematics, the rational inquiry of the Classical episteme, and the emerging human sciences had a number of intended purposes. Ideally, thinkers envisioned using Newtonian mathematics, introspective methods, and scientific observation to stabilize an era of frequent disruptions related to tensions between traditional practices and new, reform-minded state officials. There was a growing demand for the use of rational procedures, like statistics, in public administration circles, with special attention given to excesses of *laissez-faire* capitalism, "lawlessness" that required not only new governmental regulations but those derived from empirical observations. In fact, greater cryptic use of mathematics and statistics explains why, in part, classical capitalism evolved into neoclassical capitalism, the change brought on by economists mimicking methods used in the natural sciences. Moreover, the failure of previous welfare traditions produced the equivalent of a public conscience. Peter Gay notes, for instance, that Habsburg rulers often confiscated the property of expelled Jesuits, using it for public relief, while elsewhere monarchs appropriated church hospitals, foundling homes, poorhouses, and schools. These institutions were often confiscated, supervised, and scrutinized by public officials. This partial nationalization of previously religious or relief agencies was followed by a growing nationalization of education (Gay, 1977, p. 9).

The idea of employing mathematics to perfect the human condition had a southern European following. Giambattista Vico, for example, is a frequently overlooked voice in the invention of the human sciences, the Italian being a Baconian – Hobbesian natural law theorist. In his aptly entitled text *The New Science* (1725), Vico invents a science of human society, of social order, arguing that science could do for politics and nations what Newtonian physics did for natural philosophy. The power of mathematics, the physical and biological sciences, and medicine, he argued, could improve the human condition. Vico proposes a new mode of critical analysis, a method of producing patterns that reflect the way nations actually operate, a kind of political calculus. As a sidebar, Vico threads ideas of intelligence through most of his writings, using them to support his call for a new human science. For example, in a discussion of the origin of Western culture he speaks of

first men, children as it were of the growing human race, [who] believed that the sky was no higher than the summits of the mountains, as even now children believe it to be little higher than the roofs of their houses. Then as the Greek intelligence developed heaven was raised to the summits of the highest mountains, such as Olympus, where Homer relates to the gods of his day had their dwelling. (Vico, 1968, p. 5)

Like many French *philosophes*, Vico believed that intelligence and rational analysis were related, both evolutionary and progressive in nature. His earlier *De antiquissima Italorum sapientia (On the Most Ancient Wisdom of the Italians*, 1710) links mathematics to intelligence by advancing the idea that mathematical truth is nothing less than "intelligibles" (Vico, 1988, volume 1, section 2).

Mathematics also entered economic theory and daily business practices in unprecedented ways in the eighteenth century, providing merchants and governments with promises of certainty and predictability. Such assurances even guaranteed profits that helped to fund and fuel the engines of colonial expansion. In his study of the economic history of England, T. S. Ashton notes that the Enlightenment was the premier age of measurement and political arithmetic, when anything that could be quantified, weighed, or calculated was measured, and demand was high for relating precise mathematical information to an economy of "critical intelligence." Enlightenment mathematics was also essential to conceiving and creating the human sciences, the logic being that the same precise methods used in mathematics would illuminate human behavior. This assumption is at the heart of why modern thought assumes that intelligence can be measured, calculated, evaluated, classified, and placed in some kind of scaled parameters.

Hundreds and thousands of known and unknown collaborations between political and social arithmetic, state bureaucracies, and economics took a number of ideological turns during the Enlightenment, especially evident in the writings of several notable economists. During this period, capitalism evolved, translating its primarily market practices into a more fully representational symbolic system. These collaborations ultimately influenced modern capitalism by stressing the need for the systemization of value, with the worth of an object or a service transposed into a numerical representation or scale. This growing emphasis on the mathematicization of value is evidenced by the number of written reports regarding public revenue and expenditure, increases in trade and navigation, changes in methods of coinage production, and the prices of foodstuffs and other commodities. Mathematics took the political stage as figures and statistical reports informed parliamentary debates and numbers and theorems were used rhetorically to win arguments posed in treatises, pamphlets, newspaper articles, and broadsheets. By the mid-eighteenth century, public opinion began to be shaped by debate informed by mathematical evidence. Moreover, Malthus's essay on population helped to institutionalize the census and compulsory documentation of births, marriages, and deaths. Even ideas about government registries began in the eighteenth century, with mathematical data literally forming representational models of the state. In essence this unprecedented use of figures and tables extended across the sociopolitical landscape, with bills of mortality, trade and navigation reports, census tables, and parish registers becoming standardized texts. The popularity of social mathematics reveals an unprecedented interest in transposing precise social data into numerical values, that, in turn, increased the prospects for state stability, greater opportunities for profits, and more insight into the nature of human behavior.

Two important effects in Enlightenment culture resulted from the application of social mathematics, urged by economists like David Hume and Adam Smith (English *philosophes*) and the French physiocrats Quesnay, Mirabeau, Rivére, Dupont de Nemours, La Trosne, and Baudeau. First, it ultimately advanced the idea that interconnectivity could be systemized, a notion that helped to support the idea that mathematics could explain social behavior. Second, economists argued that mathematics could produce truth and wealth, an idea popularized by those who perfected mathematical analysis and enjoyed national admiration. A common analogy, in fact, linked mathematics to science in the same way that metal was thought to be the primary agent for commerce. For without hesitation many influential writers insisted that mathematics represented and created true wealth. Quesnay argued in the *Tableau économique* (1766) and in his "Grains" entry (*Encyclopédie*, volume 7, 1757) that national economies were intertwined systems of expenditures, work, profits, and consumption, understandable simply in terms of Newtonian-like "laws." This principle, in part, led to the eventual scientization of economics, an idea driven by the belief that "a knowledge of order and of the natural and physical laws should serve as the basis of economics" (Neill, 1948, p. 154).

The physiocrats were perhaps the first group of economists to combine Newton's mechanics and social mathematics and apply them to the production and distribution of goods and services. Their main focus was centered on the distribution of goods, a concept they believed to operate in the same way that universal mechanistic and natural laws did. They applied theories of mechanistic thought to other areas of social organization, assuming that since the natural tendency of mercantilism is to produce wealth, then it too could be understood as a primary means to achieve national stability. They also believed, like Bacon and Locke, that the "natural" tendency of merchants to satisfy their self-interests generated wealth that, in turn, would benefit the general population.

The physiocrats were also the first to interpret social mathematics in terms of a divinely inspired version of human intelligence. In her study of their work, Elizabeth Fox-Genovese states that "the physiocrats usually insisted upon the dictates of nature, or material conditions, as the prime determinant of human behavior, but their rhetoric cannot obscure a fundamental commitment to the ultimate role of divine intelligence. Nature realizes the plan that first existed in the eye of God." She explains that

> the Physiocrats insisted that the human animal, like all others, must eat, but that unlike the others, it stands unique in creation by its possession of an intelligence directly linking it to the deity whose purpose informs the universe . . . although they shared the physiological materialism of Diderot, they supplemented it with an idealist conception of human intelligence (as distinct from animal intelligence) as an emanation from God – literally a divine light that informs the human mind. (Fox-Genovese, 1976, p. 47)

In keeping with their age, the physiocrats believed that the deity controlling a knowable mechanical universe was also the architect of natural laws who gifted to his human creations a reflective intelligence, mathematical in nature, that produced truth, certitude, wealth, security, and an orderly political state. Regardless of the details of their arguments, the physiocrats lumped God, human intelligence, nature, and wealth together in one discursive and conceptual effect: divine-like human intelligence, reason, and mathematics produced a system of certainty, stability, and truth, the three creating unassailable value. The ideological consequence of this reasoning is obvious: human intelligence was placed squarely within a hierarchy of value that, to a large extent, structures modern thought.

The physiocrats had a figurehead. After proclaiming him the champion physiocrat, Louis XVI offered Turgot the position of Controller General in 1774. His work reflected his ideological bent: his favorite metaphors of illumination and reflection appear everywhere in his writings. The two represent Turgot's belief in the incredible power of the mind and the knowledge it produces. More importantly, this insight-production relationship framed his ideology. Turgot, the economist, was fascinated by genius and its source: "Nature," he argues, is a kind of inventory manager,

> distributing genius to only a few individuals . . . whose course is at first slow, unmarked, and buried in the general oblivion in which time precipitates human affairs, emerges from obscurity with them by means of the invention of writing. Priceless invention! – which seemed to give wings to those peoples who first possessed it, enabling them to out distance other nations. (Meek, 1973, p. 44)

Nature selects those who receive the special "gift" of enlightenment:

> There are minds to whom nature had given a memory which is capable of assembling together a large number of pieces of knowledge, a power of exact reasoning which is capable of comparing them and arranging them in a manner which puts them in their full light, but to whom at the same time she has denied the fire of genius which invents and which opens up new roads for itself. Created to unite past discoveries under one point of view, to clarify and even to perfect them, if they are

not torches which shine with their own light, they are diamonds which brilliantly reflect a borrowed light, but which total darkness would confound with the meanest stones. (Ibid., p. 51)

For Turgot, intelligence is simply nature directed; it is rare and creates "priceless" inventions. The world of genius is a society of assemblers of logic, artisans of mathesis and taxinomia, those who construct truths by making rational comparisons and arrangements and then converting them into the visibility of "full light." Nature also limits superior intelligence, and those with ordinary intelligence are like diamonds, merely reflecting the more intense light denied them. Turgot's reading of genius reflects how Enlightenment thought helped to shape modern ideas of intelligence. First, it provides a *schema* for intelligence, creating a value scale from high to ordinary intelligence. It also makes intelligence understandable in terms of class and race, and it defines superior intelligence in terms of mathesis and taxinomia, the manipulation of data to achieve absolute insight. These points helped to create the ideological framework for nineteenth- and twentieth-century "scientific" work in intelligence research, studies and, practices, as well as aiding in the construction of popular ideas about intelligence, those consumed by mass culture.

Most importantly, when Turgot links intelligence to mathematics and productivity he historicizes that combination, placing it into a narrative of sequence, order, time, and cultural progress. In *A Philosophical Review of the Successive Advances of the Human Mind* he defines history in terms of the evolution of intelligence. He traces three periods – the religious, the metaphysical, and the scientific – and argues that intelligence reaches its highest level when the anthropomorphizing of natural events and the creation of metaphysical abstractions are challenged and defeated by Newtonian methods. Turgot's equating of high intelligence to advances in eighteenth-century thought is ideologically transparent. By equating the highest form of intelligence to the high culture of Newtonian methods and Enlightenment economics, Turgot's thoughts clearly demonstrate the ideological trajectory of ideas of intelligence in service to his ideological constructions.

Many of the ideological interests of the physiocrats were taken by their next generation descendents, the *philosophes* who shared similar ideas about free trade, natural rights, the freedom of contract, individual rights, and the power of science to liberate believers or citizens from the irrationality of arbitrary religious or royal power. An influential member, Condorcet, describes their concern as being less

with the discovery or development of the truth than with its propagation, men who whilst devoting themselves to the tracking down of prejudices in the hiding places where the priests, the schools, the governments, and all long-established had gathered . . . their life-work to destroy popular errors . . . using in turn all the weapons with which learning, philosophy, wit, and literary talent can furnish reason . . . never ceasing to demand the independence of reason and the freedom of the press as the right and the salvation of mankind . . . and finally, taking for their battle cry – reason, tolerance, humanity. (Baker, 1976, pp. 228–9)

More importantly, the *philosophes* advocated using social mathematics to develop the new "human" sciences. Although the names are familiar – Rousseau, Voltaire, Montesquieu, Diderot, Leclerc de Buffon, de Condillac, d'Alembert, Helvétius d'Holbach, de la Mettrie, Malebranche, Gassendi, Leibniz, and Condorcet – the impact of their ideas on social mathematics and their effect on modern ideas of intelligence have not been adequately studied. Their views on social mathematics, in fact, created a formidable discourse by which mathematics achieved unprecedented sociopolitical power and privilege. For the first time in Western culture, the *philosophes* made mathematics an ideological tool, using it to launch and structure an epistemology ordering the human sciences. Ultimately they put mathematics to work, creating modern social and educational policy, while also institutionalizing modern social and "medical" practices.

Diderot's *Encyclopédie*, divided on the basis of human, natural, and mechanical sciences, defines "arithmétique politique" as the art of governing people ("l'art de gouverner les peuples"), in which a well versed minister could use data to perfect agriculture, enhance internal and external colonial commerce, and develop investment strategies ("un ministre habile en tirerai une foule de conséquences pour la perfection de l'agriculture, pour le commerce tant intérieur qu'extérieur pour les colonies, pour le cours et l'emploi de l'argent etc."). And in a historically significant revelation, Diderot distinguishes natural genius from the knowledge that mathematics produces. He refers to gifted ministers with a great natural genius ("d'un grand génie nature") and their lack of interest in the use of arithmetical combinations, equations, and geometrical precision. Their blindness prevents them from seeing how problems in the political and physical world can be solved by weight, number, and measure ("que le monde politique, aussi bien que la monde physique, peut se régler à beaucoup d'égards par poids, nombre, et mesure," *Encyclopédie*, volume 7, p. 678). In this passage, mathematics provides a level of knowledge that genius may not even recognize. The ideological effect here is that of a shift in or sharing of privilege, whereby mathematics is positioned *a priori* to genius, as something that produces knowledge unperceived by "natural" genius. The implication is that mathematics, and not intelligence, is a *consistent* source of truly significant knowledge; this idea, in part, is responsible for nineteenth- and twentieth-century mathematics becoming the

primary model for and means of determining intelligence. In essence, the majority of dominant modern ideas of intelligence, until the 1980s, could not be conceptualized in any way other than through mathematically representational
models. The history of this tacit intelligence, the way we now *professionally*
understand it, can, in part, be traced to Enlightenment advances in social mathematics and Diderot's belief that mathematics provides insight when intelligence
does not.

Perhaps the most intriguing take on Enlightenment social mathematics occurs
in Condorcet's *A General View of the Science of Social Mathematics* (1793). Here he
argues that social mathematics provides "us with more precise ideas and more
certain knowledge," contributing, "if it were more widespread and better cultivated, both to the happiness and to the perfection of the human race" (Baker,
1976, p. 184). Its real value, he argues, has to do with stabilizing social disorder,
helping, as it does, to "restore public prosperity . . . [and] provide for more exact
policies and methods calculated with more precision." Social uncertainty benefits from the use of reason, with the creation of an era marked by a "precision
of ideas and the rigor of proof." The value of social mathematics to solve civil
disorder is demonstrated by the rhetorical question: "how much would it not
contribute to ensure the advance of reason over this debris-covered terrain, long
shaken by violent tremors and still suffering from internal commotions." It does
that because it "teaches us how to determine the mortality rate . . . calculates the
advantages or disadvantages of a method of election . . . evaluates the advantages of a lottery . . . seeks the principles that must determine the rates of maritime insurance . . . and deals with life annuities and insurance." Moreover,

> social mathematics can consider man as an individual, the duration and relations
> of whose existence is subject to the order of natural events. Or it can be applied
> to *the operation of the human mind* . . . it weights the grounds for belief and calcu-
> lates the probable truth of testimony or decisions. . . . These various considerations
> apply to all commodities that can be utilized without being altered, or the alter-
> ations of which can be evaluated. (Ibid., pp. 186–7)

Condorcet links social mathematics to the emerging ideology in a truly comprehensive way, that is, it not only deals with large population patterns, but that
it also illuminates the "man," the "individual . . . subject to order of natural
events." Condorcet presents an idea that will influence future ideas of intelligence by asserting that although it can be applied to the outer "man," social
mathematics can also explain the inner person, and how the mind behaves. Later,
he catalogues "applications of social mathematics": "there should also be
included the technical or even mechanical means of executing intellectual

operations: such as the art of arranging historical, chronological, or scientific materials in tables or registers, or that of forming or deciphering codes, such as arithmetical machines" (ibid., p. 194). Condorcet's point validates Foucault's argument that mathesis and taxinomia were pivotal in developing the dominant Enlightenment knowledge system.

These ideas are arguably the most influential in modernizing notions of intelligence. Note that in the same ideological breath, Condorcet identifies mathematics as a tool to get into the mind, as a basis for certain beliefs, as a means of validating testimony, as having to do with "all commodities," and as something that can detail "intellectual operations." This kind of reach made it discursively and ideologically easy for mathematics to become the aperture for the testing and measuring of intelligence in the nineteenth and twentieth centuries.

Before further exploring how certain *philosophes* created new ideas of intelligence, I briefly assess how others in the group invented other new sociopolitical uses for social mathematics. This is important because it reveals a two-prong ideological Enlightenment agenda: social mathematics would be used not only to illuminate human behaviors but also to determine what institutional policies and practices would best control them.

De la Mettrie, Laplace, and Condorcet explored the social applications of mathematics more than other *philosophes*. Julien Offray de la Mettrie argued in *L'homme machine* (1748) that the "real or apparent similarity of [mathematical] figures . . . is the fundamental basis of all truths and all our knowledge" (de la Mettrie, 1997, p. 14), and Pierre-Simon Laplace (1951, p. 177) assumed that "all the effects of nature are only mathematical results of a small number of immutable laws." These testimonies to the value validity of mathematics were common during the Enlightenment, an equally typical belief being that mathematical truth could be extended to any system, natural or social, in order to understand their dynamics. Laplace argues that mathematics and probability can even determine the probability of assembly decisions and voting. In essence, political behaviors, the "general results" of popular thinking, can be "confirmed by calculus" (ibid., p. 126). Other applications include using mathematics in court decisions or to determine death and marriage probabilities (ibid., chapters 12 and 14). He also argues that there is a correlation between the benefits of institutions and the probability of events: "By the repetition of an advantageous event, simple or compound, the real benefit becomes more and more probable and increases without ceasing" (ibid., p. 149). Laplace believes that his theorem of benefits and losses proves "that regularity ends by establishing itself even in the things which are most subordinated to that which we name *hazard*" (ibid., pp. 149–50). Such a hazard, here meaning institutional instability, can be normalized by using probability analysis. This tool, Laplace assumes, creates "advantages" for institutions, produces social confidence, and can double the "strength of The State, and the sovereign himself," both of whom can gain more in legal power than they lose through arbitrary expressions (ibid., p. 151). Laplace even applies his theorem to predicting investment and moral successes: "its benefits become certain and the mathematical and moral hopes coincide; for analysis leads to this general theorem, namely, that if the expectations are very numerous the two hopes approach each other without ceasing and ending by coinciding in the case of an infinite number" (ibid., p. 154). Mathematics is even a benefit to actuarial science because it can determine monetary risks: "Indeed this kind of assurance always leaves uncertainty as to the loss which one may fear. But this uncertainty diminishes in proportion as the number of policy-holders increases: the moral advantage increases more and more and ends by coinciding with the mathematical advantage, its natural limit" (ibid., p. 155).

Laplace extends the science of calculation to school policy and the classroom:

> if we consider again that, even in the things which cannot be submitted to calculus, it gives the surest things which can guide us in our judgments, and that it teaches us to avoid the illusions which ofttimes confuse us, then we shall see that there is no science more worthy of our meditations, and that no more useful one could be incorporated in the system of public instruction. (Ibid., p. 196)

So complete, so absolute was Laplace's belief in mathematics that he argued that the only absolute model for mathematicians was divine intelligence. With Laplace's efforts, as with his contemporaries, intelligence, mathematics, and truth formed a new ideological alliance in the eighteenth century. More importantly, this alliance had the effect of humanizing what once was purely divine, with this new intelligence being a primary agency of both entities. Descriptions of divine intelligence changed during the Enlightenment, replaced by the notion of an intelligent being, with the effect of superior intelligence creating a new kind of superior human being.

De la Mettrie and Laplace's ideas cannot, however, compare to how the Marquis de Condorcet envisioned the power and utility of social mathematics, his vision eventually helping to construct the social sciences and modern ideas of intelligence. Who was Condorcet, and why might he be considered the primary architect of modern practices related to intelligence? Comte and Saint-Simon claim him to be the precursor of modern sociology, Quetelet took up where his social statistics left off, and Condorcet's idea of a rational science of decision-making influenced the work of Poisson and Cournot. According to Keith Michael Baker (1976, p. ix), Condorcet was a "prophet of social mathematics whose utopian vision extended to a universal mathematical science theoretically capable of embracing all aspects of human life and conduct." In essence, Condorcet transposed Newtonian physics into the social sciences. Condorcet argues: "if we examine the small number of facts necessary to establish the first foundations of ethics, of political, civil, or criminal legislation, or of administration . . . we shall see that these facts are as general and constant as the facts of the physical order" (ibid., p. 19). Or, as Baker observes, "as the well-made language of algebra made possible the ordering of simple phenomena through mathematicalization, so must a more elaborate analytic language order the world of complex phenomena through a philosophical calculus. Nowhere is this intimate relationship between method and language – mathematicalization and classification, more clearly revealed than in the scientific thinking of Condorcet" (Baker, 1975, p. 114).

Condorcet's goals in developing a "philosophical calculus" were clear. The scientific community had "two goals: to discover ways the scientific method could be applied to all human knowledge so as to profit from them, and, two, to find ways of codifying the scientific method, of literally reducing it to a kind of automatic template that could be applied ubiquitously" (ibid., pp. 85–6). This goal could be achieved by studying "the nature of the moral [social] sciences" so as to see that, "based like the physical sciences upon the observation of facts, they must follow the same method, acquire an equally exact and precise language, attain the same degree of certainty" (ibid., p. 86). In essence, Condorcet imparted to the human sciences the rationality of the physical sciences, hoping to create and maintain a rational political and social order. His rational social system vision was grounded in a science whose contents produced a new radically different social organization:

> the elaboration of a "social art" . . . that would command all the resources of the social sciences to realize for a given society a system of constitution, laws and administration corresponding exactly to the divisions of the political sciences . . . based on rigorous reasoning and well-attested facts, subject whenever possible to mathematical evaluation of the probabilities of social action. (Ibid., p. 201)

Cordorcet valued a *socialized* calculus of probabilities because it provided "mathematical certainty to the moral [social] and political sciences" (ibid., p. 226), an idea borrowed from Bernoulli's *Ars conjectandi*, and the application of stochastic reasoning to socioeconomic, governmental, and moral issues. Cordorcet's ideas match those in Voltaire's *Essai sur les probabilities*, both urging a "science of probabilities [that] must therefore be developed into a science of human conduct: our feeble minds must study probabilities with as much care as we have leaned arithmetic and geometry" (ibid., p. 234). Baker clarifies this new social model: "Condorcet brought to this conception of society a mathematical scientific model . . . that not only met the epistemological requirements of a science . . . but found a historical matrix in the very development of bureaucratic absolutism to which Condorcet's political theory was a response." His "social mathematics was closely associated with the expanding administrative efforts of the states. Wishing to tap to the full the human and financial resources of their societies, governments had need of accurate, extensive social statistics." Condorcet envisioned a state whose stability depended upon its ability to collect, analyze, and create policy based on precise information gathered by its citizenry:

> as the state penetrated more deeply into traditional society to bring individuals within the direct purview of public authority as citizens, so it also felt the impulse to quantify them. It was no accident that as the Revolution completed the centralizing work of bureaucratic absolutism, so it consolidated its demographic efforts by establishing a general statistical bureau. As citizens, indeed, there was a sense in which individuals were to be quantifiable and interchangeable units in a way that they were not as members of corporate social orders. Each – as Rousseau emphasized – must count for one. There is thus a fundamental continuity in administrative practice, as in political theory, between citizenship and quantifiability. (Ibid., p. 261)

Condorcet's contribution to Enlightenment thought should not be underestimated. He offered a calculus of probabilities, developed a unified mathematical conception of science, and argued for the use of demonstrational methods. He believed that together these efforts would produce a science, guided by the certitude of mathematical rules, that could triumph consistently over the contingencies of human life.

Besides translating Newtonian physics into social theory and using social mathematics to develop social policy, several *philosophes* helped to modernize intelligence, and did so in several ways. First, they elevated reason to a dominant ideological position by objectifying it, and identified intelligence as a primary human attribute. This effort was necessary if the two were to become scientific concepts. Second, the rational nature of social mathematics helped to construct a "politicized individual," a representational identity measured in various social contexts and whose freedom, in part, was tied to his or her intelligence level. In essence, one had to be smart enough to recognize and accept Enlightenment ideology, with its relating of truth to the content of the *philosophes'* political ideas. Lastly, by making intelligence objective and scientific, the *philosophes* laid the path by which intelligence would later be measured as a means of insuring social stability and economic progress. Ideological alliances between modern ideas of intelligence and the social regulatory policies of new Western nation states are explored in the following section.

The *Philosophes* and Their New Intelligence

The French *philosophes* were instrumental in contributing to the modernization of ideas about intelligence. I should like to highlight contributions made by Condorcet, Condillac, the Baron d'Holbach, Rousseau, de la Mettrie, and Diderot, the last of these thinking that intelligence was a serious enough matter to be defined in his famous *Encyclopédie*. Unlike any other prior source, Diderot's text reveals a metaphorically rich, if not ambiguous, intelligence, dressed in nine common meanings:

> this word has various meanings that can be determined by several examples. One says: this man is "gifted" with uncommon intelligence because he understands difficult things with ease. The infinite relationships that we observe in the general harmony of things announces an infinite intelligence. Milton paints us the "Eternal" descending in the night, accompanied by a cloud of celestial intelligences. A poor commentator sometimes obscures a passage rather than giving it intelligence. A father will occupy himself particularly to maintain "a good intelligence" between his children. A large politic arranges itself in all courses of intelligence . . . without intelligence, how can we understand principles? About intelligence, we have made intelligent, intelligible and we now distinguish from it two worlds, the real world, and the intelligible world, or the idea of the real world. (Lough and Proust, 1976, volume 7, part 3, p. 243)

Intelligence occupies several cultural spaces for Diderot. It is synonymous with mental agility, represents a supernatural agency, celestial forces (Milton's *Paradise Lost*), or pure information, and exists domestically when fathers provide moral insight to their children. It is also involved in larger political issues, is necessary for grasping principles, and is a means of knowing how the real world works. Diderot's intelligence combines an agile mind, divinity, information, paternalist morality, political uses, principles, and an empirical knowledge of the world in one ideological construct, consolidating mental speed, moral and divine insight, information, politics, moral codes, and material truth. These associations were made frequently throughout the Enlightenment, were then continued in nineteenth- and twentieth-century science, and now operate in current notions of intelligence, with any combination of meaning serving a variety of different ideological functions.

This variety of meanings emerged from Enlightenment philosophers who defined intelligence in terms of mathematics, political objectives, scientific applications, ordering systems, technology, quantities, and inventiveness, or by contrasting it with other mental qualities. For example, de la Mettrie thinks that intelligence is something medical, placing it squarely in a world of illnesses, idiocy, heaviness, stupidity and epidemics:

> In sickness, sometimes the soul disappears and gives no sign of life and sometimes it is so transported by fury that it appears to be doubled; sometimes imbecility is dissipated and convalescence turns an idiot into a clever man. Sometimes the finest genius becomes stupid and no longer knows himself; farewell all that splendid knowledge acquired at such cost and with so much effort. (de la Mettrie, 1997, p. 5)

For whatever reasons, "Some people's minds are heavy and stupid, while other's are lively, light and penetrating. What is the cause of this, other than, in part, the food they eat, their father's seed and the chaos of different elements swimming in the immensity of the air? The mind, like the body, has its epidemics and its scurvy" (ibid., p. 9). Rather than contrasting it to sickness, Rousseau explores intelligence in terms of how it eludes the "savage man":

> Should we want to suppose a savage man as skillful in the art of thinking as our philosophers make him; should we follow their example, make him a philosopher himself, discovering alone the most sublime truths and making for himself, by chains of very abstract reasoning, maxims of justice and reason drawn from love of order in general or from the known will of his creator; in a word, should we suppose his mind to have as much intelligence and enlightenment as he must and is in fact found to have dullness and stupidity, what utility would the species draw from all this metaphysics? (Rousseau, 1990, volume 1, p. 119)

Despite their differences, de la Mettrie and Rousseau assign value to intelligence by underscoring its opposites. On one side, intelligence and enlightenment go hand in hand: intelligence is about skillful thinking and the discovery of "sublime truth," while its characteristics are "lively, light and penetrating." And on the other side, there is nothing but savagery, dullness, and stupidity. These cultural preferences are evident, as we saw in the introductory chapter, in numerous colonial documents written during and after the Enlightenment. Moreover, Rousseau associates intelligence with reason and social "order." In either case, intelligence exists in terms of healthiness, consistency, and predictability; it is not an illness, a disease, or something incomplete, irrational, irregular, or perverse, although its absence has these properties.

De la Mettrie's reference to a "heavy" mind suggests that part of the Enlightenment mathematicalization of the mind reinforced earlier Greek equating of quantity to intelligence. This association, as I have shown, appears frequently in Western culture. De la Mettrie speaks to the idea that size matters: "In general, the form and composition of the quadruped's brain is more or less the same as man's. Everywhere we find the same shape and arrangement, with one essential difference: man, of all animals, is the one with the largest and most convoluted brain, in relation to the volume of his body" (de la Mettrie, 1997, p. 9). Similarly,

> the person with the most imagination should be considered as having the most intelligence or genius, for all these words are synonymous . . . the finest, the greatest or strongest imagination is therefore the most suitable for both science and art. I do not wish to decide whether one needs more intelligence to excel in the art of Aristotle or Descartes or in that of Euripedes or Sophocles, or if nature expended more effort in producing Newton than in creating Corneille. . . . But it is certain that their different triumphs and immortal glory were only due to imagination. (Ibid., p. 17)

Determined by quantity and size, intelligence is also a mark of inventiveness. For example, in his *Treatise on Systems*, Condillac explores genius in economics, spiritual perfection, and consistent accuracy:

> Because of an impoverished or excessive imagination, the intelligence is thus highly imperfect. . . . Although we commonly take the word "genius" to mean the highest point of perfection to which the human mind can aspire, nothing varies more than our application of this word, for each of us uses it according to his own way of thinking and the compass of his mind. To be regarded as genius by the common run of men, all one has to be is inventive. This quality is no doubt essential, but it must be combined with a right-thinking mind that consistently avoids error and that puts the truth in the most appropriate light for making it understandable. (Condillac, 1970, p. 135)

And in his *De la raison, de l'esprit et de ses différentes espèces*, Condillac explores inventive intelligence in terms of a mathematical analogue:

> Good sense and intelligence are no more than to conceive or to imagine, and differ in terms of the nature of the object that occupies us. For example, to know that two plus two make four, or to know an entire course of mathematics, is equally to conceive, but with this difference, one is called good sense, the other intelligence. Likewise, to imagine ordinary things, those common to our sight, no more than good sense is needed, but to imagine new things, especially if they are of any

extent, then intelligence is needed. The object of good sense seems related to what is easy and common whereas intelligence makes us conceive or imagine things of a newer and more compound form. (Ibid., p. 106)

Condillac investigates the relationship between invention and intelligence by asserting that:

> invention consists in knowing how to make new combinations. There are two kinds of invention: talent and genius . . . genius adds to talent the idea of a mind that is, as it were, creative. Genius invents new arts . . . superior to the genres we already know. It sees things from its own unique viewpoints. It gives rise to new fields of knowledge or . . . it opens up the way to truths never before aspired to. On truths already known, it gives a clarity and ease of which they were not previously suspected. Others can share in the character of a talented person, and they may equal and sometimes surpass him. But the character of a person of genius is original and inimitable. . . . We describe genius as extensive and vast in scope. It is extensive when it makes a great deal of progress in a genre, and vast when it combines so many genres to a degree that we have . . . great difficulty imagining that it has any limits. (Ibid., pp. 482–3)

Condorcet, too, believes that intelligence can be defined by the amount of its inventiveness:

> We shall also inquire what precisely constitutes, for each of them [new scientific truths], the talent of invention, that primary faculty of the human intelligence which has been given the name genius; by which means the mind can make the discoveries that it seeks or sometimes to be led to those which it did not seek and could not even have foreseen. (Baker, 1976, p. 249)

Part of this inventiveness is tied predictably to new technologies and new scientific ideas. Condorcet praises science as a source of intelligence: "the most important of these, perhaps, is to have destroyed prejudices and to have redirected the human intelligence, which has been obliged to follow the false directions imposed on it by the absurd beliefs that were implanted in each generation in infancy with the terrors of superstition and the fear of tyranny" (ibid., p. 250). Scientific instruments can also increase intelligence:

> The strength and limits of man's intelligence may remain unaltered; and yet the instruments that he uses will increase and improve, the language that fixes and determines his ideas will acquire greater breadth and precision, and unlike mechanics where an increase in force means a decrease of speed, the methods that lead

genius to the discovery of truth increase at once the force and the speed of its operation. (Ibid., p. 268)

When technologies are said to enhance intelligence then intelligence becomes part of how science works, so that being smart works in concert with the basic aims of science. Textual associations between intelligence and science are made throughout the Enlightenment. De la Mettrie (1997, p. 12) argues that more superior people owe this fortune to their super intelligence: "A man who owes the miracles he performs to his own genius is, to my mind, superior to one who owes his to chance." In *Sur le système du monde et sur le calcul integral* (1768), Condorcet brings certainty, scientific law, celestial dynamics, metaphysics, and mathematics together in a discussion of how a superior intelligence serves as a model for human intelligence: "the movement of bodies seems to be subject to two essentially different kinds of laws: the first are the necessary consequences of the idea that we have matter; the second seem to be the effect of the free will of an Intelligent Being who has willed that the World be as it is rather than any other way." He assesses this kind of intelligence more closely:

An Intelligence that knew the state of all phenomena at any given moment, the laws governing matter and the effect of these laws after any given period of time, would have a perfect knowledge of the System of the World. Such knowledge is beyond our power: but it is the goal towards which all the efforts of philosophical Mathematicians must be directed, and towards which they will draw closer and closer, without ever being able to hope to attain it. (Baker, 1976, pp. 104–5)

This superior intelligence is also for Condorcet a key to effective government: "the principle of the natural equality of man implied the democratic right of the still unenlightened many to participate in the formation of laws. At the same time, the principle that politics be made rational, or scientific, required that political decision-making be limited to the enlightened few" (Baker, 1975, p. 225). Condorcet identifies two institutions that produce superior intelligence: "a good method of election and an adequate level of public instruction were sufficient to ensure that the democratic choice of the people would fall upon men capable of making political decisions which would be right in the eyes of those with superior intelligence" (ibid., p. 341). Connections between intelligence and order are also made between intelligence and mathematics, with the latter enhancing the former. Baker comments on Condorcet's ideas:

Arithmetic provided the model of this process [advancement of the intellect] as well as one of its earliest and most crucial instruments, in the "happy means of representing all numbers by a small number of signs, using very simple technical operations to execute calculations that the human mind, left to itself, could never have attained." This is the first example of these methods that multiply the powers of the human mind, enabling it to extend its limits indefinitely without our ever being able to fix a point beyond which it cannot pass. The development of algebra advanced the process further by creating an instrument potentially applicable not only to the sciences of quantity but to all combinations of ideas, opening the entire universe of human knowledge to the certain and sure progress of mathematical logic. Condorcet's technical methods of processing data mathematically and his universal symbolic language of the sciences were intended to accelerate that progress immensely, multiplying the relations open to the human mind by perfecting its technology. (Baker, 1975, p. 368)

Condorcet argues that although human intelligence will never increase, the instruments it creates will advance new ideas.

Like the mystical aura of mathematics, some Enlightenment thinkers tended to mystify intelligence and genius. Cordorcet argues that "philosophy is nearly always obliged to look into the writings of a man of genius in order to find the secret thread that guided him" (Baker, 1976, p. 239). Rousseau (1990, p. 53) speaks to the mystical becoming material when genius is forced to "lower" itself "to the level of his time and will prefer to compose ordinary works which are admired during his lifetime instead of marvels which would not be admired until after his death." Nature is part of this mystification. Condillac (1970, p. 355) insists that "it is nature that inspires the man of genius; it is the muse that he invokes when he does not know where his ideas come from." Rousseau's mystification of genius is represented by metaphors of elevation and grandeur. For example, since it is born from celestial light, genius has "sparks," as in "sparks of genius" (Rousseau, 1990, p. 131) or it can be a "profound genius" (ibid., p. 147).

Interest in the mystical and material aspects of intelligence was part of a larger Enlightenment fascination with the nature of the human mind, or, more specifically, its operations, as we might expect from a group of systemizers. It is not surprising that those who politicized the production of knowledge as a mechanism for social liberation would want to know more about how the source of enlightenment, reason, and intelligence actually operated, how it was structured and how it could become a science. This ideology is nowhere clearer than in a series of observations Condorcet makes in his essay on public instruction (1791):

It is impossible for instruction, even when equal, not to increase the superiority of those whom nature has endowed more favorably . . . the superiority of the few – far from being an evil for those whose who have not received the same advantages – will contribute to the good of all. Their talents and enlightenment will become the common patrimony of society. (Baker, 1976, p. 106)

The point here is that knowledge and intelligence presumably free individuals from being dependent upon others for important socioeconomic information, and thus the more knowledge and intelligence one possesses the freer he or she is. In short, intelligence predicates independence, the point an echo of Kant's essay.

Condorcet also argues that "the class which receives better instruction will necessarily have gentler manners, a more refined sense of integrity, a more scrupulous honesty. Its virtues will be purer, its vices . . . less repulsive, its corruption less revolting, barbaric and incurable" (ibid., p. 108). Such a benefit makes it "incumbent upon society to offer each and every man the means of acquiring an education commensurate with his mental capacities. . . . No doubt a greater difference will result in favor of those endowed with greater talent and those to whom an independent fortune allows the liberty to devote a larger number of years to study" (ibid.). And therefore "society has an obligation to provide public instruction relative to various occupations. . . . In the current state of society, men are divided into various occupations, each of which requires specialized knowledge. The progress of these occupations contributes to the common good. Real equality is also promoted by opening access to them to those individuals, so destined by their tastes and abilities" (ibid., p. 109). These arguments form the cornerstone of modern education policies, evident in the "no child left behind" slogan. In a direct way Condorcet argues that "society also has an obligation to provide human instruction as a means of perfecting the human race," a goal achieved "by affording all men born with genius the opportunity to develop it" (ibid., p. 110). Here, as evident elsewhere in this chapter, the inherently problematic nature of Enlightenment ideas of intelligence surfaces. The argument that mass liberation might, in part, be dependent on the superior intelligence of the few, the gifted, or the privileged prompts an inconsistency that flies in the face of the equalitarian rhetoric of the Enlightenment.

Another problem arose when the *philosophes* took Newtonian physics and tried applying it to a mental calculus, a way of explaining mental dynamics, constant systems, and laws that would illuminate how mentality operated. How, we might ask, would one go about that kind of analysis? Or what tools would be needed to unravel the mechanics of the mind? Answers to these questions are predictable given the ideological bent of the *philosophes*. Condorcet's tool came from an all too familiar toolbox. He extolled the virtues of social mathematics and probability theory, suggesting that applications of probability "directly relate either to social interests or to the analysis of the operations of the human mind" (McLean and Hewitt, 1994, p. 13). In his *Tableau général*, Condorcet often returns to the power inherent in statistical description, describing it in terms of a social physics, a new way of defining "man," whose value lies in analyzing human intellectual operations. Baker maintains that Condorcet defined

> social sciences in terms of the whole of human action and thought. Those studies relating to the operation of the mind in itself – in logic and mathematics, epistemology and psychology – he later came to call *sciences psychologiques*, by which he meant the analysis of sensations and ideas to which his younger associates (the future Idéologues) came to give the term *idéologie*. These "psychological sciences" he distinguished . . . from those dealing with man's social relations in ethics and politics, legislation and jurisprudence, economics, demography, and statistics, for he finally preferred the term *sciences sociales*. (Baker, 1975, pp. 197–8)

Condillac's *Book on Logic* includes a passage that ties mental "laws" to a mystified superior intelligence: after many centuries

> men suspected that thought could be subject to laws. However, a happy instinct called talent, that is, a more certain and sensitive manner of seeing, guided the better minds without their knowing it. Their writings became models, and in them people tried to discover by what strategy . . . they produced pleasure and enlightenment. The more astonishing their talent, the more people imagined that these writers possessed some extraordinary technique and they looked only for simple ones. People soon believed they had figured out these men of genius. But it is not easy to figure them out. Their secret is all the more protected as it is not always within their power to reveal it. (Condillac, 1970, p. 343)

And then there is the body–mind analogy: "Now just as the art of moving large masses has its laws in the faculties of the body and in the levers that our arms have learned to use, the art of thinking has its laws in the faculties of the mind, and in the levers that our mind has likewise learned to use. Thus we must observe these faculties and levers" (ibid.). Lastly, "analysis is a method that we have learned from nature itself. And we shall use this method to explain the origin and generation both of ideas and of the faculties of the mind" (ibid., p. 344).

His emphasis on the mind has arguably made Condillac the founder of the behavioral sciences. In fact, Baker argues that "the social sciences" owe much of their grounding assumptions to "Condillac's genetic theory of mental operations." Condillac's *Traité des sensations* sculpts a symbolic statue "organized internally like us, and animated by a spirit deprived of all sorts of ideas" (ibid., p. 22). The statue is made to represent the structure and evolution of mental activity. And in his *Essai sur l'origine des connoissances humaines*, Condillac asserts that "our first object . . . is the study of the human mind – *l'espirit humain* – not in order to discover its nature, but to understand its operations, to observe in what manner they are combined and how we should employ them that we might acquire all the intelligence of which we are capable" (ibid., p. 4).

Paul Henri Thiry (1723–89), the Baron d'Holbach, occupies an intriguing place in the evolution of Enlightenment theories of intelligence. A centerist and defender of atheistic materialism, Holbach wrote *The System of Nature or The Laws of the Moral and Physical World*, a text that provides surprisingly modern notions of intelligence. For instance, he states that

> Many call those beings intelligent who are organized after his own manner; in whom he sees faculties proper for their preservation; suitable to maintain their existence in the order that is convenient to them . . . the faculty called intelligence consists in a possessing capacity to act conformably to a known end, in the being to which it is attributed. (Holbach, 1770, volume 1, chapter 5, p. 70)

Holbach makes several important points here: intelligence is uniquely human, it is a faculty responsible for human "preservation," and intelligent people act "conformably to a known end." Conformance – moral and social – eventually becomes the primary criterion in the modernization of intelligence, with science, government, and educational policy in search of compliant citizens, their conformance a mark of normal or superior intelligence.

Then by contrast Holbach argues that "He looks upon those beings as deprived of intelligence in which he finds no conformity with himself; in whom he discovers neither the same construction; nor the same faculties: of which he knows neither the essence, the end to which they tend, the energies by which they act, nor the order that is necessary to them." This quote is prophetic, especially the suggestion that a deprived intelligence is socially incompetent. As theories of intelligence evolved into the twentieth century, idiots, imbeciles, and morons were often defined clinically in terms of social, moral, or cognitive incompetence, as reflected by various levels of numerical deviation from a presumed norm. Holbach also argues that "As soon as he sees or believes he sees, the order of action, or the manner of motion, he [a human of like intelligence] attributes this order to an intelligence: which is nothing more than a quality borrowed from himself – from the manner in which he is himself affected" (ibid., p. 71). Here Holbach deconstructs traditional and Enlightenment notions of intelligence; it is neither a divine agency nor a natural phenomenon. Instead, intelligence is a kind of ordering activity that gets defined as insight, this consistent patterning being not something external but a "quality borrowed from himself," a self-reflexive metaphor of attribution.

He then extends this idea to another deconstruction of traditional assumptions about intelligence:

> Thus an intelligent being is one who thinks, who wills, and who acts to compass an end. If so, he must have organs, an aim conformable to those of man: therefore to say Nature is governed by an intelligence, is to affirm that she is governed by a being, furnished with organs; seeing that without this organic construction, he can neither have sensations, perceptions, ideas, thoughts, will, plan, nor action which he understands. Man always makes himself the center of the universe. . . . He imagines that Nature is governed by a cause whose intelligence is conformable to his own, to whom he ascribes the honor of the order which he believes he witnesses. (Ibid., pp. 71–2)

This critique of the idea that Nature is an intelligent agent is followed by perhaps the first effort at providing a history of intelligence:

> Anaxagoras is said to have been the first who supposed the universe created and governed by an intelligence: Aristotle reproaches him with having made an automaton of this intelligence . . . with ascribing to it the production of things . . . . it is for want of being acquainted with the powers of Nature, or the properties of matter, that man has multiplied beings without necessity – that he has supposed the universe under the government of an intelligent cause which he is and perhaps always will be himself the model. (Ibid., p. 73)

Holbach's point – that humans model the intelligence they ascribe to some external force – is particularly valuable for this study, supporting as it does the idea that intelligence is as much a cultural and ideologically driven construction as it may be an objective attribute or natural or evolutionary phenomenon.

While it is easy to make Nature the source and producer of "intelligent beings," assuming that "she must be herself intelligent, or else she must be governed by an intelligent cause," Holbach claims that "intelligence is a faculty peculiar to organized beings . . . to beings constituted and combined after a determinate manner; from whence results certain modes of action, which are designated under various names; according to the different effects which these beings produce" (ibid., p. 74). In a rather bold way he argues that

> It cannot be said Nature is intelligent after the manner of any of the beings she contains: but she can produce intelligent beings by assembling matter suitable to their particular organization from whose peculiar modes of action will result the faculty called intelligence . . . to have intelligence . . . it is requisite to have ideas; to the production of ideas, organs, or senses are necessary. (Ibid., p. 75)

145

Holbach's analysis of intelligence is singularly different from other Enlightenment notions of intelligence. He was the only *philosophe* to challenge the objective status assigned intelligence, a status ideologically critical in ordering Newtonian science, reason, the human sciences, market capitalism, and social mathematically based governmental practices into a new cultural myth and sociopolitical system.

This brief exploration of metaphoric illuminations in the Enlightenment has shown how the ubiquity of Newtonian apples, the deployment of social mathematics, and new ideas of intelligence contributed to the creation of new models of cultural and political order. This new system was also aided in its ideological creation by a new science and various medical assessments that ultimately helped to stabilize it. To assure such stability, another kind of illumination technology took center stage. It took form as observational practices used by those given authority and privilege to observe, diagnose, and cure or purge the irrational and the abnormal, physical bodies that could destabilize the new body politic.

12 The Clinical Gaze and Human Normalization

In addition to politicizing ideas of intelligence, human nature, and individuality, French and British *philosophes* translated Renaissance and Newtonian scientific methods into other ideological content. Observational procedures advanced by Bacon, Hobbes, Galileo, Newton, Boyle, and Locke, were, for instance, well suited for use in French mechanistic philosophy, especially given its interest in exploring and regulating social behavior in accord with new state needs. Moreover, "sensationalist philosophies of knowledge, represented by . . . Condillac, encouraged a certain empiricism of values, according an epistemological dignity to the act of observation" (Jones and Porter, 1994, p. 60).

Modern ideas of intelligence evolved from the Enlightenment politicization of certain scientific practices, especially observational ones, and, to prove that, I would like to explore the ideological aspects of Foucault's reading of the "gaze." My argument is that the modern business and "science" of intelligence (in media, advertising, research, and clinical practices) can ultimately be traced, in part, to the Enlightenment gaze.

Foucault's medical gaze begins with Bacon's and Descartes's idea that practical science makes men "masters and possessors of nature," a science

> desired not only for the invention of an infinite number of devices that would enable us to enjoy without any labor the fruits of the earth and all its comforts, but above all for the preservation of health, which is doubtless the first of all goods and the foundation of all other goods of this life. (Descartes, 1988, p. 120)

This tradition indirectly helped Enlightenment citizens to use their critical intelligence to secure power over their social and biological fate. Gay (1977, p. 12) notes that "medicine was the most highly visible and the most heartening index of general improvement: nothing after all was better calculated to buoy up men's feelings about life than growing hope for life itself." Moreover, "it was in medicine that the *philosophes* tested their philosophy by experience; medicine was at once the model of the new philosophy and proof of its efficacy" (ibid., p. 13). Examples abound for this same "efficacy," evident in modern clinical practices whereby the ideological content of various notions of intelligence reinforce a certain hegemony. For instance, Boerhaave, the Enlightenment's most famous doctor, taught medical Newtonianism and used empirical methods in his theoretical and clinical work. Enlightenment medicine also provided advances in anatomy, childbirth, and disease classification, while improving and professionalizing surgical methods. Moreover, it is not merely coincidental that the majority of the philosophical architects of the Enlightenment were medical doctors. This fact speaks to the medicalization of Western society, beginning in the eighteenth century. From the minds of doctors came the *dispostif*, the social machinery of "tangled, multilinear ensembles of vectors and tensions making up the social apparatus" of "new knowledges of human individuality," enabling institutional cooperation among the "asylum . . . the school . . . the factory . . . and the clinic" (Jones and Porter, 1994, p. 59). This medicalized "body" literally informed the body politic of eighteenth-century political culture.

These ideas, in turn, introduce us to Foucault's notion of the gaze and a "world of constant visibility" (Foucault, 1975, p. x) during the Enlightenment. The medical gaze was actually many gazes; it was as "meticulous" as it was "illuminating" or "loquacious," working to make "the invisible visible and constantly so" (ibid., pp. xi–xii). Foucault suggests that we "place ourselves . . . at the level of the fundamental spatialization and verbalization of the pathological, where the loquacious gaze with which the doctor observes the poisonous heart of things is born and communes with itself" (ibid., p. xii). From this position we can see how the gaze illuminates its own power – its making visible "the residence of truth in the dark centre of things." Most importantly, it is an "empirical gaze that turns their darkness into light" (ibid., pp. xiii–xiv). This gaze is also authoritative, "linked to the primary passivity that dedicates it to the endless task of absorbing experience in its entirety, and of mastering it" (ibid., p. xiv). For the purpose of this study,

> the gaze is no longer reductive, it is, rather, that which establishes the individual in his irreducible quality. And thus it becomes possible to organize a rational language around it. The object of discourse may equally well be a subject, without the figures of objectivity being in any way altered. It is this formal reorganization, in depth, rather than the abandonment of theories and old systems, that made clinical experience possible . . . once could at last hold a scientifically structured discourse about an individual. (Ibid., p. xiv)

Hence, the gaze engenders and dominates clinical experiences by opening "up . . . the concrete individual, for the first time in Western history, to the language of rationality" (ibid., p. xiv). This "opening" would soon prove essential to efforts to rationalize the human interior, especially the viewing, testing, and measuring of human intelligence.

This gaze is actually part of a complex medical mythology:

> The years preceding and immediately following the Revolution saw the birth of two great myths with opposing themes and polarities: the myth of a nationalized medical profession, organized like the clergy, and invested, at the level of man's bodily health . . . and the myth of total disappearance of disease in an untroubled, dispassionate society restored to its original state of health. (Ibid., pp. 31–2)

According to Foucault, each myth provides a similar medical treatment experience:

> The two dreams are isomorphic; the first expressing in a very positive way the strict, militant, dogmatic medicalization of society, by way of a quasi-religious conversion, and the establishment of a therapeutic clergy; the second expressing the same medicalization, but in a triumphant, negative way, that is to say, the volatilization of disease in a corrected, organized, and ceaselessly supervised environment, in which medicine itself would finally disappear, together with its object and raison d'être. (Ibid., p. 32)

The gaze is related to the evolution of various representations of disease, from that of a pathological essence understood apart from its concrete manifestations to the modern notion of an expression within the body, a historical transformation by which a "language of fantasy" evolves into to a world of "constant visibility." This new world of "psychological and epistemological purification" allows doctors to be "free . . . of their theories and chimeras," allowing them "to approach the object of their experience with the purity of an unprejudiced gaze" (ibid., p. 195).

The Birth of the Clinic argues that disease during the Enlightenment was repositioned discursively, removed from its prior mythic status and placed within the social realm of the body. This shift in representational domains – *identical to what happened when Renaissance thinkers humanized intelligence* – effectively changed traditional medicine modalities. The physician's work, a *pro forma* observance of some *predetermined illness*, became a clinician's gaze, a concentrated inventorying and classifying, whereby disease became something to diagnose by way of interpreting and ordering a hierarchy of symptoms. In essence, disease became a text requiring interpretation. Foucault explains this new way of seeing: "the gaze is not faithful to truth, nor subject to it, without asserting, at the same time, a supreme mastery: the gaze that sees is a gaze that dominates" (ibid., p. 39).

This emergence of the Enlightenment gaze also represents a change in how structures and spaces of visibility were understood, as well as how visibility and invisibility are related. As a consequence, new vertical spaces of obscured processes replaced the flat space of Renaissance and early Enlightenment typologies. And to make those indecipherable processes visible, the gaze penetrates the body to determine the nature or extent of illness seen now as a deviation of an orderly body. Foucault argues that the traditional model of a pathogen inserting itself into the body was replaced with the idea that the body itself becomes ill and needs to be observed and treated systemically. The gaze is part of a treating of disease in terms of "a fundamental system of relations involving envelopments, subordinations, divisions and resemblances" (ibid., p. 5). Once this new internality was reconfigured in compliance with the dominant hegemony, disease was attributed to an internal "space in which analogies define essence" (ibid., p. 6).

The *analogical defining the essential* is a critical pattern in the modernization of intelligence: its post-Enlightenment mathematicization and medicalization would have been impossible had it not been for new strategies for representing the scientific. For instance, new numerical configurations (analogical models of phenomenon) were made to represent internal physical or cognitive spaces and structures, a tradition evident in the contemporary use of CAT, MRI, and PET scans. This is precisely the case with intelligence: a presumably invisible element of the human mind was made *visible* by clinical surveillance, taking objective form as tests and activities rendered visible by various mathematical schematics. In this practice, the invisible becomes simultaneously objective and normalized in terms of the celebrated "bell curve." Foucault alludes to this transformational exchange by stating: "a true mathematicalization of disease would imply a common, homogeneous space, with organic figures and nosological ordering" (ibid., p. 13). This is precisely what happened in the early twentieth century when intelligence became something that could be mathematically represented.

So what exactly did the new clinician's gaze see, classify, and cure during the Enlightenment? Foucault insists that it was not "directed initially . . . towards that concrete body, that visible whole, that positive plenitude that faces him – the patient – but towards intervals in nature, lacunae, distances, in which there appears, like negatives, 'the signs that differentiate one disease from another, the true from the false, the legitimate from the bastard, the malign from the benign'" (ibid., p. 8). These "intervals . . . lacunae, distances" and signs of differentiation, those distinguishing the "true from the false, the legitimate from the bastard, the malign from the benign," form the basis of a future science that, in one Parisian offshoot, produced psychological scales to "Establish scientifically the anthropometric and mental differences that separate the normal child from the abnormal: of making these differences exact, of measuring them in some way so that their assessment ceases to be a matter of tact and intuition, but rather becomes objective and tangible" (Hothersall, 1984, p. 306). Here the founder of intelligence made visible and assessable, Binet, sought out "intervals, lacunae, distances," and signs of differentiation in order to "diagnose inferior states of intelligence . . . to measure general intelligence, which Binet considered to be a 'fundamental faculty,' to make correct judgments, show initiative, and adapt to circumstances. . . . Between 1905 and 1908 Binet and Simon gave these tests to large numbers of schoolchildren and arranged them in a hierarchical order based on their performance" (ibid., p. 307).

Foucault's description of the gaze and its related practices provides an explanation of how modern ideas of a clinical intelligence were methodically validated. Without this gaze and its tradition of authoritative practices, it would be impossible to identify any source for developing the clinical methods used in assessing "modern" intelligence. Fundamentally, the gaze and its ideological contexts become a parent technology of social disciplination marking the collaborative influence of the social and medical sciences on the modernization of ideas of intelligence. The gaze is ironically intelligent.

Summary of Part II

Part II of this book demonstrates how ideas of intelligence collaborated with new Enlightenment ideas about the nature of individualism, the invention of the political subject, the power of reason to create "critical intelligence," the production of modern state bureaucracies, and the power of science as a dominant epistemology. More specially, ideas of intelligence found direct alliance with four period-defining abstractions – Newtonianism, mathematics, medicine, and ideas about human behavior – all of them taking various material institutional forms as science became increasingly a means of supporting and justifying social policies and practices.

Why, however, was the age so ready to capitalize upon ideas from the social sciences, a metaphoric incubator that went on to support and study new ideas of human intelligence? Part of the answer lies in why Enlightenment social sciences were thought so valuable and why they so quickly became ideologically functional, and could function as the messaging system and content for the new society. The social sciences simply offered new opportunities for certainty, a means to precisely regulate and coordinate both individual and state behavior.

This latter virtue arose from inventors of the social sciences who were not merely metaphysical philosophers superficially interested in politics. Abstractions aside, they were actually legislators and doctors facing a number of growing social problems triggered by increasing instances of instability triggered by the new political economy. With two centuries of wars and revolutions as backdrop to his argument, Theodore Porter contrasts certain intellectual continuities of the period with "the divide of 1789," noting what the social sciences seemingly promised: "the ideological significance of the French Revolution for social science was, however, without parallel. Unruly passions, threatening political stability, inspired a pervasive sense of danger. Social science became urgent, and often more ideological, looking to the past, or to science, in order to comprehend what seemed the precarious circumstances of modernity" (Porter and Ross, 2001, volume 7, p. 22).

The ability of the social sciences to "comprehend . . . the precarious circumstances of modernity" in all their unstable cultural manifestations also extended to the individual, to the scientificization and medicalization of the human body, an object whose behavior became subject to new forms of social control. David Armstrong (1983, p. 3) argues that by the nineteenth century the human body could now be "subjected, used, transformed and improved." The goal of these practices was to surround and invest the body "with various techniques of detail which analyzed, monitored and fabricated it." A dominant Enlightenment legacy was the invention of being able to see the body in different ways and translating these views, in part, into a new political economy based on the body, in which all its aspects (gesture, structure, time, detail, movements) could be deconstructed into their component elements, analyzed, and then reformed into new notions of a now coordinated and disciplined body, more valuable in this reconstitution than the sum of the separate contributions. These efforts at the scientization of the body helped to begin the process of turning the interiority of human consciousness into something advancing the new political economy. And the primary technique for all this analysis was the *gaze*, the ultimate technology for producing *in-sight*.

I supplement Armstrong's argument by suggesting that the same ideological forces and medical practices would within the next fifty years be extended – in the spirit of such detailing – to the medicalization of intelligence, to the use of similar techniques to evaluate, monitor, and control the individual. By the early twentieth century the individual's body and mind were subject to various state systemizations. The individual, in essence, became *subject* to the *matho-medicalization* of intelligence: the "enlightenment" of the body evolved into the "enlightenment" of a mental interior. What affected and cured the body was transferred into a similar surveillance, control, monitoring, and social ordering of how well or how poorly a person reasoned. The desire to measure the interior extended to the exterior with Lavater's assumption in the *Physiognomik* (1783) that facial and physiological characteristics reflect a person's psychological nature. Ultimately the question to be answered is what ideologically needed to be in place for this evolving myth to achieve dominance as an uncontestable absolute truth.

This part of the book has identified several factors involved in the modernization of how we understand human intelligence. First, the eighteenth century translated intelligence into a purely ideological metaphor, linking it directly to reason and enlightenment. Moreover, Kant established the idea that only the truly intelligent are politically free. This was just one of many examples of the Enlightenment politicization of the individual, with intelligence becoming a metaphoric means of objectifying the mind, the controlling mechanism for ideological productions of individuality. In addition, the Enlightenment converted what the Renaissance did to ideas of intelligence into an objectified attribute, and by making it subject to scientific analysis, dominant ideas of intelligence eventually functioned as a means of shaping certain hegemonic systems. In the final analysis, the Enlightenment was busy constructing new representations of intelligence, with each having its own ideological effect. Intelligence, however, truly became modern when mainly Enlightenment philosophers transformed the idea of intelligence into a *political, virtual and critical* sign in which a universalized human attribute began to support numerous practices and institutions that regulated that attribute. If the eighteenth century *discovered* the body as an object and target of power, then the social sciences of the following centuries transferred that same dynamic to the cognitive world, where intelligence was redefined as still another kind of object and means of power.

In part III, I explore how the Enlightenment "seeing" of bodies supported the evolution of the eighteenth-century political economy, guided in part by new notions of time, gesture, and details. These ideas, in turn, became scientific and then reduced to their essential nature, analyzed, and institutionalized. These abstractions became strategies of production, helping to normalize social rules, while coordinating and disciplining bodies engaged in labor. The goal of this economy was to produce a coherent system of production that would exceed the limits of any individual production. In short, the Enlightenment developed social theories and ideological abstractions that could *together maximize output, minimize economic disruptions, and insure social stability.* These processes and their social effects extended to new ways of literally "seeing" intelligence, of developing institutionalized practices that invented and investigated a clinically accessible human interior that could help to stabilize this new political economy and the nation states it supported. Newly invented technologies, industries, and businesses functioned differently than ever before. They now acted with the competitive advantages and power of information and new forms of knowledge. No longer abstract, they functioned like a census by providing new means of demographic measurement. In essence, the evolution of modern intelligence technologies – like IQ tests and lab equipment – represents the success of surveillance devices, providing data tools for new demographic studies. Medical and clinical practices – "professional examinations" – began to *situate* and *identify* the individual, making him or her subject to the mystifying activity of converting "hidden" mental potentials into the certitude of mathematical scales and, ultimately, into a means of predicting and enabling the scales of labor so critical to economic production and state fiscal stability. During these examinations, as pencils were readied and clocks ticked away, intelligence was simultaneously being *invented and inspected*, the simple goal being the prediction and institutional facilitation of an individual's contribution to a state's socioeconomic future. Test scores – those parented discursively by a tradition of large-scale quantitative social surveys – would ideally identify defects while monitoring and determining a citizen's economic potentials and the danger he or she posed to civil government. The goals of such mind inspection technologies were nearly identical to those of body surveillance. Foucault reminds us that "these techniques represented different aspects of a *disciplinary apparatus*. Discipline involves attention to fine detail, to strict monitoring, and to the object of the disciplinary regime – the individual body – being trained to function with coordination and efficiency: through discipline, surveillance fabricates a manipulable body" (Foucault, 1975, p. 3).

More importantly, these same efforts were to be applied to a new notion of the mind. Gone essentially was Locke's metaphoric blank slate, replaced by a foundationalized, studied, codified, and even manipulated mind – in short, a mind subjected to the practices and rigors of a *science*. These efforts, in turn, required a unique ideology, a new idea of medicine, new mathematical methods, and new technologies. Their modern history indicates that new ideas of intelligence were also part of the creation of a new political economy oiled by social mechanisms heavily invested in developing a science of the body and mind. This new economy of classifying the mind and its knowledge / capital production had its advocates – Adam Smith, Quesnay, Ricardo, Turgot, and Bastiat – a group united by David Hume's observation in *Of the Balance of Trade* that "The Author of the world" desires the exchange of national commodities "by giving them soils, climates, and *geniuses*, so different from each other." This new political economy and nation state, with their scientific and Newtonian catalysis, mobilized techniques for inventing and monitoring the individual. And one such technique was to construct the clinical and the clinical professional, using observational techniques that might ultimately insure that the disorganized, the abnormal, or the incoherent could function socially in an efficient manner. And if they could not, then the very same clinical discipline would provide a means to insure that such individuals would not threaten the precarious social order of a new form of political organization. The replacement of the king with democratic capitalism was not without threats to social stability. The politicization of Newtonian mechanics offered tools of standardization and observation that could predict and help to manage disorder. This predictive feature became a ideological gold mine in the following century.

Part III

Modern and Postmodern Intelligence: Smart Architects, Smart Tools, and Smart Critiques

There is nothing about an individual as important as his IQ.
Lewis Terman, 1922

The black, the brown, and the red races differ anatomically so much from the white . . . that even with equal cerebral capacity they never could rival its results by equal efforts.
Daniel Brinton, American Association for the Advancement of Science, 1895

Our Target Visa comes with a built-in computer chip, called a *smart chip* . . . you get added benefits including exclusive access to savings through Smart Coupons.
www.target.com

13 Smart Architects and Contemporary Intelligence

Contemporary ideas of intelligence are largely derived from Enlightenment scientific methods translated into modern institutional practices. These efforts have transformed the once invisible quality of intelligence into the visibility of scales, coefficients, technologies, and treatment plans. The history of this transformation began with Darwin, Galton, Herbart, Wundt, Fechner, Sterne, and Binet, and with biological discoveries and *exact observations* transposed into insights about mental functions. Methods of scientific and mental detection, classification, and control provided new nineteenth- and twentieth-century institutions with significant social authority and power. For example, medical interventions and intelligence testing have evolved into a cooperative multi-institutional *regimen* consisting of examinations, a diagnosis (shared with the patient and family), a treatment plan, psychotherapy, medication, and consultations with other physicians. Schools, courts, and other social agencies are also involved. The power of this intervention sharply contrasts with the powerless anxiety of the "disease" to be cured. To understand the cultural implications of how something so abstract became *medically* and *politically* concrete, we need to explore the world of ideas and cultural practices that have created the *de facto* world of contemporary intelligence.

Post-Enlightenment thought grounds contemporary intelligence. For example, when Stephen Pinker (1997, p. 62) argues that intelligence is the ability to solve problems – "the ability to attain goals in the face of obstacles by means of decisions based on rational (truth-obeying) rules" – or when Anastasi argues that it is adaptive behavior, or Eysenck and Tattersall a biological element, or Sternberg a kind of overtly ideological mental "self-government," the ideological legacy of modern intellectual history is being rehearsed, with these ideas revalidating assumptions lying at the core of most scientific and social science disciplines. The fact that no *other* notion of intelligence exists – one that repudiates rationality or affirms non-linear dynamics – indicates that only habitual thinking claims the status of unitary truth by controlling the boundaries by which intelligence – *in any form* – is defined, evaluated, and made authoritative.

These boundaries can be better understood by examining a representative source. Like other textbooks, Robert Sternberg's and Benjamin Wolman's *Handbook of Intelligence* (2000) arranges already sanctioned topics and disciplinary sources in lists of mostly familiar ideas about intelligence. Their range shows the influences that hereditary sciences, developmental cognition, evolutionary biology, neuropsychology, psychophysiology, information processing, AI, sociology, emotional models, psychometrics, personality studies, and educational and public policy have played in contesting accepted notions of intelligence. What is absent – the silence of other intelligence – challenges Steinberg's claim that the book "provides what is perhaps the most comprehensive account of . . . what intelligence is, how it is assessed, how it is developed, and how it affects society and its institutions" (ibid., p. ix). Like other textbooks it does not, however, take into account poststructural theories that critique mathematics and science, the basic elements of claimed comprehensiveness.

The point is that most contemporary "inquiries" are predetermined, operating from within an *a priori* framework and residing within a boundary situating their key ideas at similar sites of social power. Would it be reasonable to suppose that a *comprehensive* textbook on intelligence might include *other* material, like the court transcripts of *Daniel Hoffman v. The Board of Education of the City of New York*, 1978? Are there last minute interviews with prisoners proven "mentally competent" as they head off to execution, and where are the thousands of stories of failure, self-abuse, depression, under-employment, unrealized dreams, and self-rejection caused by "social policies that utilize or fail to utilize mental ability" or "when opportunity is denied or misallocated due to ignorance" (Browne-Miller, 1995, pp. xiii, 190)? The ideological power of modern intelligence resides within scientific and mathematic traditions.

Early Architects of Modern Intelligence

Although Darwin and Galton are primary sources of nineteenth-century intelligence, most intelligence books ignore how economic theory prepared the Victorian public for Darwin's theory of natural selection and why it was so influential in constructing modern ideas of intelligence. The term *economic Darwinism* also explains why most contemporary ideas of intelligence are rooted in British empirical theory, itself influential in modern sciences and in ideas proposed by Adam Smith and Darwin. The relationship between economics and intelligence is often overlooked.

Smith's *Theory of Moral Sentiments* (1759) argues that humans act like economic laws; both are self-regulated. Within all of us lies an observer who regulates behavior. *The Wealth of Nations* (1776) amplifies this idea by linking intelligence to revenue, wealth, and labor. Smith argues that human skills, varied markets, and the division of labor play critical economic roles. Moreover, superior minds create new commodities by arranging existing elements into new and profitable forms. This superiority is actually a matter of economic law, with intelligence being less about genetics than material resources. Differences in intelligence are dictated by the kinds of work people do: "The difference of natural talents in different men is, in reality, much less than we are aware of; and the very different genius which appears to distinguish men of different professions, when grown up to maturity, is not upon many occasions so much the cause, as the effect of the division of labour" (Smith, 1904, book 1, chapter 2, p. 124). Smith's belief that intelligence is a matter less of genes than of jobs is consistent with late Enlightenment thought. It relocates intelligence from the world of invisibility to the material world and class inheritance.

The economic basis of intelligence cross-pollinates with Smith's ideas about labor and "social" intelligence: repetitive jobs produce little insight, with new knowledge coming from "those few who . . . have leisure and inclination to examine the occupations of other people. The contemplation of so great a variety of objects necessarily exercises their minds in endless comparisons and combinations, and renders their understandings, in an extraordinary degree, both acute and comprehensive" (ibid., book V, chapter 1, p. 179).

Associating intelligence with economics represents a pattern in the evolution of modern intelligence. There clearly is ideological significance in Smith's contributions, which reflect the confluent dominance of Enlightenment materialism and Lockean empiricism, both enabling the biological sciences to later appropriate theories of intelligence based on genetic inheritance. While Enlightenment thinkers placed intelligence and its variants within the political economy, next-century biologists and naturalists explained how intelligence evolved and how it could justify ways of distinguishing levels of intelligence.

So how did biology exert such control over the construction of new ideas of intelligence? Biology was the first science to elevate the "term intelligence . . . from lay usage to systematic scientific discourse . . . in the context of analyses of animal behavior by evolutionary biologists," those like Romanes and Thorndike interested in the difference in degree between human and animal intelligence (Danziger, 1997, p. 67). More importantly, Romanes (Darwin's assistant) references the Enlightenment association of reason with intelligence by stating: "the word reason is used to signify the power of perceiving analogies or ratios. . . . This faculty, however, . . . admits of numberless degrees; and as in the designation of its lower manifestations it sounds somewhat unusual to employ the word reason, I shall in these cases frequently substitute the word intelligence" (ibid., p. 68).

The growing authority of biological insight, particularly evolutionary and hereditary ideas, helped biological scalability to become a *normal* way of doing science:

> Because it was generally recognized that people differed in their suitability for social tasks, the argument that some were inherently unsuitable for academic work could be deployed as effectively by individual pupils accused of morally reprehensible laziness as by teachers and administrators challenged to account for poor outcomes. A discourse of differential "brightness," "cleverness," "slowness," "dullness," etc. therefore became an inevitable feature of the new system. (Ibid., p. 75)

Even more importantly, "as the fashion for giving social problems a biological interpretation reached ever wider sections of the literate population towards the end of the nineteenth century one can detect a mounting tendency to associate the traditional social labels of 'brightness' and so on with notions of biological superiority and inferiority" (ibid.).

Then there is the power of the budding icon. One could easily argue that Darwin's contribution to human understanding was at least comparable to that of Newton's celestial mechanics. Both revolutionaries offered explanations for how the real world functioned. Darwin's evolutionary theory actually put flesh on representations of intelligence. His science made intelligence absolutely human and absolutely material. Moreover, his theories have arguably had the greatest role in the history of intelligence, extending their influence to Francis Galton, James McKeen Cattell, Henry Goddard, Arthur Jensen, Cyril Burt, and scores of others, particularly those taking the side of nature in the classical "nature versus nurture" argument. Darwin opened the door for this sustained influence, agreeing "with Francis Galton in believing that education and environment produce only a small effect on the mind of any one, and that most of our qualities are innate" (Barlow, 1958, p. 43).

For Darwin, intelligence was a matter of inherent behaviors, arising first from our non-human ancestors, with the eventual gap between the level of human and non-human intelligence a difference of degree rather than kind. *The Descent of Man* (1871) contains two ideas that have singularly created the broadest foundation for modern notions of intelligence: (a) differences among species mean that each has a difference in reasoning capacity and mental powers; and (b) all organisms learn from experience, so that "intelligent" genes lingering in the gene pool advance a given species' general intelligence, especially humans'. In essence, natural selection creates its own inclusive logic, in that if all variations are inherited, so too are intellectual abilities. Hence evolution explains why intelligence varies among individuals.

Larmarckian evolutionism, Cuvier, and French science also helped to lay the groundwork for demonstrating the value of Darwin's ideas in other sciences, so that human thought could be understood in terms of multilayered cognitive activities, much as biologists and geologists used stratification. It took little time for later nineteenth-century scientists and policy-makers to treat human mental activities in terms of gradient levels of performance, and to differentiate human races in terms of different levels of intelligence. Owing to Darwin and his belief that differences between the "highest races" and the "lowest savages" were a matter of "gradations," it became standard to use a comprehensive classification to differentiate race, gender, and social class. It should be of little surprise then that when Binet began to measure intelligence, human cognition and human physical characteristics were scientifically gradable or scaled.

Darwin's ideas opened the door for eugenic theory, developed by Spencer and Galton. If Darwin's biological ideas helped to direct the formation of modern ideas of intelligence, Francis Galton's expansion of them is surely noteworthy. Galton frequently professed his dream of actually creating families of high achievers by selective breeding practices, a process that had already been in place in England for hundreds of years. Perhaps Galton read little English history. His lab in South Kensington, another point for notoriety, charged visitors for visual and auditory tests and for assessing their hand strength, reaction times, and discriminative abilities. What the tests actually validated was never scientifically explored. The lab's carnival-like atmosphere contrasted sharply with the soberness of empirical research. Galton believed that individuals with a higher intelligence had more acute physical abilities, based mostly on evidence that "mental defects" were physical impairments. His scientific logic remains unclear. Why would the frequency of impairment within a certain population necessarily be a mark of superiority for another group? Or, conversely, the very physical abilities of non-Whites or colonial subjects would certainly confuse conventional wisdom, since those populations were generally considered of lower intelligence. Or, more basically, what is the connection between the two; why does intelligence have anything to do with anything physical? Likewise, why do energy and sensitivity – two of Galton's favorite general qualities – have anything to do with intelligence? Galton thought that high levels of energy and sensory acumen were indicative of intellectually gifted individuals. The logic of those ideas remained untested.

Galton's *Hereditary Genius: An Inquiry into Its Laws and Consequences* (1892) demonstrates how science can be ideological. In this case, Galton uses science to

163

validate racist and class politics. His scientific agenda is "to show . . . that a man's natural abilities are derived from inheritance, under exactly the same limitations as are the form and physical features of the whole organic world . . . it is easy . . . to obtain by careful selection . . . a highly-gifted race of men by judicious marriages during several consecutive generations" (Galton, 1892, p. 1). Galton does not explain why genius exists even when "careful selection" has not created it. His quotes need little comment: "high reputation is a pretty accurate test of high ability"; "civilization is the necessary fruit of high intelligence"; in "any race of animal . . . the most intelligent variety is sure to prevail in the battle of life"; "the number among the negroes of those whom we shall call half-witted men is very large . . . the mistakes the negroes made in their own matters were so childish, stupid, and simpleton-like, as frequently to make me ashamed of my own species" (ibid., pp. 2, 325, 328).

Galton does not explain why "mental peculiarities of different races" (ibid., p. v) exist or how they are differentiated, or why ancestry alone would be the carrier of intelligence. Inattentive to the very empiricism he claims, Galton groups and analyses "four hundred illustrious men of all periods in history" to prove that "genius was hereditary" (ibid.). Most importantly to the future of millions of lives and thousands of deaths, to the control of countless life destinies coinciding with the development of the IQ industry, Galton claims to be the first to "treat the subject in a statistical manner, to arrive at numerical results, and to introduce the law of deviation from an average" (ibid., p. vi). His "science" serves his social ideology, for those in this objective sampling have reputations and natural gifts proving why they are judges, statesmen, military officials, literary men, men of science, poets, musicians, painters, divines, senior classics of Cambridge, oarsmen, and wrestlers, professions one rarely encounters in other races or countries with less intelligence.

Charles Spearman, William Sterne, and Karl Pearson advanced Galton's efforts in biology and statistics. Spearman invented "factor analysis" to prove that task-specific ability (s) and general intelligence (g) were applicable to determining individual intelligence. While the value of this tool is debatable, its effects are not. Spearman was arguably the first to show that the existence of general intelligence could be mathematically demonstrated, a "proof" that Binet and others accepted without question. Sterne authored the notion of an IQ, a quotient produced by dividing a person's presumed "mental age" by her or his actual age, then multiplying by 100. Karl Pearson, on the other hand, deployed statistical and probability theory in a study of genetics, inventing such now commonly concepts as standard deviation, the χ^2 or chi-square test (removing the normal distribution from its central position), the coefficient of correlation (1892), the theory of multiple and partial correlation (1896), and the coefficient of variation.

The mathematical integrity of these concepts and their accuracy have been argued at length in other studies. But here their work had one profound effect: the creation of a new kind of uncontested certainty, based on the assumption that human intelligence was objective, universal, and biological in nature, and, most importantly, quantifiable. By the beginning of the twentieth century, everything was in place, ready for that one person to bring preceding sociopolitical, economic, scientific, and mathematical thought together in the creation of an icon for the modernization of intelligence. The stage was set for a new "proof," one with tremendous cultural and political influence, a demonstration proving that individuals possess intelligence in different degrees, these differences revealing how biological fitness equates with socioeconomic success or failure and, by extension, how its measurement could prevent civil chaos, increase industrial efficiency, and identify those whose minds could create new capital. Enter Binet and the ideology of economic Darwinism center stage.

The French Architect: Binet Invents Modern Intelligence

Two icons come to mind when modern popular culture thinks of intelligence: Binet and Einstein. The first measured intelligence, and the second possessed an immeasurable intelligence. There are two Binets: the scientist working as a governmental official, and Binet the interrogator, his test questions the "objective" means for separating the intelligent from the "defective." Binet's "science" is problematic: (a) his tests do not identify the mechanisms of intelligence, of what makes a person bright or subnormal; and (b) he does not explain why certain questions are better than others, or why they and their correct responses alone constitute an objective measure of intelligence. If intelligence is a truly human universal attribute, like the capacity to remember, independent of culture and acquired knowledge, would Binet's questions be equally valid as measuring tools if his translated test were given to native Japanese, Native Americans, Tibetans, or Eskimo teenagers, to individuals whose world did not contain military officers, currency, or analogue time? Here Reuning's (1988) work with !Kung San hunters comes to mind, especially their poor performance on Western IQ and Piagetian tests despite elaborate cultural adjustments.

Binet's 1905 article in *L'Année Psychologique* is the most influential document in modern intelligence. It inaugurated something revolutionary, something conceptualized as a commodity, weaving subtle political issues and scientific research into a scientific tool justifying the state's marginalizing of "the defective." Such certification meant legitimately removing them from the community and sending them to "special" schools outside the city. Binet produced a science of mental marginalization. Most responses to his efforts have been essentially technical in nature (from within similar ideological boundaries), rather than analytical. Many professionals and writers have argued in favor of or have critiqued the methods, contents, or assumptions of a given mental test, yet there has been little effort to explore the underlying reasons behind governments' testing for defectiveness, or what the greater, unpredictable, social effects of their decisions have been. For example, have there been any consequences of governmental control of citizens on the basis of a mental standard? Has this control helped to form cultural dissatisfaction prompting social revolution (the poor and unemployed always test lower than the rich), or has there been unharvested intellectual capital (knowledge converted into capital becomes the increased tax revenues that stabilize the state) because of an error in a method, or because of misrouting a bright mind or creating a standard of normal intelligence whose bell curve represents a willing trade-off between inventiveness and uniformity? Uniformity is measurable; inventiveness does not know what time it is.

From the onset one is struck by Binet's official tone and his focus, a blend of bureaucratic and scientific language factually accounting for the history of his test. He provides a "rough sketch" of how the Minister of Public Instruction created a 1904 commission charged with developing a means to benefit the education of "defective children," pursuing the policy "that no child suspected of retardation should be eliminated from the ordinary school and admitted into a special class, without first being subjected to a pedagogical and medical examination from which it could be certified that . . . he was unable to profit, in an average measure, from the instruction given in ordinary schools" (Binet and Simon, 1916, p. 9).

Binet's solution lies in his guiding assumption that "the precision and exactness of science should be introduced into our practice whenever possible" (ibid., p. 10). While the commission goal seems worthwhile, what isn't discussed is why mental examinations alone would be the only way of identifying a defective child. Why does a key assumption remain unanalyzed: that a specific examination's content alone qualifies as the sole means for measuring intelligence, especially when the lines separating the normal from "slight imbecility" are so thin? One might assume that those respecting the "precision and exactness of science" would also insure that their method of testing was entirely accurate. Moreover, this same respect might include determining whether nervousness, hunger, distractions, fatigue, irritability, anxiety, or hypersensitivity might affect a child's test performances.

Besides ignoring the very scientific rigor it demands, Binet's method ignores how the state profits from these examinations. By identifying and ranking children in terms of established mental criteria – ways of reasoning and thinking related to how the new political economy was constructed in terms of profitable knowledge and industrial production techniques – the state actually manufactures its own "minimal class," a workforce whose *normal* mental competencies reflect as much their assimilation of a new social epistemology as they prove a universal notion of intelligence. Moreover, when testing identifies a given population, it creates a leg on the ladder of a social hegemony structured primarily on the basis of an arbitrary compliance with certain ways of knowing. In this system, the "brightest" have tended to be given the best opportunities, while the "defective," "subnormal," and "retarded" are usually marginalized into "special" schools or given "special" kinds of jobs. Does science prove the real or support social constructions of ideal class relationships? Binet's commentaries and concentration on the "subnormal" are significant. He assumes that "these inferior states are indefinite in number, being composed of a series of degrees which mount from the lowest depths of idiocy, to a condition easily confounded with normal intelligence" (ibid., p. 10).

Two questions come to mind: why is there such an "indefinite" number of subnormal categories, and what scientific experiments prove that intelligence is structured like a vertical scale, ranging from the "lowest depths" to a normal center point, and then upward to the highest number? Might it be equally reasonable to assume that if intelligence is demonstrated in different ways then a singular *scale* model of the phenomenon would prove inadequate to describe its spatial complexity? Binet's description of extreme defectiveness as something lying in the "lowest depths" tends to associate mental "defectiveness" (itself a metaphor of faulty production and imperfection) with something archetypically dark, unknown, and threatening, all the qualities requiring marginalization, containment, and continuous monitoring.

What are we to make of the "indefiniteness" of these inferior states, a surprising surplus given the absence of a near equal indefiniteness on the higher side of normal? Why is defectiveness given more separately named categories (feeble-minded, degenerate, idiot, retarded, imbecile, moron, and high and low versions within each) than normal or above normal categories? The answer, in part, comes with knowing how modern bureaucracies operate: the more subclasses represent individuals diagnosed as potential social threats, the more these "subnormal" individuals need to be contained, monitored, and ordered; the more these classifications make scientifically real what they represent, the more "technical" work is needed to monitor them, the more work is needed to treat then, and, overall, the greater is the need for supervision to insure that any changes in a person's diagnosis are quickly caught and carefully controlled with a series of scaled "interventions." Finally, the more classifications, the easier it is to operate from within the unchallenged boundary encircling these categories that

167

represent a scale of relative threat levels. Greater numbers of classifications ultimately create the *feeling* that greater order and greater control exist. Although the ability to distinguish an "idiot" from a high functioning "moron" may be good science, it is expressly political; this difference in a world of ideological compliances reinforces the ultimate value of scalability, a technocratic rational construction whose levels of differences define what is important, what we should know about the world, and what our place is in it. The scale, whether of justice, weights, temperature, or intelligence, entices us into a continual fascination with the intricacies of relative values. It is finally and ironically an ideological measurement; it is an epistemology of constructed relative space relationship points that finally help to author modernist thought.

Binet admits to a significant problem: "at the present time very few physicians would be able to cite with absolute precision the objective and invariable sign, or signs, by which they distinguish the degrees of inferior mentality" (ibid., p. 14). Binet cites efforts to solve this problem, particularly the earlier work of Dr Blin and Dr Damaye and their "first attempt to apply a scientific method to the diagnosis of mental debility." Binet outlines eighteen areas they used to test "250 idiots, imbeciles, and morons." The procedure consisted of "a pre-arranged list of questions . . . given to all in such a way that, if repeated by different persons on the same individual, constantly identical results will be obtained" (ibid., p. 28). This statement is scientifically problematic because it presupposes that standardization can be achieved by presumed identical repetition, that *exact* and identical repetition is possible, objective, and valid, and that every child's perception of every examination would be identical enough to illicit similar responses.

In reading Binet's test we need to distinguish its ideological content from its assumed ability to constitute the precise knowledge from which a measure of *objective* intelligence can be obtained. Of the eighteen areas – from "personal habits" to "trades" – ten pose questions about the state (military service, age of service, vocational schools, law, and civil government) and labor (types of jobs, or what relatives do for a living). One – "personal habits" – assumes that intelligence has something to do with social class, since it deals with "bearing, appearance, cleanliness of body and clothing." Apparently a "vest unbuttoned" or a "cravat untied" (ibid., p. 28) signals a defect. This assumption occurs more directly in the record of an examination: "The boy F . . . of nine years comes to us with his hands in his pockets, face and hands not very clean, nails bitten, countenance of little intelligence" (ibid., p. 31). This last comment echoes a distant idea, one initially offered by Aristotle with his idea that facial expressions are intelligence determinants. In what way are personal habits and vests and cravats a sign of intelligence? What kind of intelligence is worn properly? Does intelligence have a certain countenance?

There are also questions of patriotism and military service that seemingly can reveal a child's intelligence: "Would you rather belong to another country than to France, why do you prefer to be French . . . Why should one love his country . . . Would you like to be a soldier . . . What officer has the highest rank?" (ibid.). Blin's and Demaye's test questions also imply that a knowledge of labor is a measure of intelligence, with questions like "What trade does your father follow . . . Is it a good trade . . . What is a trade . . . Are there other religions than yours . . . What are they . . . What is the difference between the Catholic religion and Protestant religion . . . Between the Catholic religion and Jewish religion?" (ibid.). How labor and religious questions are related is not clarified.

There are also examples of questions that seem to have no bearing on intelligence or are open-ended or simply ambiguous: "At what age is a soldier . . . When will you be a man . . . What can it [a photograph] represent . . . Did you enjoy your breakfast . . . Is your appetite ordinarily good . . . You are never thirsty, are you . . . What did you dream last night . . . Are we far from Paris?"

Earlier he quotes from Brouardel's and Gilbert's *Treatise on Medicine*, citing their defect classifications. There is complete and profound idiocy, slight or proper imbecility, "mental instability," and "moral imbecility." The last two categories are striking: the first defines "exuberant physical mobility and intellectual mobility" in terms of "approaching imbecility," and the second asserts that "instability and perversion of instincts . . . egotism . . . a sexual development beyond their age or sexual impulses which render them dangerous" (ibid., p. 21) are signs of low intelligence. Binet refers to the problems presented by these diagnoses: "it would necessitate a long study, and probably a very difficult one, to establish the distinctive signs which separate the unstable from the undisciplined. . . . We shall set the unstable aside, and shall consider only that which bears upon those who are backward" (ibid., pp. 37–8). Science aside, these definitions and Binet's decision underscore how early twentieth-century intelligence test contents were as much guided by moral values as they were by presumed scientific objectivity, a residue evident in the contemporary belief that intelligence tests can help court officials to determine whether criminals are morally culpable for their crimes. Although the notion of "moral intelligence" has been part of the history of intelligence, its influences, logic, and effects remain largely unstudied. Moreover, the link between moral culpability and intelligence continues to be presumed rather than proved.

The first in the series of Binet's tests is entitled "Le Regard," a term that speaks to the relationship between modern ideas of intelligence and the role observational practices have played in the privileging of certain scientific methods and social agencies using surveillance tactics. Binet's test requires an examiner to watch a child's eye movement as a lighted match is waved back and forth across his or her face. Although this exercise presumably determines visual coordination acuity, the connection between it and intelligence is never discussed. There lies within this procedure an ancient bias: that a healthy body carries a healthy mind and a malfunctioning body hides a malfunctioning, troubled, or even dangerously uncontrollable mind. The waving of a match tracks a homophobia based on some vague sense of symmetry and continuity.

The remaining twenty-nine activities can be broken into three categories, testing for acquired knowledge, for *proper* behavior, and for facility with abstractions. While the majority of the exam tests for recognition of verbal and visual gestures, commands, and pictures, for comparing lengths and weights, and for recalling numerical, verbal, and object sequences, its most interesting aspects are Binet's comments and the sections dealing with "suggestability" and abstractions. For instance, in a test differentiating food from other objects, Binet states that "Although these tests succeed with very many children by appealing to their greediness, it often happens that a willful child . . . refuses to look at what is shown him" (ibid., p. 47). Later, he comments that "backward children . . . point to anything on the table" even when "they do not know the name of the object" (ibid., p. 50). Then there are the "defective," who "show an excess eagerness to designate an object, which in itself is a sign of faulty attention . . . they are incapable of suspending their judgment. This is . . . a striking characteristic of a weak mind" (ibid., p. 51). Often he notes that 'this manner of reacting would be a sign of defect were it not that one encounters the same with some normals" (ibid., p. 53). Or, again, "an individual who, when asked, to repeat 3, 0, 8, replies 2, 3, 4, 5, commits a serious error, which would cause one to suspect mental debility. But, on the other hand, it is true that all feeble-minded and all imbeciles do not commit this error, and that many young normals may commit it" (ibid., p. 54). Several times Binet observes how "ignorant" the children are: "it may happen that little Parisians, even though normal . . . have never seen a butterfly. These are examples of astounding ignorance, but we have found, what is still more extraordinary, Parisians of ten years who have never seen the Seine" (ibid., p. 59). Or "there are little Parisians who have never seen poppies or ants" (ibid., p. 61). Binet's interpretation of certain responses – children pointing to anything on the table, their eagerness, their number sequencing, or "ignorance" – fails to explore other possible meanings for these responses. He neglects the possibility that the desire to want to please is stronger than the need to be analytic, that a child's wanting to please creates a quick response, or that a girl's mimicking of mere repetition is not an indicator of inherent "defectiveness."

One of Binet's most intriguing observations lies in his comments on "suggestability." He explains its rationale. While "suggestability is by no means a test of intelligence . . . [it] produces effects which form certain points of views that closely resemble the natural manifestations of feeble-mindedness; in fact, suggestion disturbs the judgment, paralyzes the critical sense, and forces us to attempt unreasonable or unfitting acts worthy of a defective" (ibid., p. 56). This ambiguous point – testing for something that can only *simulate* defectiveness – precedes a section entitled "Snare of lines." In this test a child is repeatedly shown three pairs of unequal lines and asked if they are equal or unequal. The answer is obvious. He is then given a fourth and, "led on by the former replies . . . has a tendency, an acquired force, for again finding one line longer than the other. Some succumb to the snare completely . . . others again fall into the snare without a shadow of hesitation" (ibid., p. 59).

I quote Binet here simply to assert that a reading of his tests, like the reading of any text, reveals a significant gap between their stated purpose – that of regularizing a test created with the precision and exactness of science – and their content, particularly the choice of testing content and his commentary, both of which defy any scientific standard. I am not the first to suggest that the *appearance* of science is not science. For example, Binet fails to explain the scientific reasons why the examination of a child's hand–eye coordination, knowledge of familiar objects, words, pictures, or commands, or ability to make comparisons, define words, recite rhymes, fill in blanks, or know the meaning of questions like "When one has need of good advice – what must one do" (ibid., p. 66) yields precise intelligence measurements. Why are these specific kinds of questions, as opposed to others, capable of yielding such results? In essence, what makes our motor responses a mark of intelligence, or why does rhyme recital mimicry represent a certain level of intelligence? Why does any physical "retardation" represent a mental defect? By this standard, Stephen Hawkings could be diagnosed as having a low functioning intelligence. Binet's commentaries frequently contain moral judgments, with carelessness, greediness, laziness, ignorance, inattentiveness, dishonesty, suggestability, and immaturity listed as intelligence markers but not given any scientific analysis.

Binet's test "instrument" was unique, different from Galton's, Ebbinghaus's, and others' because of its holistic emphasis, its concentration on "higher" mental functions, and its use of a relational and statistical scale to measure ordinary tasks in terms of their intelligence content. The creation of relative rankings compared with a standard of "normal" examinees of a certain age stands as its most significant contribution. This placement within that comparison ultimately represented a transformation in the history of intelligence, producing a "medical" classification that, in turn, determined the kind of institutional treatment to be given. Binet's scale makes no claim about how the mind works. Nor does it explain individual differences of intelligence. Its sole purpose, to identify the subnormal, had a significant historical impact because Binet showed that whatever

171

intelligence is, it is knowable as something immediate, relative, statistical, and, most importantly, quantifiable, repeating the effect of Galton, Spearman, and Pearson. In essence, Binet proposed the idea that the mind could represent itself mathematically. Equally significantly, he transformed intelligence: it was no longer a thing but a kind of behavior – the ability to make and demonstrate rational *judgments* – composed of memory, attention, verbal fluency, and discriminations of objects, commands, pictures, lengths, and weights. Arguably his greatest influence was the conversion of something technical and rational into a dominant social policy and method. By "scientifically" identifying and classifying the "defective," by making their identification unambiguous, Binet's "instrument" simultaneously made marginalization a prerequisite for treatment, sanctioning the marginalization in order to create the first version of a social labor engineering tool that could identify members of the "minimal class." In *The Measurement of Intelligence*, Lewis Terman provides an ironically insightful review of Binet's accomplishment: "Binet was not concerned merely to contribute to the advancement of science: he set before himself a severely practical problem – to enable a practitioner . . . to diagnose the mental condition of a child, and to measure changes in this condition at intervals of a year or less" (Terman, 1916, p. iv). Here the emphasis is narrowly on practicality and ease of diagnosis, rather than on the social or personal effects of such efficiency.

American Architects of Intelligence

Lewis Terman entered the world of intelligence testing as a marketer who imported Binet's product to the USA, when he, Yerkes, and others repackaged in into a highly profitable, government must-have commodity: "The constant and growing use of the Binet–Simon intelligence scale in public schools, institutions for defectives, reform schools, juvenile courts, and police courts is sufficient evidence for the intrinsic worth of the method" (Terman, 1916, p. xi). Terman argues that the popularity of the test proves its *intrinsic worth*, this point being an aperture into Terman's fundamental reasoning: mental tests are valuable because they are functional. *Intrinsic* value is determined by serviceability, practicality, and efficiency. Not only does this point illuminate the ideological framing of modern ideas of intelligence – a framing begun with Bacon and progressing through the Enlightenment and into the economic Darwinism of modernism – it also quietly combines science and government policy in the same way Binet's effort did. There is significance in Terman and Binet writing science policy. The modernization of intelligence, in fact, is marked by a new kind of discourse that blends social policy and "pure" science, a body of writing that gains tremendous social authority from a new synthesis of legal and scientific power. The effect of this new discourse is obvious given the steady trend in the twentieth and twenty-first centuries toward greater collaborations between science and the law, evident, for instance, in court cases, legislative committees, and the making and enforcing of laws aided by research in the social sciences.

Terman is even more matter of fact than Binet. Why do we need these tests, he asks rhetorically. Because we need to fix the problem of low student performance: "there are many grades of intelligence . . . among those classed as normal, vast individual differences have been found to exist in original mental endowment, differences which profoundly lower the capacity to profit from school instruction" (ibid., p. 4). Here the scientific invention of gradience, especially in biology, geology, and mathematics, enters the classroom as something real, something lodged within every student, and Binet's test will be able to enter that hidden space, identifying and classifying students as one uses harvest and sorting machines. But is there not something else happening? Is it possible that these presumably internal differences are actually imprinted upon students, tattoo-like external scales formulated on the basis of the kinds of knowledge students should have at various grade levels? The issue is not functionality, whether Binet's test increased academic performance, but the construction and representation of these "grades of intelligence," what it means to say they are inherent within an individual, and what modes of power have been served by this representation. Terman explains the purpose of gradient testing as being to "take account of the inequalities of children in their original endowment and to differentiate the course of study in such a way that each child will be allowed to progress at the rate which is normal to him, whether that rate be rapid or slow" (ibid., p. 4). The solution is

> to prevent the kind of retardation which involves failure and the repetition of a school grade . . . it is a sad fact that a large proportion of children in the schools are acquiring the habit of failure. The remedy, of course, is to measure out the work for each child in proportion to his mental ability. (Ibid.)

Terman explains the value of this "remedy" by using an analogy in which the test behaves like a structural engineer who studies "materials to be used, and learns by means of tests exactly the amount of strain per unit of size his materials will be able to withstand" when making a bridge. Likewise, "the educational engineer should emulate this example" (ibid., p. 5). This comparison converts children into "materials to be used," Binet's test into a means of measuring the strength of those materials, and the "educational engineer" into a bridge engineer. The analogy equates mental tests with material science tests, suggesting that the certitude of the material sciences (of knowing exactly if a bridge will not collapse) is the same certitude of measuring a child's mind, the goal being "to acquire a scientific knowledge of the material with which we have to deal."

Terman is adamant: "Every child who fails in his school work or is in danger of failing should be given a mental examination" because it can determine if children are "feeble-minded . . . physically defective . . . merely backward . . . truants . . . incorrigibles, etc. . . . In such diagnosis and classification our main reliance must always be in mental tests, properly used and properly interpreted" (ibid.). His adamancy reaches prophetic heights with the social engineering proclamation that

> It is safe to predict that in the near future intelligence tests will bring tens of thousands of these high-grade defectives under the surveillance and protection of society. This will ultimately result in curtailing the reproduction of feeble-mindedness and in the elimination of an enormous amount of crime, pauperism, and industrial inefficiency. (Ibid., p. 6–7)

This quote contains all the elements of economic Darwinism: the biological, the economic, and state regulatory politics are fused, with tests becoming "surveillance" devices for the "production of society"; their ideological content is that of heredity politics and scientific classification methods for the "curtailing [of] the reproduction of feeble-mindedness"; they help to promote civil stability, "the elimination of . . . crime [and] pauperism"; and they fuel modern monopoly capitalism by eliminating "industrial inefficiency." This point rehearses the linkage of testing to industrial efficiency:

> A method of placing young workers which ignores each individual's aptitudes and disabilities must inevitably issue in vast preventable waste. . . . The key, then, to social efficiency is vocational fitness – a place for every man, and every man in his place. The place must be suited to the man by a careful study both of the qualifications required by the one and of the qualifications possessed by the other. (Burt, 1975, pp. 17–18)

Terman argues that mental tests also measure moral character. For instance, "it has demonstrated, beyond any possibility of doubt, that the most important trait of at least 25 percent of our criminals is mental weakness . . . physical abnormalities . . . are not the stigmata of criminality, but the physical accompaniments of feeble-mindedness." More specifically, "every study which has been made of the intelligence level of delinquents has furnished convincing testimony as to the close relation existing between mental weakness and moral abnormality" (Terman, 1916, p. 8). This last term, "moral abnormality," equates a system of values with a medical term; an over-sized heart can be an abnormality, but linking "mental weakness" to morality, in the name of science, illuminates how rich the ideological potential is of intelligence as a means of social control.

Terman justifies the moral value of mental tests by initially stating that the "students of 'degenerate' families have confirmed . . . the testimony secured by intelligence tests" (ibid., p. 9). Given this language, it is nearly impossible to challenge their validity, since the tests metaphorically gather "testimony" that has been "secured." The figurative language is clearly legalistic, given the fact that Terman is dealing with morality, with mental tests serving double duty as records of "witness testimony."

His first example of moral abnormalities (a term associating low intelligence and low morality with physical deformity) is the infamous Kallikak Family. The goal is to prove that mental deficiency is consistently hereditary, that it is the cause of criminal behavior, and that mental tests can detect potential criminality in advance. As the story goes, the Revolutionary War saw one Martin Killikak father a feeble-minded son with a feeble-minded woman. The evidence following this point – 480 illegitimate, sexually "immoral," alcoholic descendents, with 143 being feeble-minded – hinges solely upon the assumption that the mother was "feeble-minded," whatever that term means. There are other explanations: she was not "feeble-minded" by clinical twentieth-century standards, but may have had a physical ailment, or she was poor and resigned, was afraid of military men, or suffered from an anxiety disorder. Mental diagnoses were not very scientific in 1776, and hearsay is not often the best source of scientific evidence.

The remaining three examples – the Hill folk, the Nam family, the Jukes – are singled out for having a produced a presumably higher than average percentage of illegitimate offspring, including prostitutes, syphilitics, and criminals who were alcoholics, paupers, and licentious, with the Jukes cited for the "economic damage" they "inflicted upon the State of New York . . . at more than "$1,300,000 to say nothing of diseases and other evil influences which they helped to spread" (ibid., pp. 10–11). The value of these data is problematic since Terman makes no effort to validate the evidence scientifically; nor does he offer other possible causes for these behaviors, other than to attribute them to low intelligence. These causes could simply have been class status, poverty, physical illnesses, poor educational opportunities, or parental abuse. Moreover, these "kinds" of people are simply being judged, singled out for their "immoral depravity" rather than for scientifically valid reasons. This absence of anything resembling a scientific method speaks specifically to the ideological agenda of early mental testing. These populations became part of the "intelligence of difference" with the sweep of a simple phrase: "economic damage."

Terman argues that mental testing is a moral imperative. Morality, he argues, depends upon two things: "(a) the ability to foresee and to weigh the possible consequences for self and others of different kinds of behavior; and (b) upon the willingness and capacity to exercise self-restraint . . . not all criminals are feeble-minded, but all feeble-minded are at least potential criminals" (ibid., p. 11).

Ignoring the point that not all criminals can be placed in one category and that all people, in fact, can be potential criminals, not just the "feeble-minded," Terman insists that "Moral judgment, like business judgment, social judgment or any other kind of higher thought process, is a function of intelligence," and that without intelligence there is no morality: Respect for the feelings and the property rights, or any other kind of rights, of others had to be laboriously acquired under the whip of discipline: "without the intelligence to generalize the particular, to foresee distant consequences of present acts . . . morality cannot be learned" (ibid., pp. 11–12).

The point here is not whether the argument is true, but how the argument is constructed. Terman groups business, morality, and social behavior in terms of judgments, as did Binet, and then relates his arbitrary grouping to higher thought processes. But why? How is one kind of mental act indicative of "higher" or "lower" intelligence? What scale do these comparative qualities belong to and what does that scale represent? Why would a business judgment as opposed to any other kind of decision be a better mark of intelligence, in this case a higher one? "Higher" in Terman's work refers to greater frequency of conformance, while lower, as one might suspect, refers to the inability or choice not to conform. This quote is far more about honoring the claims of private property and social contract theory than a scientific investigation into the nature of intelligence or why testing is valuable for reasons other than preserving certain morality. Interestingly enough, seventy-nine years later, Hans Eysenck concludes his *New Look* at intelligence with a reference to Thomas Arnold of Rugby and his listing of "religion and moral principles . . . gentlemanly conduct . . . [and] intellectual ability" as the three most important human qualities. Eysenck comments: "moral behavior is most important; only slightly less important is the quality of being cultured, courteous and chivalrous; intelligence only comes in third. In other words, what is needed is intelligence in the service of morality and decency" (Eysenck, 1998, p. 196).

If the preservation of morality is not a good enough reason for expanding the use of mental tests then economic costs are. Terman says that, considering

> the tremendous cost of vice and crime, which in all probability amounts to not less than $500,000,000 per year in the United States alone, it is evident that psychological testing has found here one of its richest applications. Before offenders can be

subjected to rational treatment a mental diagnosis is necessary, and while intelligence tests do not constitute a complete psychological diagnosis, they are, nevertheless, its more indispensable part. (Terman, 1916, p. 12)

The indispensability of testing – its *richest* value – is tied to the "rational treatment" of "offenders" and to its managing of

the future welfare of the country [which] hinges, in no small degree, upon the right education of . . . superior children. Whether civilization moves on and up depends most on the advances made by creative thinkers and leaders in science, politics, art, morality and religion. Moderate ability can follow, or imitate, but genius must show the way. (Ibid.)

And although Terman suggests that "the handicapping influences of poverty, social neglect, physical defects, or educational maladjustment" restrict the "normal development" of "many potential leaders in science, art, government, and industry" (ibid.), he does not consider that these factors may impact test performance. He compares mental testing and its unearthing of superior children to the "primitive methods of surface mining," driven by the logic that "it is necessary to explore the nation's hidden resources of intelligence" (ibid.). The ideological creation of an economic basis for intelligence could not be more obvious.

This metaphoric argument (testing as a machine harvesting resources) turns human beings into commodities and modes of production. This is why Terman immediately argues that soon "intelligence tests will become a recognized and widely used instrument for determining vocational fitness" (ibid., p. 17). In a nod to the value of industrial surveillance, Terman notes that

it is not claimed that tests are available which will tell us unerringly exactly what one of a thousand or more occupations a given individual is best suited to pursue. But when thousands of children who have been tested by the Binet scale have been followed out into the industrial world, and their success in various occupations noted, we shall know fairly definitely the vocational significance of any given degree of mental inferiority or superiority. Researches of this kind will ultimately determine the minimum "intelligent quotient" necessary for success in each leading occupation. (Ibid.)

Matching the right employee with the right employers creates "a cheaper and more satisfactory model" with which a "psychologist" could "examine applicants for positions and . . . weed out the unfit" (ibid., p. 18).

But who or what are the "unfit?" They are "the industrially inefficient [with] subnormal intelligence." For proof, Terman explains how 50 hobos were tested. Fifteen percent tested in the

> moron grade of mental deficiency . . . the ratio of mental deficiency was ten or fifteen times as high as that holding for the general population . . . the industrial history of such subjects . . . was always about what the mental level would lead us to expect – unskilled work, lack of interest in accomplishment, frequent discharge from jobs, discouragement, and, finally, the "road." (Ibid.)

Mental tests diagnose the future and function unlike any teacher:

> When we have learned the lessons which intelligence tests have to teach, we shall no longer blame mentally defective workmen for their industrial inefficiency, punish weak-minded children because of their inability to learn, or imprison and hang mentally defective criminals because they lacked the intelligence to appreciate the ordinary codes of social conduct. (Ibid., p. 21)

A third analogy converts intelligence testing into a curative, the test being the equivalent of an efficient diagnostic tool, an elixir to heal the sick:

> just as is the case of physical illness, we need to know not merely that the patient is sick, but also why he is sick . . . we need to know the exact degree of intellectual deficiency . . . in the case of malnutrition, the up-to-date physician does not depend upon general symptoms, but instead makes a blood test to determine the exact number of red corpuscles per cubic millimeter of blood and the exact percentage of hemagloblin. He has learned that external appearances are often misleading. Similarly, every psychologist who is experienced in the mental examination of school children knows that his own or the teacher's estimate of a child's intelligence is subject to grave and frequent error. (Ibid., p. 23)

Here a mental test becomes a blood test verifying mental malnutrition. This is still another unearthing activity, this time revealing a deficiency instead of riches and resources. The test determines "degrees" of "deficiency," added degrees providing the authority that comes with added classifications and treatment variations. But, more importantly, the analogy makes mental deficiency a disease, a hidden illness that the psychologist-as-healer discovers. These unearthings are heroic; they protect us from the illness of deficiency, from those suffering from mental malnourishment.

Terman moves from the issue of why the curative is needed to the curative itself, to the composition of the test. Binet's "scale is made up of . . . problems

. . . designed primarily to test native intelligence, not school knowledge or home training" (ibid., p. 36). This point is problematic, as is the question of whether any question asked a human being can be culturally neutral. Terman outlines the test: "his intelligence scale tests [were] designed to display differences of memory, other differences in power to reason, ability to compare, power of comprehension, time orientation, facility in the use of number concepts, power to combine ideas into meaningful whole, the maturity of apperception, wealth of ideas, knowledge of common object" (ibid.). The problem, however, is that neither Binet nor Terman, nor for that matter the majority of intelligence experts, explains why any of the test components are native intelligence markers or why they are universal. Memory, reason, comparison, time analysis, number, and recognitions may be universal human capacities but what makes them primary components of intelligence? Why is memory a mark of intelligence? These questions have little to do with the cultural content of questions, but much to do with what privileges these "native markers" as intelligence markers. And in the same vein, what does Binet's scale measure? Does it identify different levels of intelligence or differences in test performances based on certain modes of knowing? Lastly, how does testing familiarization with body parts, with the naming of familiar objects and pictures, with gender identity, names, syllable repetition, with the copying of shapes, comprehension (questions about what a person does when sleepy, cold, or hungry), and with the comparison of weights, colors, and counting assume that none of these has anything to do with acquired knowledge?

Terman also defends the measurement of intelligence without completely knowing what it is:

> electrical currents were measured long before their nature was well understood . . . in the case of intelligence it may be truthfully said that no adequate definition can possibly be framed which is not based primarily on the symptoms empirically brought to light by the test method. The best that can be done in advance of such data is to make tentative assumptions as to the probable nature of intelligence, and then to subject these assumptions to tests which will show their correctness or incorrectness. (Ibid., pp. 44–5)

The problem with this analogy is that whether one does or does not measure the amount of electricity the charge still behaves as a natural phenomenon; we can see and feel it, we can be shocked by it, a current can be traced, electricity lights up a room and it makes noises. We even know to respect it. When an ohmmeter is attached to a circuit, circuit resistance can be measured; when someone is given a mental test we are not sure whether what is being measured is truly the phenomenal entity believed to be intelligence (assuming that its nature is real and objective) or is something else. Lastly, the measurement of something unknown and undefined offers itself up as a unique instance of ideological construction based on the use of metaphor that refers to an absence, a sign without a signified. The metaphor refers not to something but to a substitutive act. In this case testing displaces the signified. The measurement becomes the thing signified in the absence of the displaced signified. Measuring something that cannot be defined relocates ideological authority to the measurement. In essence, the number becomes the signified despite the absence of the signified.

Terman then outlines the history of definitions of intelligence. Darwinian echoes abound in Binet's notion that "intelligence" refers to mental processes that affect species adaptations. Terman believes Binet's idea of intelligence consisted of "three characteristics of the thought process: (1) its tendency to take and maintain a definite direction; (2) the capacity to make adaptations for the purpose of attaining a desired end; and (3) the power of auto-criticism" (ibid., p. 46). He then presents Ebbinghaus's idea that intelligence is an "intellectual ability" that "consists in the elaboration of a whole into its worth and meaning by means of many sided combination, correction, and completion of numerous kindred associations. . . . It is a *combination activity*." Meumann argued that "intelligence is the power of independent and creative elaboration of new products out of the material given by memory and the senses . . . the ability to avoid errors, to surmount difficulties, and to adjust the environment," while Stern believed that intelligence is "the general capacity of an individual consciously to adjust his thinking to new requirements; it is general adaptability to new problems and conditions of life." And Spearman, Hart, and others argued that intelligence is "a common central factor which participates in all sorts of special mental abilities" (ibid., pp. 45–7). Whether these definitions are true or not it less important for this study than their composition. These definitions speak ideologically, affirming the value of enterprise, self-autonomy, and certain scientific ideas announced during the Enlightenment and expanded during the past two hundred years. The majority of these definitions affirm the virtues of enterprise by linking intelligence to the "attaining of a desired end," to the following of a "definite direction," to being a "combination activity" and a "creative elaboration of new products," and to "adaptability to new problems." The scientific linkage appears when intelligence is defined in terms of overcoming "difficulties" and adjusting "to the environment." And the notion of "auto-criticism" speaks to both technocratic rationality and the nature of state apparatuses, both producing mechanisms of social control whereby individuals define their uniqueness in terms of self-monitoring activities.

The point of reviewing Terman's work is to suggest that by the mid-1920s intelligence found a home in the social sciences, where it became a measurable behavior. This new behavioral aspect of intelligence and its moral, enterprise, scientific, and class ideological aspects are evident in Terman's case comments. For example, in his *Intelligence of School Children* he notes that

> Intelligence of 110 and 120 IQ is approximately five times as common among children of superior social status as among children of inferior social status; the proportion among the former being about 24 percent of all, and among the latter only 5 percent of all. The group is made up largely of children of the fairly successful mercantile or professional classes. (Terman, 1919, p. 95)

These statistics simply speak to their ideological significance, linking references to the enterprising and class differences to the nature of intelligence. This is again reinforced in the statement that "the 120–140 group is made up almost entirely of children whose parents belong to the professional or very successful business classes . . . the child of a common laborer very rarely indeed . . . this is true in the smaller cities of California among populations made up of native-born Americans" (ibid., p. 96). Terman then presents a review of some of these "superior children": one girl's "social and moral traits [are] of the very best. Is obedient, conscientious, and unusually reliable for her age. Quiet and confident bearing, but no touch of vanity." Another is "a wonderfully charming, delightful girl in every respect. Play life perfectly normal." Still another has a "delightful personality and keen responses. No trace of vanity or queerness of any kind," while a "sweet girl . . . is a favorite with the young and old, as nearly perfect as the most charming little girl could be" (ibid., pp. 97–8).

Young boys fare equally well. One "superior" boy "is normal in play life and social traits and is dependable and thoughtful beyond his years." Another bright boy "gets his hardest mathematics lessons in five to ten minutes . . . since age 12 he has given much time to mechanics and electricity" (ibid., pp. 98–9), while another "when not at play . . . has the dignified bearing of a young prince, although without vanity." Terman notes that a boy with above normal intelligence is "superior in personal and moral traits as in intelligence. Responsible, sturdy . . . obedient" (ibid., pp. 100–1). Lastly, "nearly every child we have with IQ above 140 is the kind one feels, before the test is over, one would like to adopt" (ibid., p. 101). His review of children with lower intelligence underscores a dullness and a future of menial employment. Not once does Terman suggest adopting any of these children. And perhaps the most telling quote refers to the testing of some Native American children. Their low scores can be attributed to the "dullness" of their racial identity. Since they obviously were unable to "master abstractions," they needed to be segregated. The term "master abstractions" is a self-deconstructing term, ironically linking class hegemony (master) with the term – abstraction – that authorizes such control. Intelligences of difference have no cultural or spatial limits.

Although Henry Goddard preceded him, it is Terman's revision of Binet's texts (the Stanford-Binet) that marks the modernization of psychometrics. His contribution made the test *efficient*, expanding its market so that anyone could to be tested, regardless of race, age, or education, or place in specific populations. The test universalized mental classification, gaining added use and authority by creating an "IQ constant (the ratio IQ of mental age divided by actual age)." This new constant provided "proof" that an individual's intellectual potential was biologically determined and its measurement could be equated to his or her future socioeconomic status. This amazing power of precise forecasting reinscribes the Enlightenment's primary ideological production, that certainty was possible because of mathematics, science, and technology. Once Yerkes sold the Surgeon General and the United States Army on the value of mental testing, the word "IQ" began its modern journey into popular culture. The door was opened to idolize the intellect, and popular culture had only to wait a few years for an unlikely superstar with a German accent, unkempt hair, and his mystical cypher, $e = mc^2$, to appear on the streets of Princeton.

In the 1920s Goddard added a final girder to the argument that intelligence was biologically determined. He offered seemingly indisputable scientific proof. Intelligence, he argued, is a "process . . . conditioned by a nervous mechanism which is inborn: that the degree of efficiency to be attained by that nervous mechanism and the consequent grade of intelligence or mental level for each individual is determined by the kind of chromosomes that come together with the union of the germ cells" (Goddard, 1920, p. 1). The argument is that intelligence is determined by an innate neurological mechanism. Its "efficiency" and "grade" are determined by "the kind of chromosomes" organized when an egg cell is fertilized. Here is a case of "ideological swapping," a rhetorical pattern in which the language from different areas of specialization is used to prove an idea. In this case the language of industrial mechanics becomes biological proof. Words like "process," "mechanism," efficiency," and "grade" support the idea that chromosome organization determines intelligence. But what does that organization mean? Is intelligence encoded only on certain chromosomes? And, if so, how does that encoding get translated into intelligent behaviors: is intelligence encoded in the same way that hair color genes or height genes are molecularly structured? Or do more intelligent people have a high degree of intelligence proteins? Goddard's industrial metaphors are consistent with the narrative pattern of early twentieth-century definitions of intelligence. What we find in this theory of intelligence is ideological support for the creation of a economic Darwinism.

Goddard's staunch belief, based on Mendelian genetics, held that mental "defectiveness" was transmitted by a single recessive gene. This theory proves untrue in the case of obvious mental and physical impairment and as a means to justify the use of mental testing to prove that "defectiveness" was caused strictly by genetic causes.

As Goddard and Terman continued marketing the Binet scales, they modified tests by arguing that mental performances reflected an inherent and an essentially unchangeable cause. The difference was not simply a philosophical disagreement. During Terman's and Goddard's tenure as the icons of intelligence, American culture underwent significant sociocultural and national changes. The First World War and mass immigration added to a social consciousness seeking restrictive immigration laws and significant efforts to raise national intelligence, an agenda consistent with Baconian entrepreneurialism, Enlightenment rationalism and economic theory, and the ideas of Francis Galton. These efforts promoted class divisions, with investments given to the middle and upper classes to prevent the foreign laboring classes from gaining access to the middle class. Once intelligence was made conditional upon some internal and inalterable absolute, the permanence of heredity, with all its class and race consciousness, then mental testing was given scientific authority as a tool for greater social stability. The ideological significance of this metaphor of power cannot be underestimated. It was pervasive. People believed it was real. Once a potential threat could be branded with a certain number representing his or her intelligence, then racist policy produced certitude. For example, both Goddard and Terman used the argument of absolute racial intelligence, of genetic markers, to support immigration restrictions on southern Europeans, who were certainly welcomed as cheap labor but not as "real" Americans. A two-pronged social agenda issued from their biologicalization of intelligence: social programs raised the level of *national* intelligence and those that could threaten it were either sterilized or institutionalized, these actions being the basis for an "intelligence of difference" and further internal "colonial" marginalization. Goddard explains this process:

> segregation and colonization is not by any means as hopeless a plan as it may seem. . . . If such colonies were provided in sufficient number to take care of all the distinctly feeble-minded cases . . . they would very largely take the place of our present almshouses and prisons, and they would greatly decrease the number in our insane hospitals. Such colonies would save an annual loss in property and life, due to the action of these irresponsible people, sufficient to nearly, or quite, offset the expense of the new plant. Besides, if these feeble-minded children were early

selected and carefully trained, they would become more or less self-supporting in their institutions, so that the expense of their maintenance would be greatly reduced. (Goddard, 1920, pp. 105–6)

The work of early test-making eugenicists spearheaded the passage of the 1924 Immigration Restriction Act, whose effects curtailed the immigration of those trying to escape the Nazi holocaust. Neither in composition nor effect are intelligence tests ever politically neutral. They are a discourse in which the power that creates them finds immunity.

In summary, it is impossible to trace all the discursive threads that metaphors of intelligence wove into an ideological mosaic during the Binet era. The purpose here has been not to be comprehensive, but to read representative texts illustrating how the use of scientific and economic metaphors has shaped the way modern culture *lives and experiences* intelligence.

Contemporary Architects of Intelligence

Intelligence test items are to intelligence as samplings of blood pressure, body temperature, or blood chemistry are to general physiological performance. As in medicine, the goal is to find tests that are convenient, that are reliable. (Wilson and Herrnstein, 1986)

The early decades of the twentieth century saw proliferations in both theories of intelligence and the development of new test instruments. A survey of them provides an understanding of their ideological impact in modern and postmodern culture. First, we can classify these proliferations in terms of the following areas: the creation of new models of intelligence given new ideas in science, of new developmental models, and of new psychometric practices. I would like to explore those with the most significant ideological influence.

Perhaps the most dominant idea in near contemporary ideas of intelligence constitutes an expansion ideology in which previously *singular* notions of intelligence are replaced by *multiple* model theory. As scientific as they may be, many of these new multiple models are also ideological integrations of science and trends in postmodern culture. An obvious, if not exaggerated, example is the popularity of "soft intelligence," the emotional, digital, Hale Boppish neo-spiritual forms of hip-wired intelligence, mutations of the anti-material, pro-transcendental social movements begun in the 1960s and present in thousands of contemporary self-help books, websites, and cable TV shows. Emotional and spiritual notions of intelligence are also ideological, busy revalidating the idea that being truly smart or guru-like represents a cosmic linking of individual consciousness with a vast universal force, that of a higher, somewhat hi-tech, universal consciousness, an idea traceable through a number of past writers, including William Paley, deists, Emerson, Blake, Hesse, and Jung, and up to the more current cyberescapists Mark Dery explores in *Escape Velocity* (1996).

Although they may be getting closer to discovering the nature of intelligence, theories of multiple intelligences travel around postmodern culture in interesting ways. For instance, their sheer number increases the means for reinforcing the ideological basis for the Western political economy and its epistemological system. When more kinds of intelligence can be consumed for the purpose of self-production, individuals have still another way of "adding designer tag," of individuating themselves in terms of the very mass culture that produces the illusion of uniqueness. In this case a person could be a BMW driving, Ralph Lauren dressed, right-brained, musical–spatial person. This production underscores the dynamics of postmodern consumerism in which surplus commodities simultaneously cause the loss of identity and serve as the primary means of constructing another one. In this scheme, self-production functions as a commodity that becomes continuously obsolete.

The mechanics of this system underscores how intelligence has itself become a postmodern commodity, an outcome consistent with the prevalence of both economic Darwinism and prior modern intelligence practices. The gradual commodification of intelligence in the mid-twentieth century is also responsible for creating a new, post-Second World War hegemony, a unique construct that in seemingly democratizing the prior hegemony enacts a new form of social control. Although a person may not be from the perceived upper or dominant class, the availability of different kinds of intelligence (commodities and talents) allows her to produce herself as a presumably unique intelligence. Power is always about creating and protecting exclusivity and private spaces. In postmodern forms of social control, submission behaviors are no longer the sole dominion of upper-class, external force, control mechanisms. In postmodern culture the police and other system protectors have been partially replaced by habits of consumption; that is, by a focus on ourselves as being about the personal business of authentic self-production. Opposition to state policy takes time, and given increased demands at work global citizens cannot shop at the mall and still have time to demonstrate against those policies. Consumption stabilizes the state and allows governments to operate nearly free from citizen engagement other than rituals of distant politics.

The trend toward multiple forms of intelligence is worth exploring, having evolved from various sources. David Wechsler adopted a multivariate theory, arguing that general intelligence is not an absolute entity but part of a person's total personality. His effort to find a compromise between multivariate and uni-variate intelligence set the stage for a number of new psychologists to explore intelligence as a multiplicity of coordinated abilities. Howard Gardner, for instance, has essentially become a metaphor for multiple intelligences, his name heard in airport coffee shops, book stores, and university memorial unions. The popularity of multiple notions of intelligence has given postmodern rise to the idea of a kind of *dim sum* intelligence, with pop consumers picking a little of this, a little of that, claiming to have a mix of interpersonal, linguistic, and musical intelligence.

J. P. Guilford and Howard Gardner are prominent names in multiple intelligence models. My interest here is not in what their schemes represent, the value or inadequacy of their lists, but in what they reflect ideologically. Their 160 types of intelligence underscore two ideological issues: a reaffirmation of the production of technocratic rationalist-driven test criteria and the use of ideas of intelligence to support a mapping and ordering of labor classes. The social effect of multiple models of intelligence is interesting because, despite their seemingly non-traditional nature, they reinscribe the values implicit in the Enlightenment's use of metaphors of intelligence to form ideological alliances with modern capitalism, the physical sciences, and the social sciences, all in an effort to forge the infrastructure and class hegemony of the modern nation state. But how do Guilford's and Gardener's models reflect that ideological agenda?

First, Guilford's "structure of intellect" theory is a tribute to Enlightenment scientific practices. His model asserts that intelligence has three components: operations, contents, and products (Guilford, 1967). The fact that these elements operate in other venues (mathematical, economic, marketing, and industrial mass production) raises an interesting question about how modernists define intelligence. Are we to assume that intelligence is definable as a pure abstraction, a mental phenomenon independent of how cultures produce their organizing schemes, or is intelligence a metaphoric tool for shaping those organizing forms? In essence, does something else define intelligence, or is intelligence truly independent of any predetermined force or set of discursive conditions? For instance, Guildford's model is scientifically problematic because it is posed as something abstract and absolute, when it clearly isn't. This problem of how intelligence is defined as an absolute–non-absolute raises an even more significant question: how can any definition of intelligence, if indebted to metaphoric functions, claim a non-ideological status? How can any assumed abstraction or absolute, in this case a *universal* human attribute, not by its very nature be something subject to ideological engagement? The answer may lie in the possibility that nothing mentally produced escapes human social ordering or that culture is a safeguard against individual thought.

Guilford and Gardener have led the way in arguing that intelligence is not a single thing, but a mosaic of different abilities. Intelligence, in essence, is having the right internal skills that match either certain careers or metaphors for certain social epistemologies. Guilford creates sixteen sub-classifications, each indebted to values implicit in Enlightenment rationalism and science. For example, cognition, memory, divergent production, convergent production, and evaluation are subcategories of operations, while the product component consists of units, classes, relations, systems, transformations, and implications. These abilities, along with reasoning, problem-solving, decision-making, and language skills, are as much about rationalistic techniques and methods as they are about the universal nature of intelligence. Gardner (1983, 1999), on the other hand, has evolved a popular theory of multiple intelligences because it emphasizes personality, behavior, and real world experiences rather than pure abstract skills. An IQ number produces little reason for personal, continued, or inspired interest. A test, however, that tells us our "special" intelligence mix means we could be a great dancer, salesperson, engineer, or surgeon, or that our "naturalistic" intelligence means we could be a farmer or animal handler. This makes the exam more appealing, personal, and valid. Whether there are true multiple intelligences residing universally and innately in all human beings is not my focus. I am intrigued by the ideological significance of the theory, how its designer-like quality attracts consumer speculation, how it ultimately reinscribes the idea and value of knowing exactly what our intelligence is, and how it defines these new kinds of intelligences to sanction labor and job aptitudes. One wonders whether, if the biological sciences had never been invented or if existentialism had never occurred, such forms of intelligence would still be innately manifested to a greater degree in some individuals than in others.

Then there is the question of control, of what neurophysiological mechanism determines why one person would have a "higher" spatial and a lower intrapersonal intelligence mix than, say, her brother. Or why these multiple intelligences exist or what makes them possible. Do they have to do with evolutionary adaptations? Finally, multiple intelligence theories raise the question of whether they are a kind of "pin the tail on the donkey science" in which existing socioeconomic formations (cultural structures, a hegemony of highly valued careers, the class system protected by the structure, and divisions of labor) are superimposed over a metaphor called *intelligence*, ready to be branded in a certain way, signifying a corresponding strata of intelligence types. Why in Gardner's scheme are there plenty of professionally related versions of intelligences and no mention of the kinds of intelligence needed to be an excellent bricklayer, a Macdonald's employee, a service industry employee, a sanitation worker, a cesspool drainage specialist, or an offshore Visa account specialist? Multiple intelligence theories raise an interesting problem: how can intelligence be a universal, *a priori* idea if it waits – like Freud's famous mystic writing pad – to be inscribed upon by ideological values residing in new inscriptions?

Multiple intelligence theories have produced emotional, practical, social, creative, artificial, and other kinds of intelligence. As I suggested earlier, although these proliferations may get us closer to the "truth" of intelligence, they are nevertheless part of a larger modernist power dynamic in which the division of a controlling idea into derivatives reinforces the core ideology by expanding its range of consumable influence to ever increasingly larger subpopulations. This *recentrist-proliferation* mechanism is part of a surplus politics, evident, for instance, in the recent popularization of "emotional" intelligence. *Time* magazine's October 2, 1995 edition ran a cover that hooked readers with a tease, "What is your EQ?" answered with "It's not your IQ. It's not even a number. But emotional intelligence may be the best predictor of success in life, redefining what it means to be smart." Inside the story readers of the frenzied 1990s job market learned that "IQ gets you hired, but EQ gets you promoted." Here intelligence promotes the pistons of our postmodernism economy.

Time jumped on the pomo-bandwagon, responding to the phenomenal popular success of Daniel Goleman's *Emotional Intelligence* (1995), a book motivating five million readers to find out more about themselves and make more money at the same time. This popularity penetrated government services and even the corporate glass ceiling. American Express and the US Air Force, for instance, invested heavily in EQ, hoping it could solve organizational problems. According to Tony Schwartz, AmEx

> training sessions on emotional competence take place at the Minneapolis facility several dozen times a year. . . . An eight-hour version of the course is now required of all of its new financial advisers, who help clients with money management. During a four-day workshop, 20 participants are introduced to . . . an emotional-competence curriculum, including such fundamental skills as self-awareness, self-control, reframing, and self-talk. . . . The 133-question self-administered test evaluates 15 qualities, such as empathy, self-awareness, and self-control, but also includes categories that seem less obviously a measure of emotional competence – among them assertiveness, independence, social responsibility, and even happiness.

In the same article Schwartz describes how "Rich Handley, 43, an OD specialist and chief of HR development for the Air Force Recruiting Service," used a similar curriculum to achieve a higher retention rate for Air Force recruiters. Emotional intelligence has even appeared in popular culture. Readers of *Zippy the Pinhead* and *Dilbert* comics were given a steady parody diet of such soft intelligence.

These popularizations were in sync with academic and scientific versions of EQ. Note the following definitions. The first, "emotional intelligence . . . [is the] ability to perceive and express emotion, assimilate emotion in thought, understand and reason with emotion, and regulate emotion in the self and others" (Mayer and Salovey, 1997), contrasts with a similar but more global version: "the ability to perceive and express emotion accurately and adaptively, the ability to understand emotion and emotional knowledge, the ability to use feelings to facilitate thought, and the ability to regulate emotions in oneself and in others" (Sternberg, 2003, p. 263). In addition, emotional intelligence "bridges the gap between reason and emotion" (*"emotions are themselves intelligent processes"*), is "an organizational tool," and regulates: "the regulation of the emotions of others is a skill . . . possessed by . . . psychotherapists, salespeople, ministers, and con artists" (ibid., pp. 263–71).

Regardless of these various representational forms, emotional intelligence simply repurposes criteria that ground dominant conceptions of intelligence. What gets inscribed – in what appears to be a different, more personal, more vogue version of intelligence – is the ideologically familiar: words like "ability," "reason," "regulate," "accurately," "adaptively," "organizational tool," "competence," and "promoted" situate this presumably new intelligence at the center of the most dominant idea of intelligence; that is, high-level mental ability based upon and driven by abstract reasoning *even though it appears to be something else.* And whether we look at "creative intelligence" (referring to "adaptive problem solving" (ibid., p. 282), "social intelligence" (an "individual's fund of knowledge" tested with judgment, memory, word, recognition, and social knowledge (Sternberg and Wolman, 2000, pp. 359–60), "practical intelligence" ("practical problem-solving ability, adaptive behavior, and social competence" (ibid., p. 388), or "analytic intelligence" ("higher order processes used to plan, monitor, and evaluate task performance" (Sternberg, 2003, p. 63), what remains is the idea that intelligence is, as Wechlser summarized, "the aggregate or global capacity of the individual to act purposely, to think rationally and to deal effectively with his environment" (Wechlser, 1958, p. 7).

The ideological significance of other multiple theories of intelligence lies in the model appropriated to explain intelligence. Habermas's theory of "technocratic rationality" and the idea of state apparatuses provide an excellent aperture into Robert Sternberg's and David Perkin's theories of multiple intelligence. Each takes a very obvious page out of Enlightenment constitutional government, philosophical theories, and economic ideas. Sternberg's "triarchic" model, for example, is grounded in the idea that intelligence is largely a matter of mental *self-management.* Borrowing from modern Western constitutional discourse, Sternberg argues that a person's intelligence is more executive, legislative, or judicial in nature. This means the mind functions governmentally; some individuals create and formulate, others implement, and still others judge and compare. All minds, however, function regulatorily, in terms of self-government, with some intelligence being monarchic (singular goal orientation), some hierarchic (multiple goal orientation with ease of priorization), some oligarchic (equal goal orientation), some anarchic (do not follow rules and achieve goals though their own methods). This model is a uniquely American explanation of how the mind works regulatorily, not unlike Freud's now classical model of behavior based on id, ego, and superego conflicts.

The ideological basis of David Perkins's multiple theory of intelligence is no less substantial, although its sources are more covert. In suggesting that intelligence can be understood in terms of neural intelligence, experiential intelligence, or reflective intelligence, Perkins reinforces major value-given structuring components of the modernist ideology, especially those like efficiency and precision (the neurological system), the accumulation of knowledge to gain expertise (experiential intelligence as capital knowledge developing work skills), and problem-solving associated with persistence, systemization skills, and the use of imagination (reflective intelligence as degree of self-monitoring and self-managing skills). In Perkins's model reflective intelligence functions in an executive manner; as a control system it maximizes neural and experiential intelligence input.

Both of these models draw their component ideas from existing sociopolitical and economic systems, revalidating ideas that link intelligence to goals of productivity, to ways of working more efficiently and precisely, to gaining knowledge for the purpose of being a more valuable employee, and, most importantly, to a kind of autonomic and homeostastic machine that monitors and controls output, a machine that manages the input, analysis, and output production of valuable information. The ideological significance of these agency models of human intelligence cannot be underestimated. To borrow these models – to say that intelligence is monarchic in its operations or that it functions self-managerially – without assessing why these particular models are being appropriated or what sociopolitical effect they have raises serious questions about precisely what intelligence is. Whether intelligence truly exists as a phenomenon or not seems less an issue than what its supposed existence has done in the streets of material history. Asked in a bold way, is intelligence, in all its historical representations, nothing more or less than metaphoric opportunism continually about the business of reinforcing or creating a new ideological–epistemological status quo? My concern here is not with the validity of any of these multiple models of intelligence but with the absence of any effort to understand their ideological subtexts. Theories of intelligence cannot be entirely valid if they assume that their origination point resides in a historical, discursive, or ideological vacuum.

The following three areas frame current research areas in modern intelligence: new scientific models, new developmental theories, and new psychometric diagnostic tools. Applications of traditional and new sciences now stress the importance of complexity in dealing with fluid rather than static models of intelligence. Several researchers argue that task complexity ultimately dictates the assessment of intellectual performance. System theories are becoming even more widespread, with Stephen Ceci's bioecological model leading the way. Ceci's systems theory stresses the important role that biology and the environment play in intelligence: "the bioecological framework posits multiple intelligences arising out of the interplay between relevant learning regimes and specific genetically influenced predispositions for cognizing, each with its own polygenic potentiator in the form of synaptogenetic schedule" (Ceci, 1996, p. 130). A second new science theory bears even closer analysis given its ideological implications.

In an article entitled "The Evolution of Intelligence," Harry J. Jerison offers a well argued and thorough morphological account of how intelligence evolved (Sternberg and Wolman, 2000). I would like to summarize the article before exploring its ideological content. Jerson defines intelligence as "the total neural-information processing capacity in a . . . species, adjusted for the capacity to control routine bodily functions." In essence, intelligence is the equivalent to encephalization, given the fact that a "fossil record of the brain" can reveal the extent of the "evolution of the brain's information processing capacity. Relating information processing to brain size involves simple, straightforward, and unusually reliable bivariate regressions" (ibid., p. 216). This information capacity is largely "determined by the interaction of genes and environment. . . . The structure and function of mammalian brains are determined by an intricate interaction between a genetic blueprint and pre- and postnatal environments in which neurons and supporting brain tissue develop" (ibid., p. 217).

Jerison's goal is to understand "relationships between specific morphological components of the brain and specific intellectual abilities." Stating that intelligence is multidimensional, Jerison argues that

> evolutionary analysis begins with the brain's operations, which, in the control of complex behavior, involve neural systems distributed through much of the brain . . . the interconnections and interplay among the underlying neural systems that control the behavior are so extensive that their evolution probably occurred by changes in some generalized genetic instructions that regulate the development of the central nervous system. This is consistent, also, with behavior genetic analysis of human cognitive functioning. (Ibid., p. 218)

191

Interestingly, Jerison's "approach seeks an understanding of human intelligence as having evolved from roots in perhaps distantly related adaptations to other species" (ibid., p. 219).

So, what morphologically determines intelligence? "If we consider the neuron as the morphological unit for processing capacity, then the number of neurons is a measure of that capacity in any vertebrate." Intelligence, he argues, is "neural capacity . . . species with a neural network, whether or not one thinks of the species as intelligent. Intelligence is not an all-or-none trait, and its evolutionary roots may appear in distant and 'primitive' animals. These roots may represent a shared trait or suite of traits that evolved more than half a billion years ago" (ibid., p. 221). In perhaps an unintended nod to Galton and others, Jerison argues that "brain size [is] a reliable estimator of total informational-processing capacity" (ibid., p. 222). Lastly, he states that "Brain tissue is metabolically among the most expensive of bodily tissues. . . . Evolution is often thought of as an optimizing process in which costs are balanced by benefits, and the question is, What benefits were associated with the enlargement of the brain . . . to make its energetic cost worthwhile?" (ibid., p. 228). He answers his own question, insisting that "the basic reason for the brain's enlargement . . . [was] to generate knowledge of the external world, to perceive the world and understand its structure and function" (ibid., p. 231).

My quotations are aimed at revealing a continuous theme. Early in the article, Jerison presents the bible of standard intelligence markers: "speed of learning, retrieval of information from long-term memory, decision making, problem solving, symbolic communication skills, counting, spatial-relations ability, concept formation, rule learning and tool use" (ibid., p. 217). But he does not convincingly connect his points to those standard components. In essence, how does increased brain size, the amount of processing capacity, the number of neurons, and brain enlargement translate to those elements? Or, simply put, how do neurons and information processing capacity equate to intelligence? What makes them intelligence makers? In Jerison's world information processing is intelligence. But how can that be? What are the biophysiological mechanisms of translation that convert various densities of neurons to various levels of intelligence? How does density create unique insight, the stuff of "genius," or the babblings of "idiots?"

Many of the problems raised by new science approaches to intelligence also appear in some new developmental theories of intelligence. In general many of them advance surprisingly conventional ideas, those that assert that general intelligence has a substantial heritable component, that environmental factors and nutrition are important determinants of intelligence, and that heredity and environment interact. Advances in behavioral genetics indicate that genes and the environment influence the relationship among differing cognitive skills across developmental periods. Thomas and Karmiloff-Smith argue that "in the domain of atypical development, one may refer to a disordered cognitive system as having insufficient processing resources" (in Sternberg et al., 2003, p. 133). Those atypical individuals are contrasted with two other populations:

> those blessed with better cognitive abilities [who] profit . . . from the stimulation and instructions in their environments (e.g. in school) [and] those with less favorable abilities . . . those who possess better intellectual abilities and have received better education generally reach greater opportunities to gain an occupational and social position . . . those who are more intelligent and more successful in their careers [have an increased] . . . probability of success. (Ibid., p. 179)

These arguments are, in part, based on notions of *disorder,* "*insufficient . . . resources,*" and being "*blessed*" with "*better*" cognitive abilities. Each carries with it an ideological context ignored in favor of claims to scientific objectivity. To argue *scientifically* that the more intelligent will have more opportunities to be successful is a political reality, but the claim has nothing to do with the rigors of science. How can such statements be made without adequate testing of certain assumptions? This language is consistent with formal policy rhetoric, evident, for instance, in the US Office of Education definition of giftedness:

> Children and youth with outstanding talent perform or show the potential for performing at remarkably high levels of accomplishment when compared with others of their age, experience, or environment. These children and youth exhibit high performance capability in intellectual, creative, and/or artistic areas, possess an unusual leadership capacity, or excel in specific academic fields. They require services or activities not normally provided by the schools. (Sternberg and Wolman, 2000)

Specifically, emphasis is placed on "high levels," "high performance," "unusual leadership capacity," and "services" not offered by *normal* schools. No doubt some individuals more forthcoming about their curiosity are able to excel within privileged channels of constructed values, but to suggest that science discovers those "natural" abilities or that intelligence proves those differences is to accept incompleteness as an valid way of doing science and being politically fair.

Current efforts are also combining new science research with the development of new psychometric diagnostic tools. Richard Haier's essay "Brain Imaging Studies of Intelligence: Individual Differences and Neurobiology" (in Sternberg et al., 2003) exemplifies such interdisciplinary work. Haier states that the search is under way to relate genes to a high intelligence quotient, citing

Plomin, McClearn, and Smithy and their efforts to assign certain genetic markers to high and low IQs. He begins with a profound question, "where in the brain is intelligence," a query made despite the fact that "no compelling empirical reasons show that 'IQ centers' exist in the brain" (ibid., p. 186). During research efforts to achieve empirical proof, he found that "when the brain worked harder" during a PET scan test, the less well participants solved the nonverbal, *g*-loaded problems of the RAPM (a nonverbal, abstract reasoning test). After analysis, Haier claims that "We interpreted this as evidence [from various correlated scores] for a brain efficiency model of intelligence" (ibid., p. 187). He concludes his essay with a futuristic vision: "a drug to improve IQ may be elusive, but once the neurobiology of intelligence or *g* is understood, at both the low and high ends of the distribution, who knows what possibilities await in the next decade?" (ibid.).

The ideological ground of Haier's essay, based on the applied merit of work and efficiency (how do we interpret a "working" or "efficient" brain from reading PET scans?), is carried over to an interesting article written by Paul van Geert. In "Measuring Intelligence in a Dynamic Systems and Contextualist Framework" (in Sternberg et al., 2003), he refers to a study of infant cognition described as "soft-assembly" activities, in which "a concept, or knowledge in general for that matter, gets 'assembled' locally and temporally during the course of a specific action" (ibid., p. 195). Van Geert proposes quantifying intelligence in terms of order and control parameters:

> complex dynamic systems, such as biological organisms, potentially show an almost infinite number of degrees of freedom in their behavior because of the complexity of the behaving body itself. However, actual behavior is highly ordered, meaning that it can usually be described in the form of some structural whole, such as a motor pattern like walking.

How does this highly ordered behavior relate to intelligence?

> One of the consequences of these assumptions is that a property such as intelligence quotient (IQ) . . . should not be necessarily be expressed as a single number (or category). . . . It can just as well, and probably more adequately, be expressed as a range over two dimensions, namely the psychometric variable at issue (e.g. IQ) and a characteristic dimension. (Ibid., p. 201)

Given this potential, intelligence can be understood as "an order parameter – that is, a parameter that specifies a specific observable coherence property of the system's behavior." What appears to be different here is van Geert's suggestion of a "potential change in the measurement of intelligence, more precisely in the representation of intelligence scores in the form of ranges specified over a characteristic dimension" (ibid., p. 209). Despite its new scientific flavor, the article reinscribes post-Enlightenment ideology without reflecting upon the implications of that heritage. Its emphasis on order, and its attributing to all human actions and mental activities a "structural whole," are ideas similar to patterns in social science, medical, legal, philosophical, and governmental policy discourse. In these texts order is automatically a rhetorical given, a dominant metaphor, a kind of hollow template, ready to be defined in terms of specific organizations of power. Van Geert's "order parameter" is a giveaway, defined as a "specific observable coherence property of the system's behavior." This is an ideologically significant statement. Intelligence is made synonymous with order itself; it is part of a larger order and it orders. It has parameters, and when observed, intelligence is a coherent property, ordered axiomatically by the behavior of a system. This representation echoes a multitude of other historical discourses, as well as Habermas's notion of technocratic rationality. Intelligence doesn't simply help promote order; it is now order itself, an absolute, immune from any challenge because the nature of the system itself dictates that intelligence is a coherence, a structural whole, and a form of property. At the most superficial level, these ideas reinforce the idea that intelligence is measurable and true, but at the level of ideological formations, it speaks to the myth of self-authenticating power.

Before exploring how theories of contemporary intelligence take form as a series of practices and procedures, I would like to briefly review a typical introductory essay in a typical intelligence textbook. "Where Are We in the Field of Intelligence, How Did We Get Here, and Where Are We Going" (in Sternberg et al., 2003) is representative of modern approaches to intelligence that reflect the complex evolutionary and ideological history of intelligence. For instance, the essay states on one hand that "although all fields of psychology" are "perceived through ideological lenses, nevertheless few fields [intelligence studies] seem to have lenses with so many colors." The optimistic point is clarified: "visions of intelligence have often been distorted because of the imperfect lenses that researchers have used. The different views come not only from ideological biases affecting what is said but also from what defines the concept of intelligence" (ibid., p. 3). Does this mean then that *perfect* lenses would make "true" intelligence visible, undistorted by any ideological aberration? Or does this presuppose that there are ideologically neutral lenses? This point seems to ignore its own ideological lenses, reflecting an unfamiliarity with a now thirty-year-old cultural studies analysis of the nature, language, behavior, narrative dynamics, discourse mechanics, and social history of Western ideology and representational practices. Culture studies explores how knowledge and power cooperate in the production of constructed "truths" and their conformance mechanisms, "truths" privileged as being presumably free of any ideological contamination.

The essay argues for a new optimism, a new period of consolidation in which "important ideas, good or bad," are now serving "as a springboard for new ideas grown from unions of past ideas once seemingly incompatible" (ibid.). The article then surveys differences between qualitative and quantitative data, discounting its own epistemological assumptions, its obligation to interrogate the logic and implications of its own boundaries. Nowhere in the article is there a self-conscious addressing of its essential premise – that no gap exists between the concept of intelligence and the thing it to which it presumably refers. This incompleteness is also evident in the observation that

> the goal of Binet's test was to protect children from being improperly classified in school. Today, test users point out how test scores can give opportunities to children that otherwise would not get them. For example, children from lower-level or even middle-level socioeconomic backgrounds who could not otherwise finance certain levels of education may be admitted or receive scholarships on the basis of their test scores. (Ibid., p. 5)

The point is made without considering the state rationale for such *protection*, why these governmental classification systems were implemented in the first place, or why such class disparity exists. There is no analysis of why these opportunities are limited and selective, and what political reality that scarcity serves. Moreover, discussions about psychometric tools do not include any analysis of contemporary critiques of statistics and mathematics.

Its discussion of a "new integrative framework," the need for intelligence "to be situated better with respect to other related constructs, or a current "movement away from static conceptions of intelligence toward dynamic ones" (ibid., pp. 19–20) is followed by observations that highlight two patterns in the history of intelligence: its metaphoric appropriation patterns and its echoing of dominant ideologies. Both become evident with the point that "if human intelligence is a dynamic system, do we observe 'system crashes' and, if so, what do they tell us about the system's functioning? Work on the dynamics of intelligence, both in its development and in its day-today dynamic functioning, needs to move from metaphors to testable, detailed models" (ibid., p. 20). The appropriation and mixing of contemporary quantum sciences or dynamic systems and information technology (system crashes) is consistent with the history of intelligence, especially in terms of its parasitical behavior, its drawing from the strength of popular and dominant ideas in a given period and entering various hosts of power. This is clearly one of the linguistic, rhetorical, and discursive patterns by which metaphors of power behave.

Second, the article reflects the pattern of echoing the ideological by stating:

> The field of intelligence, which has been so concerned with measuring individual differences . . . has curiously favored the search for the model that applies to everyone. Perhaps it is time to put the individual at the center of our models, and one way to do this without dismissing general models is through dynamic features that allow for individual evolution.

One of the obvious patterns in post-Enlightenment thought has been that of continuous individuation, the making of a subject who, in turn, self-regulates and achieves identities by conformance to governing ideas about freedom and choice. This is particularly evident in postmodern culture, where freedom is often defined in terms of having the right to make certain consumer choices. The above agenda parallels this postmodern trend. The decision to jettison the past "mass" approach to intelligence in favor of a more designer-like concentration is indicative of contemporary practices, those meeting individual needs by limiting the range of individual experience or the potential for individual power. This individualization of intelligence has actually already been a feature of modern and postmodern intelligence. Although clinical assessment and procedures appear to be generic – the same tests or evaluation procedures – their effect is that of targeting an individual "patient" who, nevertheless, has to live with the effects of those practices.

The ideological history of the social power of ideas of intelligence would be incomplete if we did not examine the technologies that made them true.

14 Smart Tools and Modern Intelligence

The architects of modern intelligence did not merely conceptualize intelligence; their ideas shaped, forged, and converted metal, wood, paper, paint, and ink into tests, devices, and technologies. They went to market, creating a flourishing intelligence industry with all the authority of profit needed to find a place in the ideological matrix of contemporary Western culture. Companies like Houghton Mifflin, C. H. Stoelting, McGraw-Hill, The Psychological Company, Riverside Publishing, and Princeton Review were and are the most familiar, some having Dow Jones symbols. An analysis of certain laboratory devices, government reports and black-and-white photographs will provide another version of intelligence, showing how its different ideas became "real" in a world of order, profit, conquest, and promise.

Smart Tools

Modern technologies of intelligence, those invented before and during the twentieth century, were primarily measuring devices; some were made of metal and wood, some acted like machines, others had arc scales, and still others were classification documents able to trick the hidden mystery of internal intelligence out into the light of day where it could be objectively examined, evaluated, and put into social structure. The ideological power of these technologies resides in their capacity to take control of a person's intelligence and move it into the realm of science and medico-legal based bureaucracies where, manipulated and controlled by officials, it could be ranked in terms of mathematical scales corresponding, in form, to economic class scales.

The one underlying link common to these devices and tests was a largely unchallenged connection between stimuli responses and intelligence, specifically with the speed of response being a primary intelligence metric. Although Aristotle and others speak of this connection, it did not, in general, become *scientific* until Galton and Wundt presented theories based on the notion that the measuring of reaction time indicated how fast the brain worked. This is a logic based on an industrial calculus. The two did not explore the metaphoric and ideological implications of using industrial terms like "speed" and "work" to describe brain activity, nor did they explain how such response activity translates into intelligence. "Synaptic efficiency" was Galton's term differentiating the "quick" and intelligent from "slow" and poor test performers.

The first sustained scientific examination of speed and intelligence occurs in Wilhelm Wundt's *Physiological Psychology* (1969; first published 1902). Wundt's name is synonymous with experimental psychology, and he was the first scientist to create a modern psychology laboratory stocked with various devices and tools designed to measure mental events and to translate stimuli and reaction measurements into discrete mental faculties. He proved the connection between stimuli and intelligence by arguing that the "life of an organism is . . . unitary . . . therefore, we [can no more] separate the processes of bodily life from conscious processes than we can mark off an outer experience, mediated by sense perceptions, and oppose it, as something wholly separate and apart, to what we call 'inner' experience, the events or our own consciousness." Appealing to the empirical, Wundt states that "It is a matter of every-day experience that we refer certain bodily movements directly to volitions, which we can observe as such only in our consciousness" (Wundt, 1969, p. 1). And in a most direct way he surmises that

> The distinguishing characteristics of mind are of a subjective sort; we know them only from the contents of our own consciousness. But the question calls for objective criteria, from which we shall be able to argue to the presence of a consciousness. Now the only possible criteria of the kind consist in certain bodily movements, which carry with them an indication of their origin in psychical processes. (Ibid., p. 27)

Before Galton and Wundt, the Dutch physiologist F. C. Donders experimented with timing responses in milliseconds. The effort was derivative, borrowing from Charles Wheatstone's 1840 effort to measure the velocity of artillery shells. At the same time, a Swiss watchmaker, Mathias Hipp, refined Wheatstone's work and marketed an extremely accurate chronoscope. By the 1870s, technological developments were well under way for Wundt to use lab tools that could "precisely" measure physical responses reflective of mental processes. Often the emphasis on precision overshadowed the need for better scientific reasoning.

The earliest document rationalizing the inclusion of certain physical tests within a broader mental examination was written by Baldwin, Cattell, and

Jastrow ("Physical and Mental Tests," *Psychological Review*, 1898, 5, pp. 172–9). In neither that essay nor Wundt's *Physiological Psychology* is there any hard science proving that there are significant correlations between intelligence and response time. For even if speed correlates to intelligence, what does that mean? What does that connection mean, given discovered correlations, and why would they exist? Not to answer these questions is to run the risk of undermining the whole enterprise. Does the correlation exist simply because those who process information in culturally privileged ways do so with more facility than others? For the same reason that the universality of any set of questions cannot be scientifically proven, neither can the relevance of speed. At what point in a response is it considered faster or more efficient than another response? No two responses necessarily imply an identical mental construction or solution to the stimuli presented. Nor can one always assume a constant point of reference. Lastly, those who have historically advocated the speed–intelligence correlation have generally believed in the objectivity to given speed and efficiency in the correlation, an obvious point given the fact that such associations did not exist in eras preceding the Industrial Revolution. To be universal, intelligence has to be measured by transhistorical criteria. Assembly lines and mindless pistons – the byproducts of speed and efficiency – may not be the best models to scientifically measure the complex nature of universal intelligence.

Wundt's arguments and advances in measurement devices fueled interest in developing new laboratory technologies, a popularity evident in the public's response to Galton's London Anthropometric Lab. Some labs were more adequate than others. For instance, Clark University implemented a state-of-the art vision lab in 1892, while others bought a "minimal lab," a 1893 portable collection consisting of a sonometer, tuning forks, a color mixer, a Wheatstone stereoscope for vision, and a stop watch. Some labs specialized in specific areas and used special equipment. For example, interest in testing for auditory acuity meant buying the Stern tone variation device, Helmholtz resonators, or Galton's whistle. The need to time all experiments produced a lively market for time-sense apparatus, including Munsterberg, Hipp, Ewald, Sanford, Bergström, and Dunlap chronoscopes. In addition, there were devices to test memory and tactile responses.

More importantly, labs began to use combinations of sensory devices and other new tools to measure physiological responses, other than the five senses, that were considered as markers of intelligence. Kymographs (figure 14.1) were revolving drums upon which a stylus recorded responses on sheets of smoked paper. Originally used to measure blood pressure, the device was repurposed to record response times, stimulus presentations, muscle exertion, and tuning fork vibrations, linking physiological responses to intelligence. In figure 14.2, Binet

Figure 14.1 Kymograph (from Archives of the History of American Psychology, Marietta College Collection).

Figure 14.2 Binet administering a test (from Archives of the History of American Psychology, first published in *Année Psychologique*).

Figure 14.3 David Wechsler's Brunzwigia calculating machine (from Archives of the History of American Psychology, David Wechsler Collection).

and a child are engaged in an exam. Binet is focused on the kymograph drum, and the boy gazes outward. Binet's right hand rests on the boy's shoulder, an ambiguous gesture given its message, a fatherly hand inconsistent with the countenance of an evaluator, a diagnostic professional. In perspective, the kymograph separates us from Binet and the boy; it is given the representational authority of a centralized object. Binet stares at the machine, and we stare at it too; its importance is verified by Binet's preference for monitoring it rather than looking at the boy or at his virtual audience. This portrait is a drama of power: the machine commands a privileged location and a privileged role. This is a special tool; it reads what cannot normally be read. It makes visible the invisible. It is an odd machine. It is a spinning text, using a pen to write responses on smoked paper. And its story is about breaths and muscle movements. This is a text of power; it is a substitute for the original, a reproduction and a representation. It captures what could not previously be signified. Once taken off the drum and processed, the text will be more true than its source. When credibility is assigned to the text machine, a subject is born, an individual made compliant and vacant by a complex technical process. We need only look into the boy's eyes, note his facial vacuity, and compare them with those of Binet. The boy is powerless and the man administers. The child's flat affect contrasts with Binet's formal purposefulness, the scientist busy with distracting drums and smoked paper. Another drum technology, David Wechler's Brunzwigia Calculating Machine (figure 14.3), spins, computes, and harvests. Interestingly, the kymograph and the Brunzwigia are in motion, their churning of waves and calculations mixing and transforming the indeterminant into something determinant. These are machines of power translations, converting the immaterial into certitude, converting the unknown interiority of the subject into a new kind of normalized and scaled knowledge.

Figure 14.4 Wallin using an ergograph (from Archives of the History of American Psychology, J. E. Wallace Wallin Papers).

The ideological mettle of other devices can be also tested. For instance, J. E. Wallace Wallin, a well known clinician and administrator at the Vineland Hospital, used a number of tools in his work. Figure 14.4 shows Wallin using an ergograph, leaning over his desk, his eyes glued on a kymograph. As the boy's middle finger lifts and lowers a weight, the machine records the frequency and duration of his pulls. This test measures a mental characteristic, in this case the endurance of the grip being a direct measure of the child's resolve and fortitude. Figure 14.5 shows a boy blowing into a wet spirometer. This device measured *vital capacity*, or the volume of air exhaled after intense inhalation. Note that the tubing terminates in a drum that rises to various measurement points. Vital capacity was an indicator of intelligence. The child in figure 14.6 is standing on the base of a volometer, a device that measured the duration of his tip toeing. A buzzer would go off when his heels touched the base. Like the ergograph, the volometer measured persistency and determination, both a measure of intelligence. Aside from their obvious significance (machines measuring qualities not "scientifically"

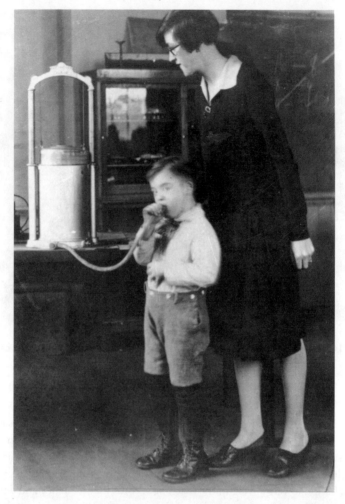

Figure 14.5 A boy blowing into a wet spirometer, a device measuring vital capacity (from Archives of the History of American Psychology, J. E. Wallace Wallin Papers).

proven to exist, let alone being intelligence indicators), these devices illustrate more profoundly how notions of intelligence are actually constructed. The point is that no idea of intelligence exists as an internal and original entity with an autogenic origin. What is clear, though, is that ideas of intelligence come into being through either simple or complex appropriation processes, and the more complex the idea, the greater the assemblage of specific characteristics required.

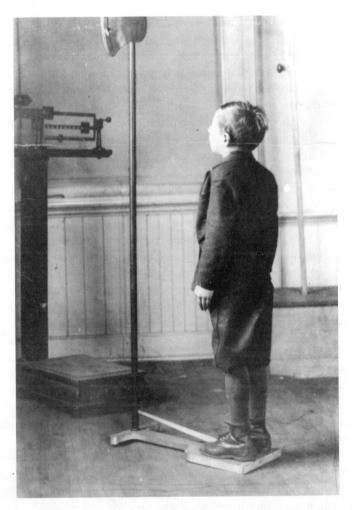

Figure 14.6   A child standing on the base of a volometer, a device measuring physical duration as a measure of mental persistence (from Archives of the History of American Psychology, J. E. Wallace Wallin Papers).

And because of this "appro-genesis," ideas of intelligence cannot exist without ideological content, functions, and values – the stuff they support – regardless of what any given theory, test, or science may argue. The science and culture of intelligence are not separate realities; the two are, in essence, part of the same woven discourse.

Ellis Island, Immigration Law, and Government Reports

Ellis Island was once a site of contested cultural power, its system and structure the convergence of historical events, philosophical ideas, social trends, capitalism, and industrial labor, and scientific, technological, and medical developments. To understand how an island harbors such complex ideological confluences, how it functioned figuratively as a contested text, I would first like to analyze an example of scientific literature dealing with immigration as a prelude to exploring the ideological role intelligence theory had on US immigration laws and other government practices.

During the early decades of the twentieth century books like *A Psychological Study of Immigrant Children at Ellis Island* (Boody, 1919), *An Analysis of Language Factors in Intelligence Tests* (Seago, 1921), and *Intelligence and Immigration* (Kirkpatrick, 1926) appeared, each announcing its own immigration agenda. The last is perhaps the most representative, marshalling biological, economic, and psychological ideas to make its impassioned arguments. Kirkpatrick's thesis is clear: "Definite limits are set by heredity, and immigrants of low innate ability cannot by any account of Americanization be made into intelligent American citizens capable of appropriating and advancing a complex culture" (Kirkpatrick, 1926, p. 2). Here intelligence is now nationalized, a metaphor of the state. His focus suggests that the power of science and psychology is that of cultural management tools. He speaks of "the need for a eugenic policy which shall include a more scientific control of immigration" (ibid., p. 3), and argues that intelligence is basically "hereditary, and it must be shown to be measurable or a least subject to estimate, in order that comparisons of the intelligence of various nativity groups can have real significance" (ibid., p. 5). In his mind, intelligence "is a group of innate capabilities by virtue of which the individual is capable of learning . . . in terms of the amount of these innate capacities with which he is endowed" (ibid.). Despite all this good science, the source of intelligence is an unknown endowment. It is an anonymous gift.

In another passage, Kirkpatrick shows how economic, psychological, mechanical, industrial, genetic, and social theory ideas are woven together to support certain ideological goals:

> intelligence can only be known by performance and types of performance suggest that there may be several . . . aspects of intelligence, which like dimensions determine volume. Certainly with the growth of intelligence there is increased power, in the sense of increased ability to learn intricate and abstruse material and to perceive complicated and abstract relationships. According to an analogy suggested by

Boring, this would correspond to the hill climbing capacity of an automobile. It is possible, however, that performance at a given level of difficulty might vary as to rapidity or speed. This would correlate to the speed of a car as determined . . . by the gear ratio. . . . General intelligence is the innate capacity fixed with the conjugation of the chromosomes in the original cell, which independently of environment determines the differences and semblances between individuals in ability to learn; the factors of power, speed, accuracy, and versatility all being taken into account. (Ibid., p. 6)

And then there is the blood of intelligence that inks immigration law: "It may be held with Brigham that the scores made on the tests by the various national groups correspond to the proportion of Nordic blood, and that the lower score of recent immigrants is due, at least, in part, to their smaller proportion of Nordic stock" (ibid., p. 17). The lack of Nordic blood is a lack of labor, a problem demanding new immigration policy: "it is almost a mistake to speak of an immigration policy of the United States save in connection with recent times, and even then the demand for a supply of cheap labor to hasten the exploitation of the natural resources of the country was the dominating consideration" (ibid., p. 106). The need for cheap labor, Kilpartrick argues, has ultimately had the effect of lowering the level of American intelligence (ibid., p. 107). Policy reform will correct the problem:

1 There should be individual selection based on scientific measurement and evaluation made as completely objective as possible.
2 Stress should be laid on what might be called the new mercantilism; a zeal for high grade immigrants (ibid., p. 112).

A closer look at immigration law will show how ideas of intelligence helped to shape provocative legislation.

US Immigration Laws

The ideological influence of science-based social policy is evident in a wide range of state and federal reports dealing with intelligence and immigration, many being narrative reports summarizing volumes of statistical tables. This use of tables speaks to Foucault's "classic" relationship between knowledge productions and formations of power. In this case, as with others cited in this book, ideas of intelligence are constructed in ideological alignments with the production of certain knowledge systems and ideologies. Differences in intelligence do not only separate individuals on psychological charts. They separate entire classes of people, those who produce "primary" knowledge from those seen either as a cheap way of getting certain work done or as threats to the production and security of knowledge and capital.

In September 1906, the New York Board of Alienists produced a report classifying intelligence along the lines of the ethnic identity of deportees. The highest number of deportees in the history of Ellis Island were the mentally "inferior"; their "defects" usually resulted in their being separated from their family and sent back. This group constitutes an intelligence of difference. According to the report appearing in *Miscellaneous Documents on Immigration 1907–1914*,

> the quality of those sent back [because of mental diseases or defects] is thus shown: of the last 100 deported we found that 16 had been insane in Europe, 45 had developed symptoms of insanity prior to landing, 15 were "always queer," 15 were of low order mentally and prone to the deterioration which came on at once after landing, and the history of 5 showed insanity in near members of the family and mental instability on the part of the aliens.

The report, like other period writings, lumped the mentally defective into one broad "mental" category, failing to distinguish real insanity from simply low intelligence, awkwardness, or odd facial gestures. In essence, "idiots" and paranoid schizophrenics were one and the same, with certain nationalities having more mental defects than others:

> insanity is relatively more prevalent among the foreign-born than among the native-born, and relatively more prevalent among certain immigrant races or nationalities than among others . . . the high ratio of insanity among the foreign-born [is attributable to] racial traits or tendencies. A further cause of mental disease is probably to be found in the total change in climate, occupation, and habits of life which the majority of immigrants experience after arrival in the United States. (Ibid.)

The federal government compiled yearly commission reports consisting of an opening summary, written by various health or immigration officials or inspectors, followed by hundreds of pages of statistical tables. Many of these reports dealt with lower intelligence issues. For example, the 1913 *Annual Report* of the Commissioner General of Immigration stated that

> it was found necessary and possible under the provisions of the immigration law to exclude 19,938 aliens during the year, amounting to 1.38 percent of the total number (1,447,165) applying for entry. The principal grounds of rejection were: likely to become a public charge, of which class 7,941 were excluded; afflicted with

physical or mental defects affecting ability to earn a living, 4,208; contract laborers, 1,624; afflicted with contagious diseases or tuberculosis, 2,564; and afflicted
with serious mental defects, 753. (Commissioner General of Immigration, 1913,
pp. 3–4)

Those with mental defects were then subclassified. The deported were the
"idiots, imbeciles, feeble-minded," those whose insanity would like make them
a public charge (ibid., p. 5).

The reports were overtly political, inventing mental defects as the underlying
cause for radical immigrant politics. What else would explain government criti-
cism? The most dangerous defect was the

anarchist of foreign birth . . . most [remain] very quiet, as a rule, until the time
limit protects him from deportation, and then he is loud and boisterous and begins
his maniac cry against all forms of organized government; excepting, perhaps,
some form of government suggested to him through his unbridled, formless, hal-
lucinari, and degenerate brain, which is always incapable of logical thought . . .
there is no room in this country for this class of mental degenerates, and there
should be no time limit to their deportation. (Ibid., p. 227)

In an interesting sidebar, the report admits that it is difficult "to ascertain whether
or not an immigrant comes from within one of these classes, especially when
the question is as to feeble-mindedness." The problem is one of inspection, of
being able to read these new aliens: "Ellis Island . . . not as fully equipped as it
should be to do this work thoroughly." Nevertheless, and rather ironically, the
writer states that

nothing is gained by closing one's eyes to this fact, on the contrary, a great deal of
harm is done . . . unquestionably a number of immigrants of this class do enter
the country every year who would be detected and excluded if the medical officers
were able to conduct a more comprehensive examination. A word as to the feeble-
minded. Not only are they likely to become a public charge on the community, but
they are also quite likely to join the ranks of the criminal classes. In addition they
may leave feeble-minded descendants. (Ibid., p. 181)

A solution to this lack of efficiency and blindness (government screening fail-
ures) came in the way of an "improvement" outlined in 1916. The "intensive
method" yielded certification of 9.37 percent of aliens as "mental defects." The
method

consisted in giving each alien a thorough examination in a private room, while the
ordinary method was a line inspection by the doctors, who looked the aliens over

as they marched before them. As was said in the last report: Certainly there could be no better or more convincing argument than that afforded by the above figures for increasing the medical force sufficiently to insure that no alien shall be admitted to the country until he has been subjected to a medical inspection really calculated to disclose his mental or physical deficiencies. (Commissioner General of Immigration, 1916, p. ix)

The language and change of procedures here further illuminate the relationship between ideology, intelligence, and immigration. First, no individual author seems to write these reports, their narrative agency being that of an omniscient matter-of-fact voice similar to official machine talk. In them the narrative tone resembles a calculator spewing out statistical improvement data. According to the writer, "improvement" occurs with greater technical control: sloppy assembly line inspection (an industrial method consistent with the alien labor being assembled) is replaced by isolation, by a quarantining of the individual body in order to inspect the mind. This shift from metallic labor to medicinal inspections represents an "advancement" through better technical systems. This change in method also illustrates how technocrat rationalism functions as a modernist trait. Mental deficiency even posed a threat to national security:

Because it is of such importance that the mentally and morally defective shall be kept out of the country, the bureau always desires to direct particular attention to the detailed statistics regarding such classes. For the exclusion of the mentally defective there is a more compelling reason than the mere risk that they will become burdens on our communities – i.e. scientific research and investigation has shown *that strains* of mental defect, once introduced, have a tendency to grow in an ever-increasing ratio from generation to generation – carried to its logical conclusion, it is a case where a "little leaven leaventh the whole lump." (Ibid., p. x)

Here ideological metaphors abound, with mental defects the figural equivalent of viruses (strains) and biblical cancers (lumps). Fear was fueled by the idea that mental defects could clone themselves, like viral diseases, and that meant the end of civilization. Intelligence, many imagined, would succumb to stupidity and biological laws.

Mullan's Report

The US Public Health Service published E. H. Mullan's *Mental Examination of Immigrants: Administration and Line Inspection at Ellis Island* in May 1917. It records how mental inspection methods functioned as social engineering technologies,

tools that met the growing need for cheap industrial labor and for national protection from subversion. This technology solved the conflict between capitalism
and the need for state security.

The document is a *comprehensive* discourse, woven together by ideas of social
Darwinism, eugenics, social science theory, scientific management, industrial
productivity models, and governmental practices. Its three-part structure
describes line inspection practices, a "weeding out process," and more thorough
examinations. Its metaphoric content consists of industrial and agrarian figures,
with "examination plants," "iron railings," "inspection lines," and "defect analysis" juxtaposed against images of "weeding out" and a "primary sifting process."
This figural mix presents an examination process by which industrial procedures
yield a strange harvest, separating those who can work from those whose
"mental condition will decidedly handicap [them] among [their] fellows in the
struggle for existence" (Mullan, 1917, p. 15). Mullan's world is clearly Hobbesian
and Darwianian. In it the steel order of industrial procedures is transformed into
the *natural* because the procedures *produce* the natural. When the sifting is fin-
ished, regularity and irregularity are identified: the good and nourishing pass
through as worthy labor, and the bad and unwholesome are rejected and
returned as unworthy.

The three-hour process was meant to determine immigrants' "mental and
physical condition . . . their fitness for admission" (ibid., p. 3). Administered by
medical and immigration surveillance staff, the process occurred in the "examination plant of the Public Health Services." This coalition of the medical, the
police, and the bureaucratic in an industrial environment – the "plant" – reveals
the relationship between metaphor and power. The appropriation of the word
"plant," particularly in America, signifies the industrialization of prior modes of
production. Literally, the fixtures, implements, machinery, and apparatus used in
industrial processes correspond metaphorically to the roots, branches, and leaves
of plants. Industrial discourse borrowed the word "plants" perhaps on the basis
that both industry and nature produced something valuable.

Mullan states that all immigrants were guided into "different inspection lines
. . . separated by iron railings." The lines, "four in number at their proximal end
and two in number at their distal end," extend "a distance of 15 feet," terminat-
ing "in a single line which is perpendicular to them" (ibid.). The language reflects
a scientific precision, moving from a general state to a specific point, from the
outer to the subject. This exactness of those spaces provides an authority carried
throughout all plant inspection activities. The words "proximal" and "distal" are
also medical terms; this association of industrial organization with medical treatment creates an ideological correspondence between the industrial, the regulatory, scientific precision, and the medical, with the first three curing unstated

211

illnesses. Social system precision acts like medicine by guaranteeing health. The correspondence also extends to the "four medical officers who carry on the general inspection" by standing at each of the "four proximal lines," while another two "stand at the extreme ends of the distal lines or just where these lines merge into two common exits" (ibid.). An attendant stands at the merging point separating those who will continue through the process from those routed to the "examination department."

The "general inspector's" duties are "to look for all defects, both mental and physical." A "quick glance" enables them "to take in six details, namely the scalp, face, neck, hands, gait and general condition, both mental and physical. Should any of these details not come into view, the alien is halted and the officer satisfies himself that no suspicious sign or symptom exists" (ibid., p. 4). One of the most "suspicious" signs was "inattentive and stupid-looking aliens." If a simple addition and multiplication answer proved wrong and mental defect was suspected, "an X [was] made with chalk on . . . the anterior aspect" on "the right shoulder." Mullan explains that "should definite signs of mental disease be observed, a circle X would be used instead of the plain X" (ibid., p. 5). The technicality of this language, "anterior aspect," combined with the nature of these codes, an X or an encircled X, underscores how immigrants were subjected to technical and systematic procedures, consistent with industrial processing methods, which ultimately reduced the marginalized to the generic. The use of an "X" was no symbolic coincidence, its encircling an even more symbolic enclosing of a generic identity further lost in a maze of technical procedures, much in the way that the future of intelligence testing made procedural compliance more significant than the individuals taking the tests. This inscribing upon the body made certain "problem" immigrants part of the state text; it singled them out as less than normal and valuable. Interestingly, these "scientific" observations produced no knowledge other than confirming existing orthodoxy.

The account continues: "The alien after passing the scrutiny of the first medical officer . . . is quickly inspected again by the second examiner . . . known . . . as the 'eye man'" (ibid., p. 7). As the immigrant came closer, "the officer" would "ask a question or two so as to ascertain the condition of the immigrant's mentality. He may pick up a symptom, mental or physical, that has been overlooked" (ibid., p. 6). This adjectival catachresis of "eye man" privileges surveillance and observation over any other mode of knowing, examination being a way that humans "act." This figure is similar to the synecdochic use of "hands" to refer to laborers, which appears in Dickens's *Hard Times*, a critique of industrial social regularization, as well as in Mullan's report: "of all the physical details in the medical inspection of immigrants it is perhaps most important to watch the hands" (ibid., p. 4). This trope-filled passage suggests how industrial processes function cognitively and organizationally, reducing meaning, value, and body parts to function, process, and productivity. The "eye man" takes a body part and makes it define the human whole. This transfer of power, this economy, speaks loud ideologically.

So what does the "eye man" look for?

> He looks carefully at the eyeball . . . to detect signs of defect and disease of that organ. . . . If the alien passes through this line without receiving a chalk mark, he has successfully passed the medical inspection and off he goes to the upper hall, there to undergo another examination by officers of the Immigration Service, who will take every means to see that he is not an anarchist, bigamist, pauper, criminal, or otherwise unfit. (Ibid., p. 6)

The physical is a window into a person's mentality: "a sizing up of the mentality is not complete without considering them. Speech, pupil symptoms, goiters, palsies, atrophies, scars, skin lesions, gaits, and other physical signs, all have their meaning in mental medicine" (ibid.). Mullan then lists what "eye man" looks for to determine the mentally defective:

> Stigmata of degeneration, facial scars, acneiform rashes, stupidity, confusion, inattention, lack of comprehension, facial expression of earnestness or preoccupation, inability to add simple digits, general untidiness, forgetfulness, verbigeration, neologisms, talking to one's self, incoherent talk, impulsive or stereotyped actions, constrained bearing, suspicious attitude, refusing to be examined, objecting to having eyelids turned, nonresponse to questions, evidence of negativism, silly laughing, hallucinating, awkward manner, biting nails, unnatural actions, mannerisms and other eccentricities.

To confirm his suspicions, questions are asked: "Where are you going? How old are you? Are you a Greek? What is your name? The majority of immigrants, however, are questioned in simple addition" (ibid., p. 8). The objective is to "enable the officer to *bring to view* the attention, alertness, reasoning ability, and emotional reaction of the alien" (ibid., p. 9). This description illuminates how rational government was operationalized and possible, particularly in its policing of health practices, its social management of poverty, its use of statistical projections, and its reinforcement of labor imperatives. Mullan's account parallels Foucault's panoptican procedures: "All that is needed, then, is to place a supervisor in a central tower . . . the panoptic mechanism arranges spatial unities that make it possible to see constantly and to recognize immediately. In short . . . visibility is a trap" (Foucault, 1995, pp. 195–6). These accounts suggest that the human mind has been a contested power site since the eighteenth century, and that any effort to bring to presumed visibility its contents, nature, and behavior is an exercise of social control and power. What Mullan's visibility tests for are qualities (attentiveness, reasoning) inherent in values residing in the modernist hegemony.

The "weeding-out process" occurred in a large room. Examiners called up detained passengers for another "brief inspection." If an immigrant was suspected of "mental abnormality," he was issued a "yellow 'hold card' . . . and . . . held over night in order to undergo a complete mental examination" (Mullan, 1917, p. 10).

The following records symptoms worthy of a yellow card:

> Six year old; cannot get child to speak. . . . Seven years old: unable to count five fingers. . . . Objects to examination; refuses to cooperate. . . . Fails in Cube and 20 to 1 tests. . . . Agitated; brought into examination room by relatives. . . . Stupid; erratic answers; wanders around the room. . . . Observe mother; child is an imbecile. . . . Emotional; noisy, boisterous, loss of self-control. . . . Clouding of consciousness; euphoric, tremor of tongue; knee jerks. . . . Alien has a peculiar affected manner. . . . Steamship's surgeon reports that alien refused to answer questions. . . . She is on the defensive. . . . Silly facial expressions. Appears to be thinking of something foreign to the examination. . . . Maria says she has been married 3 years; can sew garments but cannot cut them out. . . . Admits illegitimate child 5 months old in Ireland. Has frequent convulsions. . . . Irritable, claiming that it is her privilege to do as she pleases; went back to Ireland last December with her sister who was deported from Ward's Island (hospital for insane); another sister was deported 4 years ago; paranoid view of life; ship surgeon reported that patient would burst out into laughter without cause; also get up from dinner table and play the piano to the annoyance of other passengers. . . . Retarded; apathetic; clouding of intellect . . . reported to be acting queerly upstairs: suspect epilepsy. . . . Child is abnormally backward and has abnormal fear. She is shy and it is impossible to get any information from her. Although 10 years of age, she cannot count to 20; mother dresses her. (Ibid., pp. 11–13)

In phase three, two populations were examined: those "sent to the hospital for observation, and those . . . held in the detention room for further examination." In the latter case, "regular mental examinations are conducted in a number of rooms, each of which is provided with chairs, benches, and an examining desk which contains suitable blanks and psychological apparatus" (ibid., pp. 13–14).

Figure 14.7a and b shows immigrants standing in "proximal lines" and having their eyes inspected. Figure 14.8a, b, and c captures the *weeding out process*, the first regular exam, and the third and fourth regular exams (ibid., pp. 3–4). All three are highly ordered environments, two of which are public. Note that two uniformed governmental medical workers are always present, monitoring activ-

Figure 14.7 Immigrants being processed in "proximal lines" (by permission of the US Public Health Service, from Mullan's "Mental Examination of Immigrants: Administration and Line Inspection at Ellis Island," May 1917).

ities in rooms resembling formal hearing rooms or courtrooms. One monitor looks into the examinee's eyes, the other looks to the performance. The examinee's responses are visible to all in figures 14.8a and b, and the monitors' activities are only visible to others in figure 14.8a, the process with the most immigrants. Seemingly the more refined is the test, the less public visibility and more spatial concentration.

Each space is a stage. Something dramatic is taking place, and fate is being played out. The staging is very tribunal-like, with examinees in a spot usually reserved for defendants or criminals, each attempting to prove his or her innocence by being intelligent. The monitors act as judges. Space is barren of any distraction; everything points to the matter at hand. These restrictions create authority. Uniformities of body placement, test procedures, processing sequences, and specific mental responses produce a power that commands attention, consciousness, and conformance. The stark orderliness present in each photo minimizes the individual; the performance, rather than the person, will determine whether the immigrant stays and works or is rejected and returns home. The entire scene is a study in what Foucault would call *governmentality*, the mechanisms and systems needed for individuals to become subject to the efficient power of the modern industrial state.

The numbers are surprising. Mullan states that "from 15 to 20 percent of the immigrants are chalk-marked" (ibid., p. 6), and estimates suggest that 10 percent of all immigrants during the high migration period (1900–24) were rejected, with mental defectiveness leading the way. Rejection often resulted in the disintegration of a family. Sometimes a father, a mother, or a child was rejected.

Figure 14.9, from the US Department of the Interior (Liberty Island), offers a final and compressed representation of mental testing done on Ellis Island. All eyes are focused on the two rectangular forms. All parties are in the light, and the windows are covered over. The uniformed representative is occupied. He is testing, his left hand resting on the desk near the timepiece. He is programmed to look for and measure exact compliance. In this case, compliance orders. If all the forms fit, the man is saved from being defective. The immigrant is successful if he duplicates what he sees. Here intelligence is mimesis. A firsthand account of the rewards of such imitation reads:

> The whole experience was very frightening. They brought me up to a room. They put a pegboard before me with little sticks of different shapes and little holes. I had to put them in place, the round ones and the square ones . . . and I did it perfectly. They said "Oh, we must have made a mistake. This little girl . . . naturally she doesn't know English, but she's very bright, intelligent." They took the cross [chalk-mark] off me so we were cleared.

Figure 14.8 Immigrants participating in the "weeding out process" (by permission of the US Public Health Service, from Mullan's "Mental Examination of Immigrants: Administration and Line Inspection at Ellis Island," May 1917).

Figure 14.9 A mental test, Ellis Island (by courtesy of the National Park Service, US Department of the Interior).

This conversation with Victoria Sarfatti Fernandez, a Macedonian Jewish immigrant who arrived in 1916, took place in 1985, and was posted on the National Park Service/Ellis Island website. The criterion of faithful imitation makes for optimal industrial sense.

Yerkes's Army Tests and Mental Technologies

Prior to Yerkes's ambitious military testing project, intelligence tests were not expressly used to quantify comparative mental differences between any national or racial group. Yerkes's enterprise is recorded in a thousand-page report armed with 438 tables, most of which scale relative percentage levels of intelligence to such categories as social, racial, economic, class, geographical, or demographic classes. Yerkes gives intelligence tests a new state purpose, to solve "problems of national defense" (Yerkes, 1921, p. v), which in turn will require psychologists to "cooperate to the fullest extent and immediately toward the increased efficiency of our Army and Navy" (ibid., p. 7). His target was to identify "intellectual deficiency and psychopathic tendencies" (ibid., p. 9). Committee agreement created a policy that "all recruits . . . be tentatively classified as mentally (a) low, (b) high, (c) average, (d) irregular" (ibid., p. 10). Yerke's real goal was efficiency, his target being 20,000 tests in less than two months (ibid., p. 14).

For validation purposes, Yerkes created a control test given to medical examiners. The results were not surprising: "those who had made the higher marks in the psychological tests were the very ones who had been doing good work, developing their infirmaries, making careful recruit examinations and complying with instructions, while those who had received the lower rating had not been doing as good work" (ibid., p. 19). These "findings" are consistent with patterns in early intelligence testing, evident in Terman's work and in the use of various lab devices noted earlier, patterns in which preferred or problematic characteristics were equated with certain test or lab experiment scores.

Yerkes's project statement won government support: "to aid in segregating and eliminating the mentally incompetent . . . to classify men according to their mental ability . . . [and] to assist in selecting competent men for responsible positions" (ibid.). A few months later, his staff revised this goal: the new objectives of mental examination were

> to classify soldiers according to mental ability . . . supply a mental rating for each solider which shall assist personnel officers in building organizations of equal or appropriate mental strength; . . . assist in discovering men of superior mental ability who should be selected for officer's training camps; . . . assist in discovering and properly placing men of marked skill . . . [and] . . . assist in discovering men who are mentally inferior and who in accordance with degree of defectiveness should be recommended for discharge, development battalions, labor organizations or regular military training. (Ibid., p. 153)

Army testing procedures paralleled immigration testing by using quick visual examination techniques: army examiners stood ready to "pick out those . . . showing evident nervous or mental disturbance," with the goal of segregating "as quickly as possible cases of doubtful mental and nervous stability." When collected, exams were scored by "40 men," the work, "purely mechanical, being accomplished by an ingenious series of stencils made to fit over each form, showing at a glance the proper answer . . . nothing is left to the personal equation of the scorer" (ibid., p. 19). Like those boxes in figure 14.12 suggesting that

219

ideas of intelligence engender cognitive compliances to and replication of component values of the dominant epistemology, these "ingenious stencils" suggest an over laying, a *superimposing* of a symbolic celluloid instrument (of pure unchallengeable power to determine intelligence) over the individual who at that moment is represented by a form being evaluated for percentile compliance. By looking down at the stencil, a factory instrument of efficiency, speed, and accuracy, men in a "purely mechanical" way look for India ink dots, for marks representing elements composing intelligence and reflecting cognitive compliance with representations of it. This superimposing constitutes a doubling, a copying, a slightly sexual sandwiching measuring the seduced in terms of replicated potential.

And like Mullan's description of the purpose of immigrant testing, Yerkes's object is "to sift out those mental defective who are not qualified for military service . . . to discover men of superior ability for report to the commanding and company officers . . . [and] to discover men with marked special skill" (ibid., p. 123). Note the metaphoric pattern. These tests "sift out" the "defective," and they "discover . . . superior ability"; the first separates and grades in order to find failure, while the second discovers the most valuable. The word *discover* is consistently positive in Western culture and for obviously adventurous, romantic, gold yielding, and scientific reasons. Sifting, by contrast, exists to identify and devalue.

In sections testing for the recognition of "absurd relationships," recruits were given a Hobbesian view of the world: there were burning houses, sick people, poor sick men, accidents, murderers and robbers, the high price of food, strong men, police finding the body of a baby girl, a father sending money to his son, tardy students, low wages and workers, loss of arms, engineers, railroad accidents, young men tied up and locked in rooms, two shots killing a man, proof that God is good, a gentleman falling and breaking his neck, marriage laws, train damage, a wheel flying off a car, storms, judges hanging prisoners, and differences between kings and presidents (ibid., p. 138). These texts reveal the world of the familiar, of representations of a violent and economically depressed social world, and a natural world full of tragedies. Why is that world represented in intelligence tests? There are many possible readings. Two obvious ones come to mind: first, such a world reinforces the need for government and order, the test being an extension of that need; second, there is the implied idea that intelligence can cure such dreadfulness. This test is followed up in a memory section that has a boat striking a mine, children getting school donations, police dogs being trained, school children being killed, and the robbery of a maid (ibid., p. 142). Fear, impending war, violence, and natural disasters show why the order of the nation state is so valuable.

In the next series of questions, recruits must look for the "best" answers to the following questions:

- Why should people have to pay taxes?
- Why are people who are born deaf usually dumb?
- If you picked up a pocketbook on the road with a hundred dollars in it, what would you do to find the owner?
- Why is often a good thing for a man to have his life insured?
- Why do banks usually prefer married men for cashiers?
- Your mother is sick and has no money. You earn a dollar and are taking it to her. On the way you meet a child who cries and wants a nickel for some candy. What should you do?
- Why is a man who borrows money willing to pay interest on it?
- Why should women and children be saved first in a shipwreck?
- Why is electric light better than gaslight?
- Why should people have to get a license to get married?
- A man is 60 years old and has nobody to keep but himself. He has ten thousand dollars. What should he do with it? (Ibid., p. 143)

Another test asks that the "correct word" be inserted. Answers include a knowledge of:

body part functions, seasons, milk, anvils, who built the Panama Canal, eggs, Denver, what seven-up is played with, animals, trees, where the Declaration of Independence was signed, where the airplane was invented, forward passes, Jess Willard, who manufactures revolvers, location of main Ford factory, numbers that designate a first class batter, who was the Union commander at Mobile Bay, allies of Germany, where spark plugs are placed, what a Percheron is, a unit of electromotive force, the author of *Scarlet Letter*, bile, John Sargent, and the color of chlorine gas. (Ibid., p. 205)

And then there are multiple choice questions:

- Why ought every man to be educated? It makes a man more *useful*.
- Why ought a grocer own an automobile? It is *useful* in his business.
- Why is beef a better food than cabbage? More nourishing.
- Doctors are *useful* because they "heal the sick."
- Why is the telephone more *useful* than the telegraph? It gets a quicker answer.
- Agriculture is *valuable* because it feeds the nation.
- Purpose of education: it makes a man more *useful* and happy.

- Salary of electrical engineers: they do things which *create wealth.*
- Gold is better than iron because it is much scarcer and therefore more valuable.
- Why should all parents be made to send their children to school? Because it prepares them for adult life.
- Glass insulators are used to fasten telegraph wires because the glass keeps the current from escaping.
- Why are criminals locked up? To *protect* society. (Ibid., pp. 208, 218, 229)

These questions have a pattern, testing as they do for ideological awareness. Getting these questions correct reinforces the idea that, to some degree, intelligence is about ideological compliance. How else can we survey exam content and criteria and not see ideological compliance messaging and surveillance occurring? These content areas are not coincidental: moral law, compliance with educational laws, tax policy, stereotypes about the challenged, criminal law, property value, economic and business practices, wealth creation, labor issues, basic sciences, energy policy, social law and values of usefulness, foreign campaigns, geography, patriotic knowledge, and American history. The "intelligence" these sections test for sharply contrasts with Yerkes's definition that intelligence is "the ability to think quickly, accurately and independently; to comprehend new problems; to meet new and difficult situations; to understand and to be able to carry in mind complicated directions, etc." (ibid., p. 425). His test deconstructs its own ideological content, revealing how the modern social epistemology uses intelligence as a mode of compliance power. The test validates specifically privileged ways of knowing and conforming to social rules by making their recognition synonymous with intelligence.

The overt ideological nature of Yerkes's test becomes even more obvious in other sections that assess marginalized populations like Afro-American recruits, local prostitutes, and various "low" occupations. The rationale for such evaluations was that "the matter of elimination was not so much one of excluding the lowest from regular military service as it was one of admitting the highest" (ibid., p. 705) and obtaining external control group results. Yerkes begins by noting that

Several examiners report that it is difficult to keep up the interest of the negroes in the beta examination as it is usually given . . . a report from Camp Dodge (July 15, 1918) states "it took all the energy and enthusiasm the examiner could muster to maintain the necessary attention, as there was a decided disposition for the negroes to lapse into inattention and almost into sleep." Two factors account for this: "the relatively low intelligence of the negro beta group . . . and the fact that,

speaking English as they all did, the negroes felt the artificiality of the situation."
(Ibid., p. 705)

In plain language, the A Camp Travis report indicates a "striking inferiority in intelligence of the colored recruits" (ibid., p. 707). Such "striking inferiority" may be more about class privilege, social justice, and equal economic opportunity than the criteria being used as absolute measures of an absolute notion of intelligence.

The racism did not stop there. Yerkes endorsed an "experiment . . . of separating some of the negro recruits on the basis of skin color and comparing the intelligence ratings obtained from the lighter and darker groups" (ibid., p. 735). The results were predictable:

> The lighter class contained those whose color indicated that they were true mulattoes or persons of a larger proportionate of white blood . . . the darker class contained pure negroes. . . . The classification was made by the various examiners of the groups. . . . In alpha, the lighter negroes obtained a median score of 50; the darker obtained a median score of 30. In beta, the lighter negroes obtained a median score of 36; the darker obtained a median score of 29. (Ibid., p. 736)

The report further indicates that "the negro as compared with the white man of equal intelligence is relatively strong in the use of language, in acquaintance with verbal meanings and in perception and observation; and that he is relatively weak in judgment, in ability to analyze and define exactly, and in reasoning" (ibid., p. 738). This conclusion simply indicates that non-access to the dominant criteria defining intelligence will yield precisely such "low functioning" demonstrations. It has little to do with proving other kinds of intelligence. Yerkes's conclusion is likewise predictable:

> less than 2 percent of negroes are of A value to the military service when compared to white troops . . . about 25 percent are considered . . . too poor to make a satisfactory soldier. . . . Nearly all the negroes who rate D . . . are reported as too poor to make a satisfactory soldier. . . . In the case of white recruits a high correlation has been found to exist between psychological rating and military value. (Ibid., p. 742)

In addition to these conclusions, "percentages show that these low-grade are two or three times as likely to commit offenses as men of average intelligence, and from four to six times as likely to get into trouble as are men of markedly superior intelligence" (ibid., p. 799). The metaphor "low-grade" has a number of subtle ideological effects: it reinforces the "sifting" that separates the valuable from waste materials; it validates the power of mathematics and statistics to speak the truth and achieve certainty; and its industrial spin means poor quality.

But, more importantly, what kind of criminality does Yerkes refer to? It is prefaced by the point that the educated are intelligent and do not engage in criminal activity, in this case "purely military crimes . . . [that] discredit . . . the uniform" and reflect "disloyalty, disloyal statements, disrespect to United States" (ibid., p. 802). Here, intelligence tests produce a political harvest; they separate the intelligent and worthy citizens from minorities whose lack of intelligence makes them more likely to become criminals, and in the military the only way these criminals could operate would be to threaten American security. The ideological intentions of such sociopolitical engineering tools and propaganda cannot be ignored, despite all the claims for the validity of mathematical or scientific measurement.

Ultimately, Yerkes's scientific tests reveal the ease by which certain ideological values were affirmed and sustained with little challenge during the first two decades of the twentieth century. The exams were essentially an industrial solution to a set of socioeconomic and political state problems. The intriguing element was how the purported value of the tests literally erased any objection to them. There is little doubt that Yerkes moved intelligence testing from a diagnostic tool into a full blown tool of social power. The perceived value of Yerkes's mass military intelligence extended to other institutions in the next five decades, finding particular receptivity in public education. To understand that popularity we need briefly to highlight some significant changes in institutional dynamics.

Academic institutions underwent important changes toward the end of the nineteenth century, with space devoted to largely upper-class education shifting to become guidance centers for middle- and lower-class children. This repurposing of space also became a repurposing of information. Once the material for academic uses, knowledge and curriculum production were used as social engineering mechanisms, with textbooks and the standardization of curriculum strategies promoting and insuring state stability. What was once simply knowledge – mathematics, reasoning, and writing – was being translated into the stuff of "life skills," those essential qualities everyone needed to insure a useful and successful future. In this way, academic knowledge was recruited for use in the new social "managerial" dynamic, and knowledge became a tool to insure that the modern nation state would continue to be sustained by differences separating the education of the wealthy from that of the working class.

The use of scientifically based management tools became the dominant educational modality in modern Western culture in the late nineteenth century. Those tools, industrial and institutional in nature, had two goals: to process large quantities of middle-class students, with schools becoming industrial like "plants" or "facilities," and to regulate an orderly production behavior. The sheer difference between the number of students, administrative procedures, regularized curricula, and "special" programs distinguishing "public" from "private" education speaks, in part, to the ratio between automated systems and types of educational institutions. Examples of the early history of this industrial and scientific production of education – girl "number 24" in Dickens's *Hard Times*, Pink Floyd's "another brick in the wall" – can be traced to either Jean Itard's work with the "wild boy" of Aveyron or Edouard Seguin's strategies for educating "idiots." Both were eventually transformed into routine exercises to increase the abilities of larger student populations. Greater use of technocratic rational methods slowly institutionalized a brand of middle-class education that focused on developing the mind, the body, and moral values, with the majority of students trained to become industrial workers and good citizens. This notion of the school as a "guidance environment" comes into better focus after the Second World War, when students were taught standardized curriculum and administrators targeted "problem" children, working with the courts to prevent delinquency. Labeling a child as a "delinquent" transforms a disobedient act into a person, an identity who in failing or neglecting some duty becomes a special category. The addition of a "juvenile" delinquent is a further example of the precise classification practices of technocratic rationality. Interesting enough, the mass mental testing of students in the United States and Western Europe in the middle decades of the twentieth century echoes the goals underlying Binet's original testing: the governmental desire to identify those whose "low" intelligence constituted an ill defined threat to French political and socioeconomic security. This is why the majority of early IQ tests contained questions dealing with moral decisions, testing the assumption that moral inventory could help to insure conformance to social ideology.

This chapter has tried to bring *other* readings, *other* arguments, and *other* materials to bear upon our understanding of the determinant forces shaping the cultural history of modern intelligence. It has tried to outline modern efforts at transforming, with colonial and industrial methods, the mental world into a set of manipulated objects, procedures, and practices. This transformation of unknown value in calculable value was aided by detection, classification, and production control technologies. Each played a significant role in helping newly created social agencies to achieve the authority needed to order civil society. I have selected certain architects of intelligence responsible for these productions of intelligence, those who for the most part were influenced by the following ideas. Understanding the epistemological and ideological content of modern ideas of intelligence is impossible without knowing how economic Darwinism, technocratic rationalism, eugenics, evolutionary biology, statutory law, the demand for foreign industrial labor, immigration laws, threats to national security, and the truth value of statistics all coalesce in what transpires in every clinical, academic, or legal application of modern ideas of intelligence. It is baffling that these activities can operate with minimal consciousness as to the complex ideological forces controlling them. Being couched in various rhetorics of health, this behavior occurs with little awareness of the complex historical factors that reveal many "health practices" for what they often are: agents of social power, conformance, and repression.

15 Smart Critiques: New Sciences and New Mathematics

This chapter brings poststructural analyses of mathematics and science to a critique of dominant notions of intelligence, these ideas being generally ignored by contemporary clinicians, scientists, and social policy advocates. The disregard of the impact of contemporary critiques of traditional mathematics and science on intelligence studies parallels a similar disregard of how cultural and poststructural studies critique contemporary intelligence theories and practices. Two questions guide my inquiry: how truly "scientific" and "mathematical" are most contemporary intelligence theories and clinical practices; and what advances in science and mathematics challenge contemporary intelligence concepts?

Mathematics: What Counts in Contemporary Intelligence

In *A History of Scientific Thought* Michel Serres (1995, p. 74) imagines mathematics as an "invisible empire . . . an edifice with no parallel in history. What kind of edifice is this invention, this innovation involved in creating money and monotheism, the alphabet and metallurgy?" His interest produces another question: what role has this edifice played in constructing the social authority of modern ideas of intelligence?

Part of an answer comes with the recognition that its claim to absolute objectivity does not keep mathematics from behaving ideologically, especially since the Enlightenment. This possibility goes to the very heart of traditional theories and practices of intelligence, given their reliance on the automatic certitude assigned to mathematics. The seriousness of this matter is compounded by poststructural discoveries regarding the ideological mechanics of mathematics. Their focus on the nature of semiotics, science applications, and capitalist culture is particularly applicable. I should like to review selected critiques of mathematics and then trace them to certain historical moments in the evolution of mathematics. My goal is not to pretend to be a mathematician, but to tease out the obscure ideological relationships existing between mathematics and representations of modern intelligence.

Part of this work has already been explored by Robert Markley, Michel Serres, Ken Knoespel, Brian Rotman, Sal Restivo, and others. Knoespel, for instance, has consistently argued that mathematics is not simply about its productions, numbers, factors, and equations, but is a powerfully ideological discourse of authority and authorization. But what does it authorize, what authority does it command, and how has mathematics gained such cultural power to be the truth it signifies? The answer lies in how mathematics has been socially constructed. Like intelligence (a *real* thing *in* nature), mathematics mirrors the universe; its purity of transparence and its unmediated duplication of the real presumably preclude it from being a representational system. Galileo, for example, had no doubt that mathematics was the language science used to read the universe. Markley (1993, p. 67) explains its foregone certitude by suggesting that "mathematics has traditionally been understood as a form of originary writing, an inscription of the natural order that antedates history and the historical." Epistemologically, existentially, and mythically, mathematics defies death; its proximity to and reflection of the unchanging absolute immunizes it from the uncertainty of the natural world. As a mode of transcendental inscription, mathematics precedes time itself, apparently placing it outside the realm of representation, those orbiting divine spheres, where it garners a supreme authority that defies the chaos of nature and is far truer than the arbitrary truths of orthodox religion. Traditional representations of mathematics, as a perfection of the mind, made it an essential tool for theorists of intelligence, who historically found in its internal rationality the very criteria for a proven and demonstrable intelligence. This tautology is more than circular; it explains why modern intelligence practices and tests are primarily mathematical in content and assessment.

The history of early modern mathematics reveals how such a proximity to deity, to the originary Logos, guided the work of Newton, Descartes, Galileo, Cavalieri, Fermat, Wallis, Pascal, Huygens, Barrow, Gregory, Mersenne, Hooke, Vivani, Bernoulli, and others. It is impossible to look into their work in analytical geometry, vortice theory, principle of indivisibles, integral calculus, theory of numbers, calculus of probabilities, and three-dimensional coordinates and not see the belief that certainty about natural and human phenomena was possible. For all of them, mathematics could translate the universe into a series of laws, theorems, and equations, the latest one, Einstein's $e = mc^2$, becoming in pop culture a representation of "pure" genius, rather than signifying a specific formulation of the relationship between energy, mass, and the speed of light. Taken as a discourse, mathematics has often been presented and perceived as a chapter in the history of genius, with "mathematics the study of great men, brilliant geniuses who, by their unfathomable originality and profoundity of thought, have created in their image that which lesser men have been left simply to develop" (Serres, 1995, p. 44).

The measuring of human intelligence can first be traced to the seventeenth century, to a time when the universe became a machine, and humans needed a way to make it intelligible. Mathematics provided this intelligibility, as it did hundreds of years afterward when it was used to represent and scale the interior of intelligence that, as a kind of mechanics, directed human moral and intellectual behavior. This revolution in mathematics has played a central role in the creation and maintenance of the modern social epistemology. The mathematicization of the human, whether in early modern medicine or late Enlightenment bureaucratic practices, helped the coming to power of the social sciences from which many modern theories and practices of intelligence evolved. In essence, Renaissance mathematics and mechanics began the modern process of claiming intelligibility, the two defining themselves as the means by which understanding could take place and be measured. The more obvious point here is that this revolution *made understanding measurable*; that is, numbers, new geometrical theorems, differential equations, equality of ratio, mean proportionals, and infinitesimal analysis became ways of achieving absolute knowing. These methods did not merely produce truth, with an emphasis on the *truth*, but were the sole tools that made truth possible. An example of this was how the classic way of understanding harmonic motion in the seventeenth century was replaced by mathematical description. This shift of authority – to the modes of production – gave a primacy to these mathematical tools that even extends into contemporary work in intelligence. The bottom line is that intelligence, whatever it is, can only be accounted for mathematically. This accountability brings both intelligence and mathematics into the world of the ideological, a world shared by other mathematically privileged modes of power. This is the world the Romantics of nineteenth-century England modernist writers rebelled against. Blake's *Newton* is as much an allegory about mathematics as it is about fallen consciousness.

Mathematics became part of the new Western epistemology when it proved it could make science more precise and objective, when it became a commercial tool and an occupation, all of which feature in how intelligence became itself a thing measurable by those whose job was to measure. Scientific and commercial authority began when

> sensory perception [was] eliminated in favor of space or numbers – large, round, small, parallel. Outcome: sensory perception is eliminated in favor of

mathematical measurement. Sensations are reduced to the quantitative units of a property, and the variations within a property are brought into relation to a graded system of measurement – thermometer, musical scale, spectrum . . . distances, weights, and time. (Snell, 1960, p. 52)

Abstract mathematical power in the Renaissance coupled with the invention of new mathematical occupations. Mathematicians began to capitalize on new ways of thinking by taking them to market, to populations like the unlearned, the merchant class, instrument makers, and others who needed knowledge of practical geometry and trigonometry to make and use newly invented measuring devices. Moreover, increases in trade, early forms of colonization, and the insatiable hunger for gold all provided mathematics with a new value, its techniques being indispensable for surveying, map-making and navigation. Mathematicians began to enjoy a new social and economic status, particularly those knowledgeable in terrestrial mechanics, warfare, civil engineering, canal developments, and surveying. At the conclusion of the Renaissance, a new occupation had been culturally invented, the mathematician whose new institutional function and class made him a member of the intellectual elite. More significantly, with the advent of the scientific method and its claim to certitude, mathematical productions proved that truth could be certifiable, that the most abstract idea could, in fact, be made real. This is precisely what happened in the history of intelligence: an abstraction found various ideological incarnations, and those who performed these materializations were given unheralded authority to order the social and economic world.

Renaissance mathematicians, those bringing mathematics into the world of scientific proof, may never have thought of mathematics as a "constructed system of communication," and, as such, did not consider that "mathematics presents itself as a successful dialogue or a communication which rigorously dominates its repertoire and is maximally purged of noise." In response to Michel Serres, Markley quite rightly argues that the "ideal communication of mathematics, then, depends on the inclusion of a third term, the code, to carry the information and the rigorous exclusion of a fourth term, noise, defined as anything that interferes with the linear process of exchange." Hence its history indicates that "mathematics, as an ideal form of communication – maximum information, minimal noise – can define itself . . . in opposition to a perceived disorder that paradoxically is encoded, or anticoded, within its efforts to represent order unproblematically" (Markley, 1993, pp. 67–8). This dynamic explains, in part, why post-Enlightenment theories and practices of intelligence have so easily appropriated mathematics without much analysis, and why those appropriations have worked so well for psychology and the social sciences. The majority of modern intelligence efforts – from studies to clinical practices or from Supreme Court sterilization law to mass examinations – have been driven by political and socioeconomic "oppositions . . . to perceived disorder." This pattern is discussed in the previous two chapters, with particular emphasis on how modern "professional" intelligence practices have largely functioned as safeguards against socioeconomic and political disorder. Overlooking how mathematics encodes disorder in its production of order explains why conventional intelligence theorists and clinicians continually repurpose existing epistemologies and why, because of this disciplinarity, they cannot understand this mathematical dynamic. This blindness to how their tools construct their ideas ironically illuminates why most intelligence specialists cannot step outside the habitual either to construct different models of intelligence or to jettison the whole concept and pursue other models for understanding human cognition dynamics.

Markley argues that despite its formulas and vectors, mathematics is a rhetoric that operates contextually. In addition, its modes of representation are not as pure and unmediated as mathematicians claim, never really free from Derridean logocentricism and a metaphysics of presence. The equating of mathematics with the divine Logos and its self-legitimizing equivalence as unmediated information exchange can, however, be deconstructed. To do so Markley cites Serres's argument that its representation as

> a form of mediation between the real and the ideal, the physical world and an imagined realm of pure representation . . . mathematics *presupposes* rather than enacts a logocentric vision of communication as communion. Therefore, as a model for real characters and universal language schemes, seventeenth-century mathematics encourages views of systemic order as general and invariant and yet always in need of additional legitimization. (Ibid., pp. 68–9)

This argument has two effects: it puts into question the mathematical validity claimed by intelligence practitioners and, perhaps more importantly, it serves as a system descriptor. It identifies what continually fuels the business, social politics, and voguish controversies within the discourse of intelligence. This material side of intelligence – those new theories that ultimately generate new capital, products, services, and workers – is fueled by a two-stage, two-part construct: mathematics secures its "invariant" status by promoting the continual production of "new" variations (e.g. postmodern "emotional or creative intelligence") that then require "additional legitimization." Modern ideas of intelligence are clearly invariant, yet they possess a significant vertical and horizontal market potential, much in the same way the value of diamonds proves invariant (constant) despite the development of new markets or new designer trends. In essence there is a fundamentality to most theories of intelligence that can be manipulated to generate "new" theories and substantially lucrative practices, those used in courts, education, and business. The more subtle and delicate commercial aspects of mathematics were recognized by Arbuthnot, whom Markley quotes at length:

> Arithmetick is not only the great Instrument of private Commerce, but by it are (or ought to be) kept the publick Accounts of a Nation: . . . the number, fructification, of its people, increase of Stock, improvement of Lands and Manufacturers, Balance of Trade, Publick Revenues, Coynage, Military power by Sea and Land . . . what is it, the Government could not perform in this way, who have the command of all publick Records.

Markley deduces that "this ideologicalization of mathematics means that it becomes an expression of the emergence of the fiscal military state, a set of technologies of calculation that make the individual subservient to the command of specialized forms of knowledge" (ibid., p. 209). Although he is not speaking directly of the ideological function of modern forms of intelligence, particularly their role in advancing economic Darwinism, technocratic rationality, nation state stability, and market capitalism, Markley's point captures precisely how intelligence theories, examinations, and other practices have operated ideologically to "make the individual subservient to the command of specialized forms of knowledge." In this way, the mathematicalization of intelligence in the late nineteenth and twentieth centuries promotes another subjective technology, another state apparatus tool in which individuals are further defined as subjects. As I have suggested earlier, modern ideas and practices of intelligence have, in part, operated as social engineering technologies of calculation and conformance, producing special kinds of "knowledge" that enter the public sphere for consumption.

Markley investigates the ideologicalization of mathematics by surveying Brian Rotman's argument that:

> Capitalism and mathematics are intimately related: mathematics functions as the grammar of techno-scientific discourse which every form of capitalism has relied upon and initiated. So it would be feasible to read the widespread acceptance of mathematical platonism in terms of the effects of this intimacy, to relate the exchange of meaning within mathematical languages to the exchange of commodities, to see in the notion of a "timeless, eternal, unchangeable" object the presence of a pure fetished meaning.

According to Rotman, there is a

paradoxical double function of mathematics as both an ideal standard and a fetishized object of exchange. The ideality of mathematics . . . rests on the privileging of pure mathematics as a general equivalent and on its status as a commodity: mathematical knowledge becomes part of an exchange economy, but this knowledge must present itself as emptied of any inherent value, that is, as a fetish which can be consumed, trade, sold and commodified in what Gioux calls the "play of substitutions that defines qualitative values." (Ibid., p. 211)

Markley agrees. There is an

intimate relationship between mathematics and capitalism; this relationship is predicated on the construction of value in and through a mathematical knowledge that is both instrumental and transhistorical, that functions as a "true" and self-evident representation of theological values that are displaced into operations of the market itself. Capitalism . . . fetishizes mathematics as the means to project theological assumptions (invisible hands, for example) into a "practical" realm of exchange. (Ibid.)

Many modern sources quoted so far in this study have defined themselves as "invisible hands," their efforts being intended to measure or improve the "low" intelligence of colonial subjects or "inferior" races and ethnicities.

Mathematics is ideological because it is situated in various domains of power:

its complex series of symbolic and material exchanges involves both the practical acquisition of power and the continual fetishizing of that power as objective knowledge, as a privileged access to "reality" . . . the fetishizing of mathematics produces a dialectical essentialism: mathematics becomes an idealized location of truth and a reflexive demonstration of the reality of the world it represents and constructs. (Ibid., pp. 212–13)

Markley quotes Rotman's most intriguing critique of both mathematics and any science using it to produce truth: "what present-day mathematicians think they are doing – using mathematical language as a transparent medium for describing a world of pre-semiotic reality – is semiotically alienated from what they are . . . doing – namely, creating that reality through the very language which claims to describe it." Markley concludes by stating that

the dissemination of scientific and mathematical knowledge in the early eighteenth century may be seen . . . as part of a complex process of fetishizing individuality; it allows for both the totalizing claims of Arbuthnot's vision of social management and the means for the individual, as the possessor as well as the object of scientific knowledge, to resist those claims by accumulating his or her stock of symbolic capital. (Ibid.)

It is striking how these observations help to reveal the *other* side of intelligence, illuminating ideological aspects of intelligence normally obscured by its epistemological boundaries. These borders of technocratic rationality have obscured insight into how the modern mathematicization of intelligence has:

1 Supported the historical pattern of evaluating individual intelligence for largely economic reasons begun with the Renaissance capitalization and Enlightenment socialization of knowledge.
2 Converted intelligence into a late modern and postmodern commodity.
3 Been responsible for modern intelligence becoming a fetished meaning associated with what makes an individual presumably unique.
4 Aided the conversion of intelligence into an abstract value scalable in order to be consumed, traded, sold and commodified.
5 Helped to construct a uniquely modern notion of "social management" in which the "individual, as the possessor as well as the object of scientific knowledge," can seemingly "resist those claims by accumulating his or her stock of symbolic capital."

In essence, the theories and practices of modern intelligence operate in both worlds, functioning as a "social management tool" and as the much touted means by which individuals can escape such management because of their higher or lower intelligence. As we shall shortly see, intelligence in postmodern culture has finally become non-referential symbolic capital, the measurement of intelligence that of abstract calculations. Paul Benoît has observed that "calculation is the essential foundation not only of the sciences but also of technology and economic activity" (quoted in Serres, 1995, p. 246). As we shall see, the most dominant notions of contemporary pop culture intelligence, those that promote the vision of genius entrepreneurs and their *smart* products, use calculations to market the virtue of calculation in these very calculating "bottom line" times.

The use of mathematics in the social sciences and its connection with theories of intelligence and commerce owes some of its historical legacy to how seventeenth-century mathematicians quantified and classified probability. This interest delivered game theory probability into the world of commerce because of perceived connections between games of chance and economic trends derived from earlier merchants who likened the dynamics of games to the world of commercial activities. This association has had a long history and is still popular today. How many games of *Monopoly* have been sold, a game with ideological content?

Investment redistribution is a prime example of correspondences between games and markets, as well as profit share forecasting and risk trading. In all of these, economic risk is comparable to the same kinds of risks appearing in games: in both venues outcomes are determined by unplanned or random events. This new mathematical interest may also have helped to form representations and institutionalizations of individualism, given the fact that commercial forecasting produced a person who had to plan, who amassed information in order to lessen the vagaries of random events. Evidence of this developing mathematical–commercial–individual paradigm comes with the work of Christian Huygens and Niklaus Bernoulli in numerical value expectation and the applications of calculus probability to practical problems.

Other practical applications of mathematics to probability studies and capitalism came with the invention of mechanized industries. This new paradigm of production for the first time authored an equating of those who built engines of production with ingenuity. From the earliest seconds of the Industrial Revolution to our latest Information or Digital Age inventions, "captains" of industry have always been treated as geniuses, the correlation between wealth and intelligence obvious. Increased mechanization and new kinds of mechanical power – those evident in windmills, driving wheels, manufacturing pumps and presses, driving wheels, geared pulleys wheels, cams, and ratchets, and transportation and production systems (from rudders to production control technologies) – had the effect of regulating life in terms of mechanical processes. Arguably this new way of living made it fairly easy for the creation, evaluation, assessment, and implementations of intelligence testing to be created, deployed, and evaluated in a highly mechanistic fashion. Reading test examiner "how to" manuals shows how truly regulated and mechanistic the mass administration of tests was.

These practical applications of mathematics stand in sharp contrast to both its mythic and semiotic nature, the latter the basis for Brian Rotman's critique of mathematics and its scientific applications, his work having a direct application to how mathematics works ideologically as a tool in modern intelligence studies, practices, and capitalistic uses. His "Towards a Semiotics of Mathematics" (1988) begins with the poststructural question of "what is the nature of mathematical language" (p. 1) and concludes that

> what is salient about mathematical assertions is not their supposed truth about some world that precedes them, but the inconceivability of persuasively creating a world in which they are denied. Thus instead of a picture of logic as a form of truth-preserving inference, a semiotics of mathematics would see it as an inconceivability-preserving mode of persuasion – with no mention of "truth" anywhere. (Ibid., p. 34)

In his semiotic analysis of mathematical signs Rotman asserts that mathematical

> signs seem to be constructed . . . so as to sever their signifieds, what they are supposed to mean, from the real time and space within which their material signifiers occur; and the question of secondary, of whether mathematics is "about" anything, whether its signs have referents, whether they are signs *of* something outside themselves, is precisely what one would expect a semiotics of mathematics to be in the business of discussing. (Ibid., p. 4)

Rotman notes that those who interrogate the foundations of mathematics agree that whatever mathematics is it can be understood in formalist, intuitionalist, or platonic terms. While intuitionists "deny that signifiers . . . play any constitutive role," that "mathematics is a species of purely mental construction," and Platonists believe that it can "discover and validate objective or logical truths," formalists think that

> mathematics is a species of game, a determinate play of written marks that are transformed according to explicit unambiguous formal rules. Such marks are held to be without intention, mere physical inscriptions from which any attempt to signify, to mean, is absent . . . formalism . . . reduces mathematical signs to material signifiers which are . . . without signifieds. (Ibid., pp. 4–5)

What bearing do these different notions of mathematics and Rotman's conclusion have on the history of ideas about intelligence, particularly more contemporary ones? And, more importantly, why hasn't the discipline taken into serious consideration the implication of these ideas, given how they undermine the validity of any theory or practice of intelligence based on mathematics, statistics, and their *a priori* rationality? I ask these questions only to identify the use of mathematics as an ideological mechanism in the construction of intelligence.

First, mathematics is profoundly problematic on all counts. Choices lead nowhere. His study leads us inevitability to the question of fundamental referentiality. If mathematics severs all relations to its signifieds, if its signs represent nothing outside themselves, if it is only a mental construct, or if its "marks" have no inherent intentionality, no capacity to mean anything, then what does its claim to the discovery of "objective or logical truths" mean? How can mathematics make that claim, how can it know when it has achieved such discovery, and how does it know if its discoveries are truly "objective" if on all counts its representational dynamics have no internal or external reference? These questions are particularly significant when aimed at the mathematics implicit in many theories and practices of modern intelligence.

I should like to argue that it is precisely this lack of mathematical referentiality that functions ideologically in most mathematically dependent models of intelligence. Throughout this study I have argued that the word "intelligence" is an open-ended trope, a sign with an almost unlimited potential for producing politically functional signifieds. If taken from this position and placed in Rotman's argument, my thesis is further validated by another language, not tropic, as in a metaphor, but literally figurative: *signs that calculate or equate*. In these two worlds of significance, intelligence does not have to mean anything, its play or range of continuous undecidability an ideological godsend, invariant at the level of sign, yet able to be shaped into any needed meaning. Hence an IQ of 81 or 67 or 135 functions consistently with all three fundamentals of mathematics. Being produced by formalistic, intuitional, and platonic models of mathematics, these scores gain the authority that comes with formal rules, cognitive universals, and objective truth, although, in the problematics discussed above, they have no referentiality to the phenomenal world. Like all poststructural signs, IQ scores are signifiers with inherently direct signifieds, the gap being the source of power construction and manipulation. In this light, Rotman's conclusion makes perfect sense. To paraphrase and slightly alter his point, those in the business of mathematicizing intelligence believe in the validity of what they do

> because they are persuaded to believe; so that what is salient about [the mathematical basis of modern intelligence] is not their supposed truth about some world that precedes them, but the inconceivability of persuasively creating a world in which they are denied. Thus, instead of a picture of logic as a form of truth-preserving inference, a semiotics of [how mathematical signs behave ideologically in intelligence theory/practices] would see it as an inconceivably-preserving mode of persuasion – with no mention of "truth" anywhere. (Ibid., p. 34)

In essence, what does the mathematical world of intelligence refer to? Its history is far more about rhetorical designs – making us all believe such a thing can be measured – than about proving that its mathematics possess the objectivity it claims.

The following nullify the validity of mathematical models used to validate intelligence theory and practice. Research shows that little effort has been made in the intelligence communities to deal seriously with their implications. There are seven formal points:

1   Contradiction-free theorems do not insure absolute proof of consistency.
2   Confidence in any formal mathematical system is based on incomplete inductions.

3 Formal systems are not complete enough to encompass all of mathematics.
4 Naive set theory (Cantor or Frege) has not been addressed by the intelligence community.
5 Mathematical consistency cannot be rigorously proven within any formal system whose consistency is inherently unproven and dubious.
6 Mathematical consistency is a consequence of the presumed truth of its axioms. Defining a set of axioms as true is no guarantee of a formal proof of their consistency.
7 Mathematics creates its productions of reality, asserting its claims of objective truth by means of the very language which claims to describe truth.

Mapping the history of mathematics in Western culture reveals a good deal of the evolution of Western thought, from Platonic and Pythagorean worlds of thought to the more rational, empirical, and practical world of modern mathematical applications. The itinerary from instrumentality to realism is complicated given its ideological implications. In transitions from hypothetical theories and mathematical calculations to analyses of the laws behind the real phenomenal world we recognize how in modern history the validity of calculations proves theory validity. This pattern is precisely where the modern and postmodern world of intelligence currently resides; various versions prove the existence of intelligence rather than the inverse or, for that matter, any other method of understanding the phenomenon. The complexity of this precondition reveals just how truly significant is its ideological power.

Contemporary Intelligence and the New Sciences

Here on earth, once it was formed, systems of increasing complexity have risen as a consequence of the physical evolution of the planet, biological evolution and human cultural evolution. The process has gone so far that we human beings are now confused with immensely complex ecological, political, economic, and social problems. When we attempt to tackle such difficult problems, we naturally tend to break them up into more manageable pieces. That is a useful practice, but it has serious limitations. When dealing with any non-linear system, especially a complex one, you can't just think in terms of parts or aspects and just add things up and say that the behavior of this and the behavior of that, added together, makes the whole thing. With a complex non-linear system you have to break it up into pieces and then study each aspect, and then study the very strong interaction between them all. (Murray Gell-Mann, 1995)

Murray Gell-Mann's work on linear and non-linear systems raises a question about the validity of traditional ways of doing science. This concern is particularly appropriate for the largely traditional scientific methods and theories informing the majority of work done in intelligence studies. In fact, one of the truly major weaknesses of modern theories of intelligence is a failure to adequately respond to or incorporate new critiques and methods of science. This section traces those critiques that have a significant bearing.

There are four "new" sciences that challenge some of the premises underlying both traditional and more contemporary theories of intelligence: complexity theory, quantum mechanics, chaos theory, and catastrophe theory. I should like to outline them to show how they impact on our common understanding of intelligence.

Complexity theory

The first premise of complexity theory is that dynamic systems exhibit inexplicable behaviors whose significance cannot be determined by the tools and methods of traditional scientific analysis. These behaviors occur in living systems as well as in more abstract ones like the stock market, earthquake predictions, tsunamis, or chess games. Human consciousness and thought processes can be treated as a complex neurological system. Part of exploring it means having to identifying its structure and behaviors. It would be easy if the brain was a clock or a bee hive, both having complex structures but highly repeatable and predictable behaviors. The brain, however, is both behaviorally and structurally complex, a complexity compounded by the fact that its meanings depend on both its codes (information and transmission) and its contexts. In essence one cannot study human thought without being aware of how language and meaning are bound up with the whole process of communication (part of the system). Hence the complexity of the brain cannot be treated in isolation, as if it were a mere element of the system. System complexity is inherent simultaneously in the system, in the properties of the system, and its relations with other systems.

A second consideration suggests that the informality of the word "complex" tends to overshadow the need for a true science of complexity that would transpose informality into a determinate syntax and symbolic vocabulary. In essence a true science of complexity would be "fuzzy" free.

Complexity theorists have identified the major components of this new science. First, it would require a means of exacting determinate predictability. Simple systems have a higher degree of predictability for obvious reasons, whereas more complex ones have more complicated predictability challenges.

The second component, connectedness, is a recognition that while simple systems have small numbers of interactive parts, more complex versions may have indeterminate numbers of variable connective relations, some with near infinite feedback loop transactions. The third element stresses how the control of complex systems is scalable, with simpler systems have a more easily identified, concentrated source of order and more complex versions defying the notion of a single control authority, with control a diffusive property. The more multiple and decentralized the authority, the more complex the system, with behavioral dynamics corresponding in complexity to the number of and relationships among controlling units. A dictatorship, for example, can be contrasted with the Internet, representing significant differences in the architecture and function of authority. Theorists use the term decomposability, the fourth component, to refer to the frequency, strength, and duration of component interactions. The more complex the system the less chance there is that components can be decomposed into fragmented subsystems without experiencing an irretrievable insufficiency of the very data that are the system.

Given this overview of complexity, I would like to quote from some contemporary intelligence theorists and their ideas of complexity:

> Some of the most well-known scholars in the study of intelligence are forecasting a change in how intelligence will be understood in the future. The transition will be marked by a movement away from unitary to multiple kinds of intelligence and "from static conceptions of intelligence toward dynamic ones," especially in the areas of "intellectual development . . . learning potential . . . and interactions between genetic and environmental components of intelligence." (Sternberg et al., 2003, pp. 18–20)

If we contrast my brief account of complexity with this quote, then what kind of complexity is being forecasted by this apparent change? The answer to this question is unavailable given the absence of research into how complexity theory affects modern theories of intelligence. In fact, the irony is that those efforts that include complexity theory in their work are essentially no different than most traditional and contemporary research. Theories in the history of intelligence have consistently envisioned, treated, or measured intelligence in terms of a simple system. Consequently, efforts by contemporary theorists to treat intelligence as a complex system represent a major contradiction, since those efforts are guided by a simple systems model. Second, complexity theory shows how a simple system approach to intelligence proves inadequate given the dominance of linear dynamic models. Proof that most theories are based on a simple system model is evident in the following considerations:

1   Its historical assessments presume that intelligence is predictable.
2   Most notions of intelligence assume that intelligence has a small number of elements, with few connections to other elements affecting its unpredictability.
3   A concentrated source controls simple systems, which in the case of intelligence theories is represented by rationality, the mechanism guiding the construction of intelligence theories and used as its primary assessment criterion (as opposed to multiple decentralized authority elements in complex systems).
4   Most theories of intelligence are based on a very limited set of interactions among very limited numbers of components, whereas complex processes have multiple interactions and unlimited components.

These ideas suggest that the majority of intelligence theories will have a difficult time becoming complex system theories, and that the history of intelligence clearly demonstrates that intelligence has uniformly been conceptualized as a simple system. Most importantly, research into brain neurophysiology and contemporary cognitive studies indicates that if intelligence is part of how the brain works, then no simple system theory of intelligence can be accurate in accounting for complexity. Despite its adolescence, complexity theory not only provides a better means for understanding the complexities involved in those behaviors we commonly define as intelligence, but also reveals, in the most serious of ways, the inadequacy of traditional and contemporary simple systems constructions of intelligence.

The uncertainty principle and the problem of measurement

Modern physics, particularly theories related to quantum mechanics, has not been given adequate consideration by intelligence theorists. The cost of this oversight is that there is a failure to answer some significant challenges that quantum theory poses for traditional theories of intelligence. In fact, quantum theory undermines the entire set of assumptions upon which most theories of intelligence, those of individualism, the possibility of rationalism, and the accuracy of objective measurement, rest. The failure to answer these challenges simply undermines the validity of many theories of intelligence. I would like to briefly explore how the "new science" does that.

In 1927, Werner Heisenberg advanced the notion of the uncertainty or indeterminacy principle, which simply states that an object's velocity and position can never both be measured exactly at the same moment, either in practice or in theory. Moreover, the idea of an exact position or number to represent something, together with its exact velocity, has essentially no corresponding meaning to the natural object or phenomenon being measured. The impact of this idea on the notion that intelligence is an accurately measurable natural phenomenon is obvious. The significance of the uncertainty principle is rarely brought to consciousness in the daily life of intelligence, in habitual and obligatory clinical practices and tests whose habitual applications simply prevent awareness that such a principle exists. Arguably, a sampling of a thousand random clinicians of intelligence would yield a very low percentage of awareness of the import of Heisenberg's theory on the value and validity of their work.

Measuring a person's intelligence presumes that what is being measured – the person's abilities at that time and his or her "intelligence" – is constant, and that the actual measuring tools and methods are equally constant. And while it might be relatively easy to measure the velocity and position of the space shuttle, doing the same for an individual's performance on an intelligence test is problematic given the complexity, minuteness, and abstract observations involved in the test environment. This relation of size complexity to uncertainty in physics is engendered in the rule that the product of the uncertainties relative to velocity and position is equal to or greater than a minute physical quantity. And with a little stretch, we can speculate that any effort to measure anything potentially unstable, whether an electron or any of thousands of complex variables operative during any assessment of intelligence, can only result in the measurement of something whose state is unpredictable. If this is true, then measurements based on the assumption of correlations between objects and their behavior have no testable validity. Heisenberg's theory of the quantum mechanical world applies to any measuring act, even human intelligence. To ask a Popper-motivated question: how can I know that the measurement of my performance on an intelligence test was valid, given the quantum premise that whenever any measurement is made, some aspect of the system doing the measurement has been disturbed?

The concept of measurement in a more general way has become problematic with the advent of quantum mechanics. Whether we rehearse that problematic as it was played out in the Schrödinger's cat paradox or the Einstein–Bohr debates, the very nature of measurement has undergone significant analysis in the twentieth and twenty-first centuries. And whether the problem concerns the postulate of collapse or dynamic principle inconsistencies, it nevertheless transcends the world of physics and applies to philosophical traditions supplying blood to the heart of most theories and practices of intelligence, namely Cartesian and Lockean notions of observation as the creation of inner reflections, on the one hand, and more modern post-Kantian views of observation as a quasi-externalized physiological process. In either case, any assertion of the validity of intelligence assessment is subject to the quantum critique that either of these traditions of observation is invalid. When Heisenberg argues that speculations ignoring the concrete to get to the "real" truth are problematic or that the law of singular causality is invalid, he indirectly challenges the very foundations of modern theories of intelligence that assume that the real truth of human identity is constant, that it can be measured and is knowable in terms of various kinds of causality, e.g. that those with "low" intelligence are more likely to be criminals and come from minority populations. And while modern physics has moved into a new science, into describing connections between various perceptions and how they can be true, the majority of intelligence studies are wrestling with ghosts, busy with the old business of still constructing theories to prove that singular or multiple forms of intelligence exist as something "real" and "true." Perhaps some of the epistemological metareflectivity of the new science may drift over into the study of intelligence, and – the issue of science aside – first reveal its highly ideological history before being able to transcend it.

Chaos and catastrophe theories

One could argue that of all the new sciences chaos theory might prove most valuable to intelligence research. The reason is that chaos theory alone argues that underlying all the apparent disorder or random data emitted by a given system there is nonetheless a fundamental order. Chaos theory has produced a number of vogue terms like the butterfly effect, sensitive dependence, self-similar, and fractals. The theory stresses that an apparently insignificant or minute change at the point of initiation can drastically affect the long-term dynamic of a given system. This idea certainly impacts the validity of an intelligence evaluation, with any variable, noise (system feedback), or unperceived inaccuracy inherent in the instrument affecting the outcome. However, in most cases, what appears as random behavior can be graphed to reveal laws of chaotic dynamics: static versus periodic behaviors. Variables never change or the system manifests an indefinite self-looping; hence Lorenz's famous equation that definite order is validated by a continuous spiral. The Lorenz attractor suggests that order is never ultimately repeatable, even if it appears so periodically. There has been little research into how the basic tenets of chaos theory and fractal structures might offer new ways of understanding what intelligence is or isn't, or whether it behaves as a system – internally within the brain or externally as a variable in how culture operates.

In the 1960s, Rene Thom formulated catastrophe theory, which, like chaos theory, attempts to study, classify, and predict phenomena dynamics characterized by seemingly abrupt behavior shifts stemming from relatively small changes. Thom suggests that discrete catastrophes are bifurcations of different equilibria elements, or fixed point attractors. Classifications of different catastrophes are based on the number of varied control agents being emitted. Presently, the theory has been applied to such different phenomena as the stability of ships at sea and fight-or-flight behaviors expressed by animals or prison rioters.

If they can be applied to such real-world systems as the branching of trees, the Pacific Rim economy, blood vessels, or predictive mapping of social violence, then what prevents the application of chaos and catastrophe theories to intelligence in a comprehensive manner, treating intelligence as a complex or chaotic system rather than simply as a "thing," as it has since the fifteenth century? One could certainly assume that the self-similarity dynamics of chaos systems, for instance, might attract psychometricians looking for patterns in evaluation data or the significance of correlations between economic class and levels of intelligence. Would a fractal structuring of these assumed correlations prove anything? Moreover, if many modern sciences have incorporated these new sciences in their theorizing and experimentation, as physics and biology have done in the study of subatomic and ecological microsystem dynamics, then those interested in the nature of human intelligence might be served, in one way or other, by doing something similar. The disciplinary world of modern intelligence studies has prevented us from seeing how these new sciences might impact such research, while, at the same time, they have been responsible for overlooking ideological flux and patterns in the ideational history of intelligence. There is nothing preventing us from treating ideological dynamics in terms of these two new sciences.

Conclusion

The future of intelligence studies proves as interesting as its past, a largely trans-
formative future given that intelligence is subject to political, ideological, technological, and biological forces, the four partners in the evolution of human
consciousness and culture.

The future of intelligence will combine the past and the yet uninvented. Evidence for this appears in recent efforts at a neo-techno-transcendentalization of
intelligence, focused less on the individual and traditional supernatural forces
(e.g. Zeus or God) than on a mix of the technological, the collective, and a new
age global consciousness or *collective intelligence*. The idea is based on the notion
that organic life and technology forge a unified, absolute, and integrated intelligence. H. G. Wells's idea of the "world brain" and Pierre Teilhard de Chardin's
"noosphere" come to mind. In *Collective Intelligence* (1994) Pierre Levy says that
this new smart is an information economy transformed into a social economy
driven by the *sharing* of significant knowledge. This sharing creates a virtual community. Others, like Howard Rheingold (2002), Robert David Steele (2002), and
Howard Bloom (2000), offer similar ideas like "public intelligence," "intelligence
minutemen," and "national intelligence" to envision a new society ordered by
intelligent people parlaying information in a goal to globalize democracy.

Collective intelligence holds the promise of destroying the secrecy of information that traditionally has served "selfish" interests. It evolves a more liberated
public, their freedom no longer dependent on those who use their wealth-power
to control intelligence. While Rheingold argues that "smart mobs" use information and communication technologies to increase human cooperation, Bloom
believes that humans are part of a larger organic whole, rather than being robots
engaged in "selfish gene" competitions. The evolutionary biologist argues that
sociality originated when the universe came into being. His book asks us to
explore how perceptual, evolutionary, emotional, and biological mechanisms
have created a meta-human, social learning machine. Collective intelligence has

full organic membership, a collective mind representing all species. Bloom posits the idea that modern connectivity technologies are correlatives of what makes humans biologically unique, our evolutionary history proof that the worldwide web was already programmed in the moment organic life appeared on the planet. Here muscle fibers become ethernet wire.

Collective intelligence has generated some intriguing, less mainstream theories, those guiding the Green Party, the Global Greens, and anti-globalists, and those of Ted Szuba. The Polish mathematician argues in *Computational Collective Intelligence* (2001) that informational structures and human beings can be relationally modeled in terms of complex "information molecules." These units resemble abstract forms of mathematical logic. And finally there are more radical intelligence collectivists like those surveyed in Mark Dery's *Escape Velocity* (1996) and those whose real life mass suicides took place in San Diego in 1997. The 39 followers of the Heaven's Gate "religion" believed in a bricolage, microchip spiritualism of theosophical, Christian, extra-terrestrial, and collective intelligence ideas. Their suicide was a rendezvous absorption into the oneness of a techno-alien Intelligence.

The technological future of intelligence also brings into focus the cultural significance of cyborgs, androids, and artificial or virtual intelligence. Alien machine intelligences are favorite characters in postmodern science fiction films and cyberpunk novels, giving cultural studies critics a good deal to talk about. Names like Philip K. Dick, Donna Haraway, K. W. Jeter, Björk (Cunningham's video for "All Is Full of Love"), *Borg*, Katherine Hayles, Rodney Brooks, and Ray Kurtzweil populate this community. George Dyson (1998) also promotes a future vision of intelligence, arguing that it is inherently a collective entity, its goal to amass neurons in order to produce a global collective intelligence, an objective human interconnectivity that technologies are proving to be true. In essence, no human tool is a mistake: their evolution is a map of human destiny. Intelligence works to objectify itself as a collective because "evolution is an intelligent process and intelligence an evolutionary process. . . . Technology, hailed as the means of bringing nature under control of our intelligence, is enabling nature to exercise intelligence over us" (Dyson, 1998, p. 228). The future is a techno-wilderness:

> We have mapped, tamed, and dismembered the physical wilderness of our earth. But, at the same time, we have created a digital wilderness whose evolution may embody a collective wisdom greater than our own. No digital universe can ever be completely mapped. We have traded one jungle for another, and in this direction lies not fear but hope. For our destiny and our sanity as human beings depend on our ability to serve a nature whose intelligence we can glimpse all around us, but never quite comprehend. (Ibid., p. 228)

The future of intelligence, like its past, seems unable to escape the ideological, even though the American Psychological Association (1996, p. 40) suggests that such a future

> does not need politicized assertions and recriminations: it needs self-restraint, reflection, and a great deal more research. The questions that remain are socially as well as scientifically important. There is no reason to think them unanswerable, but finding the answers will require a shared and sustained effort as well as a commitment of substantial scientific resources. Just a commitment is what we strongly recommend.

Part of that commitment means asking new questions and creating a new agenda significantly different from those suggested above: what kind of science is the science of intelligence; does it have an ideological basis that ultimately affects its scientific assumptions; what would a science that moves intelligence studies from evaluation and classification to proactiveness look like; and has its history brought intelligence to a new phase, the creation of a new discipline closer to a phenomenological interest in how knowledge gets produced and valued?

And perhaps as something guilty of historically robbing significant members of a population of their potential, intelligence might find a substitute in the word *interest*. What kind of future might it be if, rather than being *tested*, children, workers, and anyone needing to be *invested in* were given the opportunity to use whatever tools were needed to fulfill their destinies? If our Enlightenment legacy is correct – that intelligence alone defines the human as a unique species – then perhaps developing a *humane* science of knowledge production in our social, legal, economic, and educational institutions might better validate efforts to stabilize such a historically slippery and ideologically prone metaphor.

Bibliography

Adams, R. (1994) *Leibniz: Determinist, Theist, Idealist*. Oxford: Oxford University Press.

Adas, M. (1989) *Machines as the Measure of Men: Science, Technology, and Ideologies of Western Dominance*. Ithaca, NY: Cornell University Press.

Adas, M. (1991) Scientific standards and colonial education in British India and French Senegal. In T. Meade and M. Walker (eds), *Science, Medicine, and Cultural Imperialism*. New York: St Martins Press.

Agassiz, E. C. (1887) *Louis Agassiz: His Life and Correspondence*, two volumes. Boston: Houghton Mifflin.

Agazzi, E., Gruender, D. and Hintikka, J. (eds) (1981) *Probabilistic Thinking, Thermodynamics and the Interaction of the History and Philosophy of Science*. London: D. Reidel.

Alembert, J. L. R. (1765) *Encyclopédie ou dictionnaire raisonné des sciences, des arts et des metiers, par une société de gens de lettres*. Neuchâtel: Faulche et Cie.

Alexander, H. (ed.) (1956) *The Leibniz–Clarke Correspondence*. New York: Philosophical Library.

Althusser, L. (2001) *Lenin and Philosophy and Other Essays* (trans. B. Brewster). New York: Monthly Review Press.

American Psychological Association (1996) *Task Force Report on Intelligence*. Washington, DC: American Psychological Association.

American Psychological Association Task Force on Intelligence (2003) *Human Intelligence: Historical Influences, Current Controversies, Teaching Resources* (ed. J. A. Plucker) (www.indiana.edu/~intell).

Anstey, P. (2000) *The Philosophy of Robert Boyle*. Routledge, London.

Aristotle (1915) *Works of Aristotle* (trans. W. D. Ross). Oxford: Oxford University Press.

Aristotle (1981) *Aristotle's On the Soul (De Anima)* (trans. H. Apostle). Grinnell, IA: Peripatetic Press.

Aristotle (1986) *Aristotle: Selected Works* (trans. H. Apostle and L. Gerson). Grinnell, IA: Peripatetic Press.

Aristotle (1995) *Aristotle: Selections* (trans. T. Irwin and G. Fine). Cambridge, MA: Hackett.

Armstrong, D. (1983) *Political Anatomy of the Body: Medical Knowledge in Britain in the Twentieth Century*. Cambridge: Cambridge University Press.

Ashton, T. S. (1965) *An Economic History of England: The Eighteenth Century*. New York: Barnes and Noble.

Bacon, F. (1861) *The Works of Francis Bacon, Baron of Verulam, Viscount St Albans, and Lord High Chancellor of England*, 15 volumes. Boston: Brown and Taggard.

Bacon, F. (1960) *The New Organum and Related Writings* (ed. F. Anderson). Indianapolis: Bobbs-Merrill.

Bailey, C. (1964) *The Greek Atomists and Epicurus*. New York: Russell and Russell.

Baker, K. M. (1975) *Condorcet: From Natural Philosophy to Social Mathematics*. Chicago: University of Chicago Press.

Baker, K. M. (ed.) (1976) *Condorcet: Selected Writings*. Indianapolis: Bobbs-Merrill.

Barlow, N. (ed.) (1958) *The Autobiography of Charles Darwin*. London: Collins.

Barnes, J. (1993) *The Presocratic Philosophers*. New York: Routledge and Kegan Paul.

Barthes, R. (1976) *Mythologies* (trans. A. Lavers). New York: Hill and Wang.

Baudrillard, J. (1994) *Simulacra and Simulation*. Ann Arbor: University of Michigan Press.

Baugh, A. (ed.) (1967) *A Literary History of England*. New York: Appleton-Century-Crofts.

Beare, J. (1906) *Greek Theories of Elementary Cognition: From Alcmaeon to Aristotle*. Oxford: Clarendon Press.

Benton, B. (1987) *Ellis Island: A Pictorial History*. New York: Facts on File.

Bergin, T. and Fisch, M. (eds) (1968) *The New Science of Giambattista Vico*. Ithaca, NY: Cornell University Press.

Berkeley, G. (1710) *The Principles of Human Knowledge*. Oxford: Oxford University Press (1996).

Berry, J. W. (1974) Radical cultural relativism and the concept of intelligence. In J. W. Berry and P. R. Dasen (eds), *Culture and Cognition: Readings in Cross-cultural Psychology*. London: Methuen.

Berry, J. W. (1992) *Cross-cultural Psychology: Research and Applications*. New York: Cambridge University Press.

Bevington, D. (ed.) (1998) *The Complete Works of Shakespeare*. Chicago: Longman.

Binet, A. (1911) *Method of Measuring the Development of the Intelligence of Young Children*. Baltimore: Williams and Wilkins.

Binet, A. and Simon, T. (1916) *The Development of Intelligence in Children*. Baltimore: Williams and Wilkins.

Bloch, M. (1977) *Land and Work in Medieval Europe*. London: Routledge.

Bloom, H. (2000) *Global Brain*. New York: Wiley.

Boas, M. (1966) *The Scientific Renaissance 1450–1630*. New York: Harper Torchbooks.

Bond, D. F. (1965) *The Spectator*. Oxford: Clarendon Press.

Bonner, R. and Rimer, S. (2000) Executing the mentally retarded even as laws begin to shift. *New York Times*, August 7.

Boody, B. M. (1919) *A Psychological Study of Immigrant Children at Ellis Island*. New York: Arno Press.

Bos, H., Palm, L., Sneiders, H. and Visser, E. (eds) (1989) *New Trends in the History of Science*. Amsterdam: Rodopi.

Bibliography

Bourdieu, P. (1979) *Outlines of a Theory of Practice.* Cambridge: Cambridge University Press.

Bouwsma, W. (2000) *The Waning of the Renaissance, 1550–1640.* New Haven, CT: Yale University Press.

Boyle, M. and O'Rourke (1998) *Sense of Touch.* Boston: Brill.

Braudel, F. (1982) *Civilization and Capitalism, 15th–18th Centuries* (trans. S. Reynolds). New York: Harper & Row.

Braverman, H. (1974) *Labor and Monopoly Capital: The Degradation of Work in the Twentieth Century.* New York: Monthly Review Press.

Brigham, C. C. (1923) *A Study of American Intelligence.* Princeton, NJ: Princeton University Press.

Broca, P. (n.d.) Sur le capacité des crânes parisiens des diverse époques. *Bulletin Société d'Anthropologies,* 3.

Browne-Miller, A. (1995) *Intelligence Policy: Its Impact on Social Admissions and Other Social Policies.* New York: Plenum Press.

Brucker, G. (1966) *Renaissance Florence.* New York: Putnam.

Buffon, G. and Le Clerc, L. (1862) *A Natural History, General and Particular, Containing the History and Theory of the Earth, a General History of Man, the Brute Creation, Vegetables, Minerals, & DC, & C* (trans. W. Smellie). London: T. Kelly.

Burckhardt, J. (1990) *The Civilization of the Renaissance in Italy* (trans. S. Middlemore). New York: Penguin.

Burke, P. (1989) *The Italian Renaissance: Culture and Society in Italy.* Princeton, NJ: Princeton University Press.

Burt, C. (1918) Individual psychology and social work. *Charity Organisation Review,* 253.

Burt, C. (1921) *Mental and Scholastic Tests.* London: P. S. King and Son.

Burt, C. (1975) *The Gifted Child.* London: Butler.

Burton, R. (1989) *The Anatomy of Melancholy.* New York: Oxford University Press.

Butler, J. (1993) *Bodies that Matter: On the Discursive Limits of "Sex."* New York: Routledge.

Calvin, J. (1963) *Institution de la Religion Chrestienne.* Paris: Libraire Philosophique.

Calvin, J. (1978) *The Cambridge Economic History of Europe.* Cambridge: Cambridge University Press.

Cameron, E. (1991) *The European Reformation.* Oxford: Clarendon Press.

Cardano, G. (1968) *De Vita Propria (The Book of My Life).* New York: E. P. Dutton.

Cassirer, E., Kristeller, P. and Randall, J. (1948) *The Renaissance Philosophy of Man.* Chicago: University of Chicago Press.

Cassirer, E., Kristeller, P. and Randall, J. (1951) *Philosophy of the Enlightenment.* Princeton, NJ: Princeton University Press.

Ceci, S. J. (1996) *On Intelligence: A Bioecological Treatise on Intellectual Development.* Cambridge, MA: Harvard University Press.

Ceci, S. J., Sternberg, R. J. and Grigorenko, E. L. (eds) (1997) *Intelligence, Heredity, and Environment.* New York: Cambridge University Press.

Cervantes, M. de (1992) *The Ingenious Gentleman Don Quixote de la Mancha* (trans. C. Jarvis). Oxford: Oxford University Press.

Chambliss, J. J. (1971) *Enlightenment and Social Progress: Education in the Nineteenth Century*. Minneapolis: Burgess Publishing Company.

Chase, A. (1977) *The Legacy of Malthus*. New York: Knopf.

Cipolla, C. (1967) *Clocks and Culture, 1300–1700*. London: Collins.

Clark, G. and Dear, M. (1984) *State Apparatus: Structures and Language of Legitimacy*. Boston: Allen & Unwin.

Clavelin, M. (ed.) (1968) *The Natural Philosophy of Galileo: Essays on the Origins and Formation of Classical Mechanics*. Cambridge, MA: MIT Press.

Cleve, F. (1949) *The Philosophy of Anaxagoras*. New York: Kings Crown Press.

Clough, C. H. (1976) *Cultural Aspects of the Italian Renaissance*. New York: Columbia University Press.

Cohen, B. I. (1978) *Isaac Newton's Papers and Letters on Natural Philosophy*. Cambridge, MA: Harvard University Press.

Cohen, B. I. (1980) *The Newtonian Revolution*. Cambridge: Cambridge University Press.

Commissioner General of Immigration (1913) *Annual Report of the Commissioner General of Immigration*, June 30. Washington, DC: Government Printing Office.

Commissioner General of Immigration (1916) *Annual Report of the Commissioner General of Immigration*, June 30. Washington, DC: Government Printing Office.

Comte, A. (1856) *The Positive Philosophy* (trans. H. Martineau). New York: Calvin Blanchard.

Condillac, E. de (1970) *Oeuvres Complètes*. Geneva: Slatkine Reprints.

Condillac, E. de (1982) *Philosophical Writings of Etienne Bonnot, Abbé de Condillac* (trans. F. Philip). London: Lawrence Erlbaum Associates.

Conrad, J. (1971) *Heart of Darkness*. New York: Norton Critical Edition.

Cope, E. D. (1887) *The Origin of the Fittest*. New York: Arno Press.

Crombie, A. C. (1959) *Medieval and Early Modern Science*. New York: Doubleday Anchor.

Curley, E. (ed. and trans.) (1985) *Collected Works of Spinoza*. Princeton, NJ: Princeton University Press.

Curley, E. (ed. and trans.) (1994) *Spinoza Reader A: The Ethics and Other Works of Benedict de Spinoza*. Princeton, NJ: Princeton University Press.

Curtin, P. D. (1964) *The Image of Africa: British Ideas and Action, 1780–1850*. Madison: University of Wisconsin Press.

Da Bisticci, V. (1926) *Le Vite dei Huomini Illustri: The Vespasiano Memoirs, Lives of Illustrious Men of the XVth Century* (trans. W. George and E. Waters). London: G. Routledge.

Danziger, K. (1997) *Naming the Mind: How Psychology Found Its Language*. London: Sage.

Darwin, C. (1871, 1896) *The Descent of Man and Selection in Relation to Sex*. New York: D. Appleton and Company.

de la Mettrie, J. O. (1997) *Machine Man and Other Writings* (trans. A. Thomson). Cambridge: Cambridge University Press.

De Soto, H. (2000) *The Mystery of Capitalism: Why Capitalism Triumphs in the West and Fails Everywhere Else*. New York: Basic Books.

Deleuze, G. (1988) *Foucault* (trans. S. Hand). Minneapolis: University of Minnesota Press.

Bibliography

Demming, W. E. (1994) *The New Economics: For Industry, Government and Education*. Cambridge, MA: MIT Press.

Derrida, J. (1978) *Edmund Husserl's Origin of Geometry: An Introduction* (trans. T. Leavey Jr). New York: Hays.

Dery, M. (1996) *Escape Velocity*. New York: Grove Press.

Descartes, R. (1988) *Descartes: Selected Philosophical Writings* (trans. J. Cottingham, R. Stoothoff and D. Murdoch). Cambridge: Cambridge University Press.

Descartes, R. (1991) *Philosophical Writings of Descartes* (trans. J. Cottingham, A. Kenny, D. Murdoch and R. Stoothoff). Cambridge: Cambridge University Press.

Dobbs, B. J. T. and Jacob, M. (1995) *Newton and the Culture of Newtonianism*. Atlantic Highlands, NJ: Humanities Press.

Duplessis, R. (1997) *Transitions to Capitalism in Early Modern Europe*. Cambridge: Cambridge University Press.

Dyson, G. (1998) *Darwin among the Machines: The Evolution of Global Intelligence*. Reading, MA: Perseus.

Earle, P. (1974) *Essays in European Economic History 1500–1800*. Oxford: Clarendon Press.

Earle, P. (1989) *The Making of the English Middle Class: Business, Society, and Family Life in London, 1660–1730*. London: Methuen.

Enenkel, K., de Jong-Crane, J. L. and Liebregts, P. (eds) (1998) *Modelling the Individual*. Amsterdam: Rodopi.

Evans, B. and Waites, B. (1981) *IQ and Mental Testing: An Unnatural Science and Its Social History*. London: Macmillan.

Eysenck, H. (1998) *Intelligence: A New Look*. London: Transaction.

Feyerabend, P. (1975) *Against Method*. London: New Left Books.

Ficino, M. (1989) *Three Books on Life* (trans. C. Kaske and J. Clark). New York: Center for Medieval and Early Renaissance Studies.

Fick, M. L. (1939) *The Educability of the South African Native*. Pretoria: South African Council for Educational and Social Research.

Fisher, D. and Scher, L. (1997) *Articulations of Difference: Gender Studies and Writing in French*. Palo Alto, CA: Stanford University Press.

Foucault, M. (1965) *Madness and Civilization: A History of Insanity in the Age of Reason* (trans. R. Howard). New York: Vintage.

Foucault, M. (1975) *The Birth of the Clinic: An Archeology of Medical Perception* (trans. A. M. Sheridan Smith). New York: Vintage.

Foucault, M. (1977) *Counter-Memory, Practice* (ed. D. Bouchard). Ithaca, NY: Cornell University Press.

Foucault, M. (1979) Nietzsche, genealogy, history (trans. D. Bouchard and S. Simon). In *Language, Counter-Memory, Practice*. Ithaca, NY: Cornell University Press.

Foucault, M. (1980) *Power/Knowledge: Selected Interviews and Other Writings 1972–1977* (ed. C. Gordon). Brighton: Harvester Press.

Foucault, M. (1994) *The Order of Things: An Archeology of the Human Sciences*. New York: Vintage.

Foucault, M. (1995) *Discipline and Punish: The Birth of the Prison*. New York: Vintage.

Foucault, M. (2001) *Fearless Speech*. Los Angeles: Semiotext.

Foucault, M., Dreyfus, H. and Rabinow, P. (eds) (1983) The subject and power. In *Michel Foucault: Beyond Structuralism and Hermeneutics*, 2nd edn. Chicago: University of Chicago Press.

Fox-Genovese, E. (1976) *The Origins of Physiocracy: Economic Revolution and Social Order in Eighteenth-century France*. Ithaca, NY: Cornell University Press.

Fox-Keller, E., Jacobus, M. and Shuttleworth, S. (1991) *Body Politics: Women and the Discourses of Science*. New York: Routledge.

Frazer, A. (ed.) (1981) *Berkeley's Complete Works*. Oxford: Oxford University Press.

Friedländer, P. (1969) *Plato. The Dialogues: Second and Third Periods*. Princeton, NJ: Princeton University Press.

Galileo (1953) *Dialogue on the Great World Systems*. Chicago: University of Chicago Press.

Galileo (1962) *Discoveries and Opinions of Galileo (Siderius Nuncius and Saggiatore)* (trans. S. Drake). Berkeley: University of California Press.

Galton, F. (1892) *Hereditary Genius: An Inquiry into Its Laws and Consequences*. London: Macmillan.

Galton, F. (1907) *Inquiries into Human Faculty and Its Development*. New York: Dutton.

Galton, F. (1909) *Memories of My Life*. London: Methuen.

Gardner, H. (1983) *Frames of Mind: The Theory of Multiple Intelligences*. New York: Basic Books.

Gardner, H. (1999) *Intelligence Reframed*. New York: Basic Books.

Gates, B. (1999) *Business @ the Speed of Thought: Using a Digital Nervous System*. New York: Warner Books.

Gaukroger, S. (1995) *Descartes: An Intellectual Biography*. Oxford: Clarendon Press.

Gay, P. (1977) *The Enlightenment: The Science of Freedom*. New York: W. W. Norton.

Geertz, C. (1973) *The Interpretations of Cultures*. New York: Basic Books.

Gell-Mann, M. (1995) *Complexity*. New York: Wiley.

Gilman, S. (1988) *Disease and Representation*. Ithaca, NY: Cornell University Press.

Gilson, E. (1960) *The Christian Philosophy of St Augustine*. New York: Random House.

Gliddon, G. and Nott, J. C. (1854) *Types of Mankind*. Philadelphia: Lippincott.

Goddard, H. (1919) *Psychology of the Normal and Subnormal*. New York: Dodd, Mead.

Goddard, H. (1920) *Human Efficiency and Levels of Intelligence*. Princeton, NJ: Princeton University Press.

Goddard, H. (1940) *Feeble-mindedness: Its Causes and Consequences*. New York: Macmillan.

Goldthwaite, R. (1995) *Banks, Palaces and Entrepreneurs in Renaissance Florence*. Cambridge: Cambridge University Press.

Goleman, D. (1995) *Emotional Intelligence*. New York: Bantam.

Gould, S. J. (1987) *The Mismeasurement of Man*. New York: Norton.

Guilford, J. P. (1967) *The Nature of Human Intelligence*. New York: McGraw-Hill.

Guthrie, W. K. C. (1962–81) *A History of Greek Philosophy: The Earlier Presocratics and the Pythagoreans*. Cambridge: Cambridge University Press.

Habermas, J. (1971) *Towards a Rational Society*. London: Heinemann.

Bibliography

Hall, A. R. (1962) *Scientific Revolution 1500–1800: The Formation of the Modern Scientific Attitude*. Boston: Beacon Press.

Hall, A., Scott, J. F., Tilling, L. and Turnbull, H. (eds) (1959–77) *The Correspondence of Isaac Newton*. Cambridge: Cambridge University Press.

Hallie, P. (1966) *The Scar of Montaigne*. Middleton, MA: Wesleyan University Press.

Hamilton, E. and Huntington, C. (eds) (1982) *Collected Dialogues of Plato*. Princeton, NJ: Princeton University Press.

Haraway, D. (1991) *Simians, Cyborgs, and Women: The Reinvention of Nature*. New York: Routledge.

Hardy, G. (1938) *Histoire de la colonisation française*. Paris: Larose.

Hegel, G. (1900) *The Philosophy of History* (trans. J. Sibree). New York: Wiley.

Heilbroner, R. (1985) *The Nature and Logic of Capitalism*. New York: Norton.

Helvétius, C.-A. (1988) *De l'espirit* (ed. J. Moutaux). Paris: Fayard.

Helvétius, C.-A. (1989) *De l'homme, de ses facultés intellectuelles et de son education* (ed. G. Montaux and J. Montaux). Paris: Fayard.

Henry, J. (1997) *The Scientific Revolution and the Origins of Modern Science*. London: St Martin's Press.

Herrnstein, R. and Murray, C. (1994) *The Bell Curve: Intelligence and Class Structure in American Life*. New York: Free Press.

Hobbes, T. (1962) *Leviathan, or The Matter, Form and Power of a Commonwealth Ecclesiastical and Civil*. London: Scientia Allen.

Holbach, P. H. T. (1770) *The System of Nature*. New York: Garland (1984).

Hothersall, D. (1984) *History of Psychology*. Philadelphia: Temple University Press.

Hume, D. (1739) *A Treatise of Human Nature*. New York: Longman.

Hume, D. (1748) *An Enquiry Concerning Human Understanding* (www.rbjones.com/rbjpub/philos/classics/hume/echu071.htm).

Hume, D. (1777) *Of the Balance of Trade*, in *Essays, Moral, Political, and Literary* (http://socserv2.socsci.mcmaster.ca/~econ/ugcm/3ll3/hume/trade.txt).

Hunter, M. (1995) *Science and Shape of Orthodoxy*. London: Woodbridge.

Hunter, M. (ed.) (1998) *Archives of the Scientific Revolution*. London: Boydell Press.

Hyma, A. (1951) *Renaissance to Reformation*. Grand Rapids, MI: Eerdmans.

Im Hof, U. (1994) *The Enlightenment*. Oxford: Blackwell.

Jacob, J. R. (1998) *The Scientific Revolution: Aspirations and Achievements, 1500–1700*. Atlantic Highlands, NJ: Humanities Press.

Jacob, M. (1997) *Scientific Culture and the Making of the Industrial West*. Oxford: Oxford University Press.

Jacob, M. (ed.) (1994) *The Politics of Western Science 1640–1990*. New York: Humanities Press.

Jameson, F. (1991) *Postmodernism, or, The Cultural Logic of Late Capitalism*. Durham, NC: Duke University Press.

Jessup, T. and Luce, A. (eds) (1969) *The Works of George Berkeley*. New York: Greenwood.

Jeter, K. W. (1998) *Noir*. New York: Bantam.

Johnson, M. (1996) *An Archaeology of Capitalism*. Oxford: Blackwell.

Jones, C. and Porter, R. (1994) *Reassessing Foucault: Power, Medicine and the Body*. London: Routledge.

Kant, I. (1781) *Critique of Pure Reason* (trans. N. Kemp Smith) (www.arts.cuhk.edu.hk/Philosophy/Kant/cpr/).

Kant, I. (1790) *Critique of Aesthetic Judgment* (trans. J. Creed Meredith) (www.mnstate.edu/gracyk/courses/phil%20of%20art/kant%20selections.htm#46).

Kent, D. (1978) *The Rise of the Medici Faction in Florence*. Oxford: Oxford University Press.

Kirkpatrick, C. (1926) *Intelligence and Immigration*. Baltimore: Williams and Wilkins.

Knight, I. (1968) *The Geometric Spirit: The Abbé de Condillac and the French Enlightenment*. New Haven, CT: Yale University Press.

Kretamann, N., Kenny, A. and Pinborg, J. (eds) (1982) *The Cambridge History of Later Medieval Philosophy*. Cambridge: Cambridge University Press.

Kristeller, P. O. (1964) *The Philosophy of Marsilio Ficino* (trans. V. Conant). New York: Columbia University Press.

Kristeller, P. O. (1980) *Renaissance Thought and Arts*. Princeton, NJ: Princeton University Press.

Kulstad, M. (1991) *Leibniz on Apperception*. Munich: Hamden.

Landes, D. (1983) *Revolution in Time*. Cambridge, MA: Harvard University Press.

Langhoff, V. (1990) *Medical Theories in Hippocrates: Early Texts and the Epidemics*. Berlin: de Gruyter.

Laplace, M. de P. S. (1951) *A Philosophical Essay on Probabilities* (trans. F. W. Truscott and F. L. Emory). New York: Dover.

Laudan, L. (1977) *Progress and Its Problems: Toward a Theory of Scientific Growth*. London: Routledge & Kegan Paul.

Le Roy, L. (1944) *De la vicissitude ou variété des choses en l'univers* (ed. B. W. Bates). Princeton, NJ: Princeton University Press.

Leibniz, G. W. (1989) *Philosophical Essays* (ed. R. Ariew and D. Garber). Cambridge, MA: Hackett.

Levin, D. M. (1993) *Modernity and the Hegemony of Vision*. Berkeley: University of California Press.

Levy, P. (1994) *Collective Intelligence: Mankind's Emerging World in Cyberspace*. New York: Plenum Press.

Liebraum, J. (1995) Dentist's murderer gets death penalty. *Houston Chronicle*, February 9.

Lindberg, D. and Westman, R. (eds) (1990) *Reappraisals of the Scientific Revolution*. Cambridge: Cambridge University Press.

Linnaeus, C. (1758) *Systema naturae per regna tria naturae, secundum classes, ordines, genera, species, cum characteribus, differnetiis, synonymis, locis*, 10th edn. Holmiae: Laurentii Salvi.

Locke, J. (1975) *An Essay Concerning Human Understanding* (ed. P. Nidditch). Oxford: Clarendon Press.

Locke, J. (1980) *Second Treatise on Government* (ed. C. B. Macpherson). Indianapolis: Hackett.

Lough, J. and Proust, J. (eds) (1976) *Diderot: Oeuvres Complètes*. Paris: Hermann.

Lynn, R. and Vanhanen, T. (2002) *IQ and The Wealth of Nations*. Westport, CT: Praeger.

Bibliography

Lyotard, J. F. (1984) *The Postmodern Condition: A Report on Knowledge* (trans. G. Bennington and B. Massumi). Minneapolis: University of Minnesota Press.

McClellan, J. and Dorn, H. (1999) *Science and Technology in World History*. Baltimore: Johns Hopkins University Press.

Machiavelli, N. (1965) *Machiavelli: The Chief Works and Others* (trans. A. Gilbert). Durham, NC: Duke University Press.

McLaughlin, M. M. and Ross, J. B. (eds) (1977) *Portable Renaissance Reader*. Penguin: New York.

McLean, I. and Hewitt, F. (eds) (1994) *Condorcet: Foundations of Social Choice and Political Theory*. London: Elgar.

Makeig, J. (1995) Retarded teen convicted of killing dentist for car. *Houston Chronicle*, February 4.

Malebranche, N. (1997) *The Search After Truth* (ed. T. Lennon and P. Olscamp). Cambridge: Cambridge University Press.

Malthus, T. (1960) Essay on the principle of population. In *On Population* (ed. G. Himmelfarb). New York: Modern Library.

Manetti, G. (1975) *De dignitare et excellentia hominis* (ed. E. R. Leonard). Padua: Antenore.

Mann, N. and Syson, L. (eds) (1998) *Image of the Individual: Portraits in the Renaissance*. London: British Museum Press.

Markley, R. (1993) *Fallen Languages: Crisis of Representation in Newtonian England, 1660–1740*. Ithaca, NY: Cornell University Press.

Maurer, A. (trans.) (1964) *Medieval Philosophy*. New York: Random House.

Mayer, J. D. and Salovey, P. (1997) What is emotional intelligence? In P. Salovey and D. Sluyter (eds), *Emotional Development and Emotional Intelligence: Implications for Educators*. New York: Basic Books.

Meek, R. (1973) *Turgot on Progress, Sociology and Economics: A Philosophical Review of the Successive Advances of the Human Mind, On Universal History [and] Reflections on the Formation and the Distribution of Wealth*. Cambridge: Cambridge University Press.

Miscellaneous Documents on Immigration 1907–1914. Washington, DC: Government Printing Office, 1911.

Molho, A. (1981) *Florentine Public Finances in the Early Renaissance*. Cambridge, MA: Harvard University Press.

Montaigne, M. de (1968) *The Complete Works of Montaigne* (trans. D. Frame). Palo Alto, CA: Stanford University Press.

Morse, M. (1998) *Virtualities: Television, Media Art, and Cyberculture*. Bloomington: Indiana University Press.

Mullan, E. H. (1917) *Mental Examination of Immigrants: Administration and Line Inspection at Ellis Island*. Reprint No. 398 (May). Washington, DC: Government Printing Office.

Murphy, E. (1996) *Leadership IQ*. New York: Wiley.

Murphy, J. J. (1974) *Rhetoric in the Middle Ages*. Berkeley: University of California Press.

Neill, T. P. (1948) Quesnay and physiocracy. *JHI*, April 2.

Newton, I. (1687) *Philosophiae Naturalis Principia Mathematica* (trans. F. Cajori). Berkeley: University of California Press (1947).

Newton, I. (1704) *Opticks, or A Treatise of the Reflections, Refractions, Inflections, and Colours of Light.* New York: Dover (1952).

Nicholas of Cusa (1970) *The Vision of God* (trans. E. Gurney Salter). New York: Ungar.

Nicholas of Cusa (1972) *Opera omnia, iussu et auctoritate Academiae Litterarum Heidelbergensis.* Hamburg: F. Meiner.

Nicholas of Cusa (1981) *Of Learned Ignorance* (trans. J. Hopkins and A. Banning). Minneapolis: University of Minnesota Press.

Nietzsche, F. (1987) *Philosophy of Nietzsche* (trans. H. Zimmern). New York: Modern Library.

Norena, C. (1970) *Juan Luis Vives.* The Hague: Martinus Nijhoff.

O'Meara, P., Mehlinger, H. and Krain, M. (2000) *Globalization and the Challenges of a New Century.* Bloomington: Indiana University Press.

Ornstein, M. (1928) *The Role of Scientific Societies in the Seventh Century.* Chicago: University of Chicago Press.

Pardo, J. C. (1992) *Economic Effects of the European Expansion, 1492–1824.* Stuttgart: Steiner.

Pascal, B. (1995) *Pensées and Other Writings* (trans. H. Levi). New York: Oxford University Press.

Pearson, E. S. (1978) *Studies in the History of Statistics and Probability.* London: Charles Griffin & Co.

Peltonen, M. (ed.) (1996) *The Cambridge Companion to Bacon.* Cambridge: Cambridge University Press.

Perez-Ramos, A. (1988) *Francis Bacon's Idea of Science and the Maker's Knowledge Tradition.* New York: Oxford University Press.

Perkins, D. (1995) *Outsmarting IQ: The Emerging Science of Learnable Intelligence.* New York: Free Press.

Petrarch (1975) *De vita solitaria* (ed. G. Martellotti). Turin: Trauben.

Pinker, S. (1997) *How the Mind Works.* New York: Norton.

Plotinus (1948) *Essence of Plotinus: Extracts from the Six Enneads and Porphyry's Life of Plotinus* (trans. S. McKenna). New York: Oxford University Press.

Pope-Hennessy, H. (1966) *The Portrait in the Renaissance.* London: Chatto.

Popkin, R. H. (1974) The philosophical basis of modern racism. In J. P. Anton and C. Walton (eds), *Philosophy and the Civilizing Art.* Athens: Ohio University Press.

Popplestone, J. A. and MacPherson, M. W. (eds) (1999) *An Illustrated History of American Psychology,* 2nd edn. Akron, OH: University of Akron Press.

Porter, T. M. and Ross D. (eds) (2001) *The Cambridge History of Science.* Cambridge: Cambridge University Press.

Potter, T. (1986) *The Rise of Statistical Thinking 1820–1900.* Princeton, NJ: Princeton University Press.

Power, H. (1966) *Experimental Philosophy.* New York: Johnson Reprint.

Prak, M. (ed.) (2001) *Early Modern Capitalism: Economic and Social Change in Europe 1400–1800.* New York: Routledge.

Rasch, W. and Wolfe, C. (eds) (2000) *Observing Complexity: Systems Theory and Postmodernity.* Minneapolis: University of Minneapolis Press.

Bibliography

Restivo, S. (1992) *Mathematics in Society and History*. London: Kluwer Academic.

Reuning, H. (1988) Testing Bushmen in the central Kalahari. In J. W. Berry and S. H. Irvine (eds), *Human Abilities in Cultural Context*. New York: Cambridge University Press.

Rheingold, H. (2002) *Smart Mobs: The Next Social Revolution*. Cambridge, MA: Perseus.

Robinson, H. W. (1949) *Notes and Records of the Royal Society, Volume 7*. London: Royal Society.

Roche, J. R. (1998) *The Mathematics of Measurement: A Critical History*. London: Athlone Press.

Rotman, B. (1988) Towards a semiotics of mathematics. *Semiotica*, 72(1/2), 1–34.

Rose, N. (1990) *Governing the Soul: The Shaping of the Private Self*. London: Routledge.

Rousseau, J.-J. (1990) *The Collected Writings of Rousseau* (ed. C. Kelly and R. Masters). Hanover, NH: University Press of New England.

Rousseau, J.-J. (1964) *First and Second Discourses* (trans. J. R. Masters and R. D. Masters). New York: St Martin's Press.

Runes, D. (ed.) (1951) *Spinoza Dictionary*. New York: Philosophical Library.

Sarason, S. B. and Doris, J. (1979) *Educational Handicap, Public Policy, and Social History*. New York: Free Press.

Schlagel, R. (1996) *From Myth to Modern Mind: A Study of the Origins and Growth of Scientific Thought, Volume 2*. New York: Peter Lang.

Schmitt, C. (ed.) (1998) *The Cambridge History of Renaissance Philosophy*. Cambridge: Cambridge University Press.

Schwartz, T. (2000) How do you feel? *FastCompany*, 35 (www.fastcompany.com/online/35/emotion.html).

Seago, D. W. (1921) *An Analysis of Language Factors in Intelligence Tests*. Baltimore: Williams & Wilkins.

Senate Record Vote Analysis, 101st Congress, 2nd Session, May 24, 1990, Page S-6883, Vote No. 107. Omnibus Crime Bill, Capital Punishment – "Right and Wrong" Standard.

Serres, M. (ed.) (1995) *A History of Scientific Thought: Elements of a History of Science*. Oxford: Blackwell.

Shapin, S. (1996) *The Scientific Revolution*. Chicago: University of Chicago Press.

Shaviro, S. (2003) *Connected, or What It Means to Live in the Network Society*. Minneapolis: University of Minnesota Press.

Shepherd, M. (ed.) (1999) *Friend to Mankind: Marsilio Ficino*. London: Shepheard-Walwyn.

Shuger-Kuller, D. (2000) *Habits of Thought in the English Renaissance: Religion, Politics, and the Dominant Culture*. Berkeley: University of California Press.

Siraisi, N. G. (1990) *Medieval and Early Medicine Medicine: An Introduction to Knowledge and Practice*. Chicago: University of Chicago Press.

Smith, A. (1904) *An Inquiry into the Nature and Causes of the Wealth of Nations*. London: Methuen and Co.

Snell, B. (1960) *The Discovery of Mind: the Greek Origins of European Thought*. New York: Harper.

Sprat, T. (1959) *History of the Royal Society* (ed. J. Cope and H. Jones). London: Royal Society.

Stanton, W. (1960) *The Leopard's Spots: Scientific Attitudes toward Race in America, 1819–1859*. Chicago: University of Chicago Press.

Steele, R. D. (2002) *New Craft of Intelligence*. Carlisle Barracks, PA: Strategic Studies Institute, US Army War College.

Sternberg, R. (1988) *The Triarchic Mind: A New Theory of Intelligence*. New York: Viking Press.

Sternberg, R. (1990) *Metaphors of Mind: Conceptions of the Nature of Intelligence*. New York: Cambridge University Press.

Sternberg, R. (2004) Culture and intelligence. *American Psychologist*, 59(5), 325–38.

Sternberg, R., Lautrey, J. and Lubart, T. I. (2003) *Models of Intelligence: International Perspectives*. Washington, DC: American Psychological Association.

Sternberg, R. and Wolman, B. (2000) *Handbook of Intelligence*. Cambridge: Cambridge University Press.

Stewart, M. A. (ed.) (1979) *Selected Philosophical Papers of Robert Boyle*. Manchester: Manchester University Press.

Stewart, T. (2001) *The Wealth of Knowledge: Intellectual Capital and the Twenty-First Century Organization*. New York: Currency.

Stigen, A. (1966) *The Structure of Aristotle's Thought*. Oslo: Universitetsforlaget.

Štigler, S. (1986) *The History of Uncertainty before 1900*. Cambridge, MA: Harvard University Press.

Sutherland, J. (1956) *Defoe*. London: Longman.

Szuba, T. M. (2001) *Computational Collective Intelligence*. New York: Wiley.

Talbot, M. (2003) The executioner's IQ test. *The New York Times Magazine*, July 29.

Terman, L. (1906) Genius and stupidity. In *Pedagogical Seminary*.

Terman, L. (1916) *The Measurement of Intelligence*. London: Harrap.

Terman, L. (1919) *Intelligence of School Children*. Boston: Houghton, Mifflin & Company.

Themistius (1996) *Themistius: On Aristotle, On the Soul* (trans. R. Todd). London: Duckworth.

Tilly, C. (1990) *Coercion, Capital, and European States AD 990–1990*. Oxford: Blackwell.

Tweyman, S. (ed.) (1993) *René Descartes: Meditations on First Philosophy*. New York: Routledge.

Vico, G. (1968) *New Science of Giambattista Vico* (ed. T. Bergin and M. Fisch). Ithaca, NY: Cornell University Press.

Vico, G. (1988) *On the Most Ancient Wisdom of the Italians: Unearthed from the Origins of the Latin Language: Including the Disputation with the Giornale de'letterati d'Italia* (ed. L. M. Palmer). Ithaca, NY: Cornell University Press.

Vives, J. L. (1782) *Valenti Opera Omnia*, eight volumes (ed. G. Mayans and Siscar). Valencia.

Vives, J. L. (1987) *Early Writings* (ed. C. Fantazzi, E. George and C. Matheeussen). New York: E. J. Brill.

Voltaire, F. M. A. de (1952) *Notebooks* (ed. T. Besterman). Geneva: Institut et Musée Voltaire.

Waller, R. (ed.) (1971) *Posthumous Works of Robert Hooke*. London: Frank Cass.

Bibliography

Weber, A. S. (ed.) (2000) *Nineteenth Century Science: A Selection of Original Text*. New York: Broadview Press.

Weber, M. (1988) *The Protestant Ethic and the Spirit of Capitalism* (trans. T. Parsons). Gloucester, MA: P. Smith.

Wechlser, D. (1958) *The Measurement and Appraisal of Adult Intelligence*, 4th edn. Baltimore: Williams and Wilkins.

White, L. (1962) *Medieval Technology and Social Change*. Oxford: Clarendon Press.

Wilderspin, S. (1840) *The Infant System for Developing the Intellectual and Moral Power of All Children from One to Seven Years of Age*. London: Simkin and Marshall.

Wilson, J. Q. and Herrnstein, R. J. (1985) *Crime and Human Nature*. New York: Simon and Schuster.

Wilson, L. G. (1970) *Sir Charles Lyell's Scientific Journals on the Species Question*. New Haven, CT: Yale University Press.

Wippel, J. and Wolter, A. (eds) (1969) *Medieval Philosophy: From St Augustine to Nicolas of Cusa*. New York: Free Press.

Wittgenstein, L. (1961) *Tractatus Logico-Philosophicus*. London: Routledge & Kegan Paul.

Wollstonecraft, M. (1972) *A Vindication of the Rights of Woman* (www.bartleby.com/144/4.html).

Wood, A. (ed.) (2001) *Basic Writings of Kant*. New York: Modern Library.

Woolf, H. (ed.) (1961) *Quantification: A History of the Meaning of Measurement in the Natural and Social Sciences*. Indianapolis: Bobbs-Merrill.

Wundt, W. (1969) *Physiological Psychology* (trans. E. B. Titchener). New York: Kraus Reprint Co.

Yerkes, R. M. (ed.) (1921) *Psychological Examining in the United States Army*. Memoirs of the National Academy of Sciences, Volume XV. Washington, DC: Government Printing Office.

Zenderland, L. (1998) *Measuring Minds: Goddard and the Origins of American Intelligence Testing*. Cambridge: Cambridge University Press.

Zuboff, S. (1990) *In the Age of the Smart Machine: The Future of Work and Power*. New York: Basic Books.

Index